Youth and marginalisation:
Young people from immigrant families in Scandinavia.

the Tufnell Press,
London,
United Kingdom

www.tufnellpress.co.uk

email contact@tufnellpress·co·uk

British Library Cataloguing-in-Publication Data
A catalogue record for this book is
available from the British Library

paperback ISBN   *1872767680*
ISBN-13   *978-1-872767-68-0*

Printed in England and U.S.A. by Lightning Source

Youth and marginalisation: Young people from immigrant families in Scandinavia

**Gestur Gudmundsson,
Dennis Beach
and
Viggo Vestel**

Contents

Authors

Dennis Beach is Professor of education at the universities of Gothenburg and Borås in Sweden. His main research interests lie in the field of sociology of education. He has a particular interest in issues of policy and politics in education. He has authored and co-authored numerous books and articles in these areas and is currently chief editor of the journal *Ethnography and Education*.

Frédérique Brossard Børhaug is Associate Professor of Education at NLA School of Religion, Education and Intercultural Studies, Norway. Her field of specialisation is intercultural education. She works on ethics and anti-racist education in French and Norwegian multicultural school contexts. A recent contribution (2012), How to better combine equality and difference in French and Norwegian anti-racist education? Some reflections from a capability point of view. *Journal of Human Development and capabilities.* Routledge. 13(3): 397-413.

Katrine Fangen is professor in Sociology at the University of Oslo. She has conducted research in the areas of youth research since 1990 and migration research since 1999. Her research focuses more specifically on processes of inclusion and exclusion, identity work, subcultures, transnationalism, political and civic involvement and right-wing extremism. A recent article is, (2013) Young Adults of Ethnic Minority Background on the Norwegian Labour Market: the Interactional Co-Construction by Employers and Customers, *Ethnicities,* 13(5) (co-author Erlend Paasche).

Ivar Frones is Professor of Sociology at the University of Oslo, and senior researcher at The Norwegian Center for Child Behavioural Development. His work covers a variety of areas, with an emphasis on childhood, youth and social exclusion. His numerous publications cover a variation of perspectives, such as digital divides, media use, marginalisation, cultural trends, consumption, and life course development. His most recent publication (with Ragnhild Brusdal) is entitled, The purchase of moral positions: an essay on the markets of concerned parenting, *International Journal of Consumer Studies* 2013, 37(2): 159-164.

Gestur Gudmundsson is professor in Sociology of Education at the University of Iceland. He has primarily researched into youth culture, youth education and social exclusion/inclusion of young people, youth unemployment, youth without upper secondary education, youth with immigrant background. A recent article: (2013) Quality Spirals and Vicious Circles among Children of Immigrant Entrepreneurs: How Immigrant Entrepreneurs' Resources are Remoulded by the Second Generation, *Young—Nordic Journal of Youth Research* 21(2): 173-191.

Jonas Lindbäck is a doctoral student in Youth Studies at the Department of Education, Communication and Learning at the University of Gothenburg. His primary research interest is in youth, identity and education. His forthcoming doctoral thesis focuses on youth from schools in immigrant-dense and disadvantaged urban neighbourhoods where half of all the students do not obtain sufficient grades for upper secondary school. The relation of this situation to the students' everyday life and the hierarchically structured urban space is of specific interest.

Henry Mainsah is a Senior Researcher at the Centre for Design Research at the Oslo School of Architecture and Design. He has a Ph. D. in Media and Communication from the University of Oslo. His current research focuses on social media, design, youth and civic life. He has published in journals such as the *European Journal of Cultural Studies*, and in edited volumes such as *Media in Motion: Cultural Complexity and Migration in the Nordic Region*. Elisabeth Eide and Kaarina Nikunen (eds) (2010) London: Ashgate.

Åsa Möller is currently working towards completion of a Ph. D. in pedagogical work at the Department of Department of Education, Communication and Learning at the University of Gothenburg. Her areas of interest include diversity issues, race and racism, critical pedagogy, knowledge construction, and normativity in education and learning.

Sune Qvotrup Jensen is an associate professor in Sociology at Aalborg University, Denmark. He has pursued a broad range of research interests including gender and masculinity, intersectionality, urban studies, ethnography, social problems, cultural analysis and subcultural theory. His most recent work includes *Stemmer fra en bydel : Etnicitet, køn og klasse i Aalborg Øst [Voices from a district: Ethnicity, gender and class in Aalborg East]*, Aalborg Universitetsforlag 2012 (together with Ann-Dorte Christensen).

Ove Sernhede is professor at the Centre for Urban Studies and the Department of Pedagogy, Communication and Education at Goteborg University. He has been involved in research on different aspects of youth culture and music, urban studies, Afroamerican culture, psychoanalysis and social pedagogics. He is the author of several books and articles. Among them, *AlieNation is My Nation* (Stockholm: Ordfront 2002/2007).

Viggo Vestel is a senior researcher and social anthropologist, working in the Section for Youth Research at NOVA (Norwegian Social research) in Oslo. His research interests cover migration, multicultural neighbourhoods, popular culture, the semiotics of class, and political articulation. He has written several articles in refereed journals, and contributed to several books. Vestel has been member of the editorial collective of *YOUNG – Nordic Journal of Youth research*.

Introduction

Excluded youth in itself and for itself—Young people from immigrant families in Scandinavia

Gestur Gudmundsson

The Nordic countries are widely perceived as the home of egalitarianism and minimal social inequalities, and critics of social injustice often look to this region for positive alternatives. In the migration waves of the last decades the Nordic countries are often seen as decent hosts, who adhere to the principles of multi- or interculturalism and not least emphasise that young people from immigrant families should get a fair chance in an egalitarian educational system. In terms of practices in education, on the labour market, in housing and in various other areas, there are however, to say the least, some rather dark sides to this picture.

This anthology looks at the experiences of youth from immigrant families in relation to education, housing and cultural production against a common background of Nordic Welfare Societies. Most of the chapters are based on intensive ethnographic work in immigrant communities and in schools in immigrant-dense areas, but other (both quantitative and qualitative) methodological tools are also used. Theoretically we have learned from a variety of approaches: from critical studies on subcultures and resistance, from urban studies on territorial stigmatisation, from critical perspectives on racism and postcolonialism, and from classical sociology and various other sources.

Taken together, the chapters show that youth with immigrant backgrounds in the Nordic countries encounter various processes of exclusion, not least in school, and experience many of the effects of territorial stigmatisation of the immigrant-dense areas they live in. Inclusion and multiculturalism are key words in Nordic educational policy, but analyses of curricula, teaching practices and experiences of young people show that these goals to a high degree remain abstract and are far from being realised. Educational practices are segregated from other experiences of young people from immigrant families and for a large part of them, these practices do not open any roads for equal participation in society. For large segments of the young immigrant population, viable *capabilities* (Amartya Sen) are found in cultural responses based on resistance against processes of marginalisation and on a search for forms of expression that suit their experience of being stigmatised and excluded.

This anthology is a result of four years of cooperation between researchers of youth from immigrant families in Sweden, Norway, Denmark and Iceland. The research network has discussed each other's research projects intensively and repeatedly and sought inspiration by arranging larger seminars with invited international guests who have analysed the situation of youth with immigrant backgrounds in French, British and American cities. Most of the articles are based on ethnographic research in the cities of Gothenburg, Oslo and Copenhagen (three of the four biggest cities in Scandinavia), but other methods are also mobilised, such as comparative discourse analysis of curricula and the combination of quantitative and qualitative methods.

The network has an interdisciplinary profile. The authors work within the academic fields of cultural studies, youth studies, urban studies, sociology, education and anthropology. Discussions in the network and the editing process have simultaneously aimed at strengthening the specific approach of each article and at making them understandable across the interdisciplinary field of research on young people with immigrant backgrounds. The authors of the anthology are firmly based in the Nordic, interdisciplinary tradition of youth studies, which means not least that cultural expressions and social background are neither examined separately nor is one reduced to the other. Some contributors focus more on culture, others on social background but all consider that both sides are at work and intertwined.

We will shortly present the chapters in the book and the specific key concepts and theories that are at play in each of them. However, first, the twin concepts of social exclusion and inclusion will be briefly presented. Like the ethnographic approach these concepts are central in our common box of intellectual tools. They are more directly on stage in some articles, whilst in other articles they remain rather more in the background.

The conceptual pair of social exclusion and social inclusion has been a part of the sociological vocabulary since the middle of the twentieth century. Talcott Parsons (1951) used this conceptual pair to analyse contradictory developments in the situation of immigrants. In his analysis, *exclusion* means that minority groups as a whole are denied economic, social and/or cultural privileges enjoyed by the rest of society. Later some favoured member of the minority group may gain access to these privileges and become *assimilated*, but the problem of exclusion is not solved until the minority group as a whole gets access to positions and full participation in society without having to give up its own culture—a situation that is covered by the concept of *inclusion*.

The concept pair of exclusion-inclusion moved to the centre of social theory during the 1990s without much reference to Parsons but rather as a remedy against the oppressive implications of the integration concept that had dominated discussions and analyses of underprivileged groups. Critical theorists like Erving Goffman (1961) and Michel Foucault (1975) informed an understanding of exclusion as more or less misrecognised aspects of power relations. The concept of inclusion was often (re)launched to direct attention to the responsibility of privileged groups and the need for institutions to change in order to give room to newcomers and the underprivileged.

During the last decades social scientists have increasingly pointed out that social groups and individuals can simultaneously meet processes of exclusion and inclusion in a differentiated and segmented society. Immigrants may be included into certain subspheres of the economy and the educational system but highly excluded from other subspheres, some residential areas may be characterised by exclusion and others by inclusion, and similar differentiation can take place in the different sections of culture, leisure and social and political life. Such mechanisms may meet different groups with immigrant background in different ways.

In the history of migration it is well known that new groups of immigrants often find niches in an otherwise closed occupational structure, and that in some cases such niches turn out to be dead-end streets while in other cases they become gateways to wider opportunities. It is often reported that girls from immigrant families appear more included than boys in the educational systems in general. Some educational tracks, like medicine, natural and technical science and business and economics seem to include fewer obstacles for many groups with immigrant background than humanities and social sciences that are more strongly and tacitly embedded in the inherited culture of the host country. However, few studies focus on the prices of inclusion, when young people with immigrant background are successfully included in certain realms of work and social life but excluded from others and at the same time often painfully alienated from their family and ethnic peers.

The multiplicities of social exclusion and inclusion of immigrants are in most research reduced to a few measurable variables, especially educational achievement, position on labour market, income and residence. These are important indicators but they are also used because they are available and their validity can and should be questioned. Furthermore they can only in a very limited way point to the mechanisms that lead the one way or the other. An important step is taken in the article of Fangen and Frønes who draw up some general patterns of exclusion and inclusion from a quantitative approach and then examine through qualitative material some of the processes and mechanisms that lie behind such outcomes.

Mechanisms of exclusion and inclusion are often cumulative and much international research has pointed to residential segregation as a factor that reinforces other mechanisms of exclusion. In terms of social capital such segregation minimises bridging social capital and isolates the bonding social capital of the neighbourhood. It has been documented in research and journalistic inquiries on how residential segregation often becomes a decisive factor that turns the multitudes of inclusive and exclusive processes into a vicious circle: young people with an immigrant background, who have completed education that usually gives access to employment, are often turned down by employers because they have the wrong address. Such experiences teach their younger siblings that it is useless to pursue education. Often, dramatic events are necessary to turn the general attention to this exclusion, and often such attention only confirms widespread convictions that it is the population of the 'ghettos', the *'banlieues'* and other such areas that is the problem. The vicious circle of exclusion is reinforced and takes the form of *territorial stigmatisation* that labels the immigrant inhabitants of certain areas as troublemakers that do not want to adjust to the norms, laws and aspirations of their new country.

The egalitarian aura of the Nordic countries may lead some outsiders to believe that such extreme forms of exclusion cannot happen in these welfare countries, but the fact is that all the Nordic countries have immigrant-dense parts of town that show similar signs of stigmatisation as those found in other European countries. In many Nordic towns such areas were built as a part of the victorious march of welfare state planning in the 1950s and 1960s. They provided the rising working class with decent housing and good facilities for cultural and leisure activities and spurred their social mobility. Gradually, however, other aspects than social mobility became prevalent: these areas were segregated from the rest of the city and looked down on from middle class areas; the more mobile part moved away and left those with limited education and low status jobs, if any. Gradually, a new population group with aspirations of social mobility moved into these areas. These were mainly immigrants and their descendants, but now the spiral of mobility had turned downwards and many of the inhabitants experience their neighbourhood as chains that keep them in inferior positions.

This territorial stigmatisation is an important part of the background of several studies presented in this volume. Åsa Møller shows how a school, which intends to be inclusive, writes off the experiences of their pupils in their own neighbourhood and indicates that most valuable experiences are found outside. Jonas Lindbäck and Ove Sernhede show how the innovative offerings of an Upper Secondary School in such an area attracts students from other parts of town, where they can add to their own cultural capital, while the homegrown students look outside of their neighbourhood in hope of getting a slice of the established cultural capital.

Such crossings do not necessarily soften the division of the city between social groups; through the narratives of young people from both groups Lindbäck and Sernhede show how the city's spaces and people are described, categorised and positioned in stigmatising ways that affect the image of these spaces and their inhabitants and how people relate to them. Åsa Möller shows how the school recommends 'Swedishness' as the inherited native culture and argues that social differences become racially constructed and need to be deconstructed. Möller provides such a deconstruction based on *postcolonialism* and *critical race theory*.

Not only school practices but also the national curricula are in need of being critically examined, as shown in Frédérique Brossard Børhaug's comparative examination of French and Norwegian curricula as ideological key documents for school practice. The Norwegian curricula openly state that the school shall fight any form of racism and discrimination in school and society by promoting democratic values. On the other hand, the Norwegian cultural heritage, founded on Western humanistic and Christian values, is presented as a shared body of references. Thus, the curricula also stresses a universalist approach based on human rights to the detriment of a differentialist argumentation promoting the cultural rights and capabilities for youth with immigrant background, so the educational policy cannot be characterised as multicultural or intercultural.

Exclusion and inclusion are not sufficient as overarching concepts for migrant studies and the chapters in the anthology especially make use of the concepts of *resistance* and *creativity*. Here, as well as in our emphasis on ethnographic methods, our studies are indebted to the tradition of sub-cultural studies and theories of Chicago scholars and the well known Birmingham school tradition of cultural sociology.

Sune Qvotrup Jensen points out that those who have criticised the Birmingham school have tended to ignore its basic force, which is to study cultural responses in relation to social conditions. His study of hip-hop culture in immigrant-dense areas in Copenhagen, demonstrates that hip-hop provides youngsters of immigrant background, who are on the edge of exclusion, with tools to express, elaborate and unite in resistance and creative responses to their problematic social situation. For most of them this leads to higher self-esteem, for many it leads to careers in cultural activities, and it contributes strongly to a collective platform. Dennis Beach and Ove Sernhede discuss the hip-hop culture in broader terms, its ambivalences about crime, misogyny, commercialism and resistance, and dig into their rich material of ethnographic studies to show how this multi-faced cultural form provides possibilities for creativity and autonomous learning activities that challenge residential stigma and other forms of exclusion.

Henry Mainsah examines how minority youth in Norway use other channels of creativity, specifically for instance social networking sites, in relation to issues of identity construction, voice, and transnational social networks. Here young people with immigrant background can cross not only geographic and political borders but cultural and linguistic ones as well. They learn to navigate in different contexts of transnational social networks and experiment with the articulation of different identity moments, and Mainsah emphasises how they learn to tackle being members of multiple worlds and having multiple layers of identities.

These and other notions are brought together in the concept of *youth* which is over-arching and in some articles so self-evident that it is not worded. Youth is a social and cultural concept, opposed for instance to the most frequent uses of the adolescence concept as a term for a stage in psychological development. Sometimes the weight of the youth concept is laid on transition from childhood to adulthood, sometimes on a specific stage of shielded growth and experimentation, as in Erikson's moratorium. In this anthology youth refers roughly to the age sixteen to twenty-five years-old, as the age when young people in the Nordic countries gradually receive the rights and obligations of independent individuals and citizens—although some are kept longer in a continued dependent situation as unemployed.

Youth is a heavily loaded social construction, which has been associated with risks and promises in various ways. As Fangen and Frønes point out, youth is not least understood as the life phase in which future inclusion or exclusion is established; the increase in youth marginalisation is likewise seen as a fundamental challenge in post-industrial societies. Beach and Sernhede find that in the Marxist sense, in the common media representation and in schools, according to our analyses suburban youth are in a sense generally to be viewed as a *class-in-itself*: objectified, exploitable and often vilified, downtrodden and symbolically exploited in the mainstream media and common understanding. Brossard Børhaug finds a similar objectification in the national curricula of France and Norway and the analyses of Möller and Lindbäck/Sernhede of educational practices reveal that this objectification is not only a form of expression. It is also carried out in schools.

Turning the attention to *youth cultures* Qvotrup Jensen evokes the other half of the Marxist class concept, the *class-for-itself*, in understanding youth sub-cultures as creative collective responses to a shared social situation. He finds that hip-hop offers a way to ascribe value to ethnic/racial minority status through a conscious identification with the marginal position of urban black USA that offers a repertoire to reflect and comment upon experienced marginality and ascribed otherness. Hip-hop is often postmodern in identity-play and aesthetics, but by no means de-politicised, and Quotrop Jensen discards the tendency of post-subcultural approaches to decouple structural conditions from the understanding of contemporary youth culture. He adheres instead to the neo-Birminghamian understanding that subcultures are sometimes still about a collective answering of shared situations—but also that these situations are *intersectional*. The analysis of Beach and Sernhede implies this same argumentation, and so do other articles that report on young people's attitudes and actions. Mainsah's analysis of internet communication furthermore reveals that even when young people are only meeting in cyberspace they, 'are capable of actively resisting and creatively negotiating resisting dominant discourses of place, identity, and belonging in society'.

References

Foucault, M., (1977) *Discipline and Punish. The Birth of the Prison*, Harmondsworth: Penguin.

Goffman, E., (1961) *Asylums: Essays on the Social Situation of Mental Patients and other Inmates*, Garden City: Anchor Books.

Parsons, T., (1951) *The Social System*, Glencoe: Free Press

Chapter 1

Structural barriers and individual agency: A mixed-methods approach to school-work transitions among young adult immigrants and descendants

Katrine Fangen and Ivar Frønes

Introduction

The transition from education to work in our times is not necessarily a linear process, and many youth researchers use concepts such as extended youth phase and characteristics like unpredictability to describe this (e.g. (MacDonald et al., 2005, Kennely et al., 2009). The next step after finishing the mandatory school years is not given. Earlier school performance sets limits to what choices are available. Socio-economic background in general and social capital in particular also influence the perceived availability of different tracks. Furthermore, what track one chooses during the youth phase has important consequences for future inclusion or exclusion.

Having access to education and employment is obviously a critical factor in the lives of young people, but even though Norway has a system which encourages equal opportunities, statistics show that young immigrants in Norway, as in Europe in general, face greater barriers than do young people from the majority population (see e.g. Feliciano and Rumbaut, 2005, Olsen, 2009). Children of immigrants born in Norway, on the other hand, often perform at the same level as the majority population (Olsen, 2009); and young people of certain country backgrounds, like for example Indian, are at the top in school achievements in Norway, as in the UK (Henriksen, 2007, Fry et al., 2008). Nevertheless, in most European countries a picture of ethnic inequality generally emerges (Kalter and Kogan, 2006).

In this chapter, we will use both quantitative and qualitative data in order to highlight some factors that are important for the range of possibilities and barriers affecting young immigrants' and descendants' school-to-work transitions. Statistical data explain the importance of socio-economic variables in the continued marginalisation of some groups of young people. Qualitative data based on life-stories illustrate how structural and relational factors serve as a context that hinders or helps young people in making their choices regarding work and education.

Terms like *dropouts* illustrate the official view of young people who do not complete the high school/upper-secondary level. However, it is not unequivocal that those who quit school after the mandatory nine years are marginalised from the labour market: a recent Norwegian study shows that boys working at the age of seventeen to eighteen years-old were as likely to be working at the age of twenty-five years-old as boys who had finished the upper-secondary level (Frønes, 2010). This illustrates that having completed the upper-secondary level as such seems not to be the only important factor, but whether the young man was involved in something, whether it was in work or in schooling.

Life-course analyses emphasise that modern societies require *planful competence* (Clausen, 1991). The ability to plan and to act upon one's environment is not just a function of socio-economic background; social capital and other contextual resources are also important (White and Wyn, 1998, Raffo and Reeves, 2000). Both *planful competence* and social capital influence educational attainment (Dinovitzer et al., 2003). Social factors thus operate in interaction with individual factors. Quantitative data prove that *social background* correlates with future life course trajectories; however, qualitative data are needed in order to identify the importance of individual agency for exclusion or inclusion.

Methods and data

The perspective of life course analysis includes the interplay of structural and institutional contexts on the life paths of groups and individuals. This is captured in quantitative studies as patterns of relationship between factors. Summing up recent development on studies of resilience, Schoon and Bynner (2003) underline that young people may move in and out of the risk category through the life course. Such transitions between inclusion and exclusion are available through life-story data, which also makes it possible to identify the interplay of different factors and the impact of agency in an individual's life.

The macro level and the use of population registers
Through quantitative analysis based on all young non-Western immigrants and Norwegian-born with immigrant parents from the Norwegian population registers, we seek to identify the strength of some of the various *background* factors that influence the life-course development. We look for factors that strongly shape the outcome. Logistic regression, which indicates the probability

of certain outcomes related to high or low values on specific variables, suits this perspective. The tables present the odds ratio for outcomes. The odds ratio (the Exp[B]) is the ratio of the odds of an event occurring in one group to the odds of it occurring in another group, with the probabilities expressed as a ratio.

The probability ratio of today being Monday (or any other day) is, for example, one to six. When Exp(B) is 1, the chance of an outcome is 50%; a very high or low odds ratio indicates that one group has a much higher or lower chance of something than another group. The odds ratios can easily be translated into percentages of chance for something to happen to a group, related to the combinations of values of all variables. This implies, for instance, that the chances of getting a high school diploma can be calculated for groups with low or high values on a variety of indicators of social, economic, and cultural capital.

The population registers[1] refer to the whole population. Some registers are relatively new, like registers of school grades, implying that the relationship between e.g. grades at compulsory schooling and achievements at upper secondary level only can be studied among some age cohorts. Our study is based on data of all immigrant children in Norway born 1986-1988 (in one table 1987-1991). Age groups are adapted to the combination of registers. All children in the analysis are either born in Norway, or they have arrived Norway at the age of nine or younger.

Two indicators of risk of future marginalisation are chosen: dropping out of school at the upper-secondary level and being charged with crime. OECD (2012) underlines education as the gateway to employment and inclusion. Educational failure is consequently seen as the road to social exclusion. A risky life style involving crime is likewise understood as an indication of possible future exclusion. McNally and Telhaj (2007: 28) argue that becoming a young offender is, 'a one-way ticket to further exclusion'. In our analysis these two indicators are related to a set of factors of social background.

The biographical level and the life stories

The quantitative data gives us insight in important indicators of social exclusion, but life-story interviews are necessary in order to find out how young people of ethnic minority background actively relate to barriers and opportunities, and how their plans are affected by both strong and weak ties to other persons in their surroundings (cf., Granovetter, 1973). In order to study how young

---

1　Register-based statistics in the Nordic countries. Review of best practices with focus on population and social statistics. United Nations, New York and Geneva, 2007.

people of ethnic minority background plan and how significant others affect
their choices, the second part of this chapter is based on analyses of semi-
structured life-story interviews with young people from a variety of ethnic and
socio-economic backgrounds taken from fifty qualitative interviews collected in
Norway for a European comparative project of young adult immigrants (eighteen
to twenty-six year-olds) and descendants of immigrants (EUMARGINS).[2]
We have strategically selected cases from this sample that might illustrate the
complex dynamic of inclusion and exclusion within a life story. Such transitions
between inclusion and exclusion over time are not possible to study merely with
quantitative data. Most of the interviews were conducted by research assistants
and master's degree students in their twenties and early thirties, thus more or
less the same age as the interviewees (some interviews were also conducted
by Fangen, who was the project coordinator). Some of the interviewers were
themselves immigrants or descendants of immigrants. The case presentations
are given as closely as possible to how the interviewees presented themselves in
the interviews; direct quotations are given in italics.

Factors influencing school achievement

Scandinavian longitudinal studies show that social background is mediated
through educational achievements, but also that failure at school exerts an
autonomous influence on the risk of future social exclusion (Berlin, Vinnerljung,
and Hjern, 2011). Table 1 shows factors influencing the level of grades achieved
when finishing compulsory schooling. All of the factors indicate the level of
economic, social, and cultural capital, but point to different aspects of the social
background of the young person. Having had the first child as a teenager is an
indication of social and cultural background, not only an indication of early
motherhood as such. The factor termed *employment* of father and mother is a
dichotomised version of an index based on years of employment and relative
income per year; as such it indicates the level of integration into the labour
market. High value on the employment index is related to high education or high
competence, as well as to years of employment. This is a more fruitful indication
in this context than education as such, since the majority of the parents have
low formal education, and are often working in a sector not related to their
education or training. All variables are dichotomised.[3]

2   The total sample is two hundred and fifty life-story interviews from seven countries.

3   Employment indicators are dichotomised into the two highest and lowest quartiles; not in
    employment is included in the category of low employment. For mothers the cut off is set as

Table 1. Logistic regression: likelihood of getting over/under 40 grade-points upon finishing compulsory schooling. *Independent variables; mother's and father's position in the labour market, whether the mother had her first child as a teenager or has been single for a period, and the gender of the child. Children born, 1987-1991*

	B	Sig.	Exp(B)
Father's employment at 40	.204	.000	1.226
Mother's employment at 35	.564	.000	1.758
Mother been/not a single mother for a period	-.231	.000	.794
Mother had children before age of 20	-.716	.000	.489
Gender	.735	.000	2.086
Constant	-2.262	.000	.104

Nagelkerke R Square = 0.088

The dependent variable in table 1 is getting over/under 40 grade-points[4] when completing compulsory schooling. (The average grade-point level in Norway in the period was well above 40 for girls and less than 40 for boys; about sixty per cent of boys and 40 per cent of girls in this age group have fewer than 40 points on the national level.) Table 1 indicates that the chance of getting good grades is positively related to both father's and mother's integration into the labour market, and negatively related to having a mother who had her first child as a teenager. Girls have a higher probability of good grades than boys. Odds ratios can be transformed into probabilities expressed as percentages. If both parents are not well integrated into the labour market, and the mother had her first child as a teenager and has for a period been a single mother, only 12 per cent of the boys and 23 per cent of the girls are likely to have 40 points or more. If the mother has never been a single mother, had her first child at 20 years-old or older, and the parents are well integrated into the labour market, the figures would be 40-three per cent for boys and 60 per cent for girls. Configuration of social background factors influence grades at primary school, but do not determine educational achievements.

between being employed or not, among men the cut of is between the two highest and lowest quartiles.

4   Grade points in compulsory schooling refer to an indication of total grades at school.

Factors influencing drop out at the upper secondary level

OECD (2012) underlines that the finalisation of upper secondary level is an indication of the future of the individual as well as of the nation or region. In Table 2, the dependent variable is dichotomised into completed upper-secondary level/did not complete upper-secondary level. The independent factors are identical to table 2, but two factors are added; having ever been charged with crime, and grades at compulsory schooling, dichotomised into over/under 40 grade point.

Table 2. Logistic regression: the likelihood of having completed upper-secondary education. *Independent variables: mother's and father's position in the labour market, whether the mother had her first child as a teenager, the sex of the child, and grade-points when finishing compulsory schooling. Children born 1986-1988, educational level spring 2009.*

	B	Sig.	Exp(B)
Father's employment at 40	0.203	.016	1.226
Mother's employment at 35	0.097	.188	1.101
Mother been/not been a single mother for a period	-0.395	.000	0.674
Mother had children before age of 20	0.320	.000	1.378
Gender	0.113	.074	1.120
Ever been charged with crime	-0.998	.000	0.369
Grade points	2.144	.000	8.531
Constant	-2.965	.000	0.052

Nagelkerke R Square = 0.043

Factors influencing school drop-out ratios

In sociological theorising of social class, parental influence often appears as a transmission of the habitus and capitals of classes (see, e.g., Bourdieu, 1984). Later studies on socialisation underscore the importance of active parental support and monitoring, as illustrated by the middle-class praxes of upbringing termed 'concerted cultivation' (Lareau, 2003). The development of the capacity for life-course planning, critical in today's educational society, is an essential part of middle-class upbringing. Individual capacity for navigation and planning is likely to be more important for young immigrants moving into the unknown than for middle-class youth with their middle-class habitus and naturalised knowledge about dominant styles and codes. The success of South-Asian immigrants in USA is related to their stressing of hard work and achievements. In fact 39 per cent of Asian-Americans said that parents from their subgroup put too much pressure on their children related to school achievements, thus indicating the role of family culture (Pew Research Centre, 2012).

Table 2 shows that father's and the mother's level of integration into the workforce increases the chances of further schooling only to a modest degree when other factors like educational achievements are controlled for. The mother who has had her first child as a teenager influences further schooling negatively. But as the odds ratios show the factor that influenced the likelihood of finalising upper-secondary level of education the strongest when other factors controlled for, is the grade level when leaving compulsory schooling.

The interplay of factors can be illustrated by the chance of finalising upper-secondary level related to various combinations of social background factors; if the parents have low labour participation, and if the mother had her first child at a young age, has been single for a period and the child has less than 40 grade points, 34 per cent of both boys and 46 per cent of girls among these cohorts will have finished upper-secondary education. With a *low* score on background factors but high scores on grade-points, this increases to 83 per cent of boys and 88 per cent of girls. Among the few boys charged with crime, 17 per cent had finalised upper-secondary level. Almost no one with over average grade level had ever been charged with crime. If the parents were integrated into the labour market, if the mother never was single or a teenage mother but the child had under 40 grade points, the percentage finalising upper-secondary level would be about 51 per cent for boys and 54 per cent for girls; when social resourceful background is combined with good grades almost everyone (90 per cent and 91 per cent) finalised upper-secondary level. Socio-economic status influences grades at school, but when controlling for the other factors, grade-points exert strong influence on the chances for further education.

Grades, when finalising compulsory schooling, are the end result of a long and complex socialisation process. The impact of the grade-level from compulsory schooling indicates that a series of factors rooted in the family culture, local context, sub-cultural gender patterns and characteristics of the individuals influence school achievements; and that these factors are of great importance related to immigrant youth, who in general will be in a weaker position than other groups in terms of general economic, social and cultural capital.

Indicators of risk for social exclusion; the probability of being charged with crime

The statistics on being charged with crime presented here include all kinds of possible crimes, but are nonetheless an indication of risk. Table 3 shows a logistic regression of the relationship between background factors and being charged with a crime. The indicator is operationalised as having been charged/never been charged, with any sort of crime.

Table 3. Logistic regression; risk as indicated by probability of being charged with crime. *Covariates; mother's and father's employment/position at the labour market, whether the mother had her first child as teenager, sex/gender, and grade points when leaving compulsory schooling. All immigrant children born 1987-1991, crime registered before 2009*

	B	Sig.	Exp(B)
Father's employment at 40	−0.141	0.257	0.868
Mother's employment at 35	−0.094	0.364	0.911
Mother been/not been a single mother for a period	0.426	0.000	1.531
Mother had children before age of 20	−0.475	0.000	0.622
Gender	−1.626	0.000	0.197
Grade points	−1.615	0.000	0.199
Constant	2.997	0.000	20.027

Nagelkerke R Square = .174

The importance of school grades as relates to crime may be rooted in grades being an access road to the future that is blocked for those who leave school, and good grades may be an indication of distance to the street culture. Resilience, a good outcome despite risk, can be rooted in individual capacities, in interaction with specific significant others, or in institutional contexts supporting and encouraging talents and capacities. Behind the statistical patterns there is complex interaction between individual life courses, groups, and social contexts. The importance of grades also illustrates the importance of agency; agency is shaped by processes involving individual factors and the structures of local contexts.

Table 3 shows that the factors influencing being charged with crime are primarily gender and level of grade points when completing compulsory schooling; the mother having the first child as a teenager also exerts influence when other factors are controlled for. Grades are related to social background, but the level of parental employment has little direct influence on the chance of being charged with crime when school grades are brought into the equation.

Grades when finishing compulsory schooling are influenced by social background factors, but not at all determined by them. The effects of background factors are largely mediated through grades, even if teenage motherhood as such influences the risk of marginalisation. If the mother had her first child as a teenager; had spent at least a period as a single mother; the child had less than 40 points when finalising compulsory schooling; and the parents were low on integration in the labour marked: then 35 per cent of the boys and 9 per cent of the girls had been charged with crime. With 40 grade points or more, the percentages charged with crime were 10 per cent for boys and 2 per cent for girls. If the mother did not have her first child when she was under 20; the parents were low on integration in the labour market; and the child had 40 points or more at compulsory schooling: the percentages charged with crime were 4 per cent for boys and 0 per cent for girls. With under 40 grade point the figure was 18 per cent for boys and 4 per cent for girls.

Grades are an indication of life-course processes, not only of position in the educational system as such. Being charged with crime correlates with social background factors. But the correlation between grades and being charged with crime when other factors are controlled for, indicates that criminal behaviours are rooted in local contexts and individual characteristics.

Patterns and mechanisms of inclusion and exclusion

The analysis above refers to all young people in Norway with an immigrant background (including both immigrants and descendants). The reason why we do not bring in *ethnicity* as such is not only because what is referred to as *ethnic factors* often are just the amount of relevant cultural and social capital and the history of the various immigrant groups, but also because of the strong variation in the social background of young immigrants. *Ethnic background* indicated by the national background of the family, for instance, is primarily a very crude indication of social and cultural factors that vary considerably within each ethnic category.

The patterns indicate that cultural and social capital is mediated through educational achievements. But poor grades are an indication of future exclusion independent of social background factors. The autonomous effect of education and the autonomous effect of being involved in crime indicates the importance. Educational failure or success is a result of the interplay of individual agency and contextual factors, not a delimited factor related to social background or the educational institutions as such.

The relationship between factors of social background and life course is contingent, not determined. Studies of resilience show how children may manage in spite of severe conditions (Luthar and Sigler, 1991). Factors facilitating resilience range from genetic profiles to significant others in the environment. Behind the statistical patterns there are a variety of individual roads leading to social inclusion and exclusion.

Paths to exclusion and inclusion;
The influence of environments, families and peers
Social resources (or the lack thereof) in families and neighbourhoods influence individual life courses (Fangen, 2010). Relationships with parents, siblings and peers can encourage certain educational or vocational paths, but can also pull in another direction than the one a young person aims at. Kenan was born and raised in a North-Eastern suburb of Oslo. His parents came from Turkey to Norway during the 1970s. Kenan's father was fourteen to fifteen years-old when he came to Norway. Kenan looks up to him, describes him as, 'a fighter who doesn't give up very easily'.

Kenan expresses a wish to be seen as someone who acts properly and who does not involve himself in crime, but it seems that the environment he lives in is a major pull factor in the wrong direction. According to him, it is an area where many criminals live. He states that, 'those who are between eighteen and twenty-four are always driving fancy cars by the [shopping] centre. They just stop there, give you dirty looks, and speak their own language.' Kenan, in his presentation of himself, on the one hand points out that he has a big smile that charms people, but on the other hand, if they try to hit him he is familiar with self-defence. 'I have worked out, and I am quite large. I weigh a hundred kilos. I hit tons. I can pass just two to three strikes, and he's dead. And I know pretty well where to hit', he states. However, Kenan underlines that his motivation for working out is not to defend himself. On the contrary, he thinks he would have been more aggressive if he had not worked out: 'working out makes me relaxed, and I smile to people.' When asked whether he has been involved in criminal groups, Kenan says it is a difficult question and then remains quiet for a long time. The interviewer then asks whether it is common for young people to get involved in a criminal crowd. Kenan responds:

> It is common. Do you know how it starts? [They say:] 'Hey, come here. Why are you giving us dirty looks?' 'I didn't give you dirty looks, I didn't

do anything.' Then another one comes over and says the same: 'hey, he gave us dirty looks' and hits him with the elbow. If he's tough, he gets up and says, 'Come on! Come!' then the other one says, 'you are tough! Why don't you join our gang?' do you understand? But when you push someone, and he gets up and runs off, they think, 'no, forget about him.' That's how one gets involved in criminal groups.

This is how other young people in the neighbourhood might serve as social capital pulling in the wrong direction. As Kenan describes it, it is easy to be dragged in by the social influence of these tough guys, and hard to stay aloof of it. Kenan has had several brief stays in prison. He says he has a lot of friends with good lawyers, and once a lawyer helped him get out immediately. 'When you have a big, strong lawyer who also is well known, they don't touch you, you know', Kenan says. Despite these references to having been involved in criminal acts, Kenan states that he will work with anything that brings in money as long as it is not criminal. When asked which groups he does not want to be a part of, Kenan says gangs. 'Because when you are doing business and are seen with them it's a bad example'. He adds: 'I try to live like a Norwegian. Follow the laws. So I've called the police several times saying this and that has happened.'

When he is with his friends, they often are a group of thirty to forty people. Kenan tells us about his friends that, 'seventy per cent of them are from abroad. Twenty per cent of them are Norwegians. And they are mainly girls. Perhaps two per cent of them are boys. And the rest of them are just Turkish.' He rarely hangs out with ethnic Norwegian youth in his spare time. Kenan says that this is mainly due to cultural reasons. He tells a story about an ethnic Norwegian colleague who asked if Kenan had a sister and then started to do, 'bad talk'. This resulted in Kenan, 'hitting and almost killing him'. He states he will not tolerate conversations like, 'do you have a sister? Let me have her?' and that he would gladly risk twenty years in prison for reacting to such comments.

He did manage to complete upper-secondary school, but does not want to pursue further education; instead he works a day job. 'My only priority [now] is to do business', Kenan states. Kenan dreams of owning a holding—a five to six floor office building where he will be the, 'big boss' of 300-400 people with a helicopter on the roof.'

In addition to the bad influence stemming from his peer group, Kenan's family background is part of the explanation why he does not prioritise school and education. His father currently runs a shop and has invested a great deal in Turkey. Kenan states that after opening the shop, his father was the first *immigrant* who bought a Mercedes C500. 'He was one of the richest ones before. He is still rich,' Kenan explains. Similar to his father, Kenan gambles and plays a lot of poker on the internet and abroad. Kenan spends his money on 'having style'—mentions he has a watch worth 10,000 Euro, but he does not like bragging about such things. 'People who see it know. But only idiots brag. It's not my style', he says.

Omar is another young man of Turkish descent living in the same neighbourhood as Kenan, but who has managed to distance himself more from the criminal elements in his environment. He says that one reason for this is that his parents have been very strict with him, which is related to the fact that Omar's brother was in prison for two years. Earlier, Omar's parents disapproved of Omar's style of clothing—what he calls yoyo style, 'like 50 Cent'. He says his father got frantic and yelled a lot. Omar says that his mother has told him that his father, 'used to be kind', but that he changed a lot when he came to Norway and both of Omar's older brothers committed criminal acts. Omar explains his brother's previous criminal acts as based on the group of people around him. Omar believes that after witnessing the changes in his son, his father decided that Omar should not become like his brother. Omar explains that it means a lot to him that his parents are proud of him. He is closest to his mother and shares everything with her particularly since she does not tell his father when the children have done mischievous things. Sometimes he even helps his mother financially.

As for the neighbourhood influence, Omar himself concludes that the neighbourhood is bad. There is a lot of vandalism and yelling from the apartments. He went to a school with pupils mainly of an ethnic minority background. In the weekend he goes out, relaxes with his friends and goes to the cinema. Six months back, Omar spent more time with friends from different ethnic backgrounds. But recently he has found himself spending more and more time with his cousins. He says he feels more drawn to his family and that after one starts working there is less time for many friends.

Omar's father was a politician in Turkey. He came to Norway as a labour migrant, in order to earn more money. Due to an extended period of illness, he is currently on social allowance. Omar's mother is a housewife. His brother runs a grocery store, where Omar had his first job. Omar has worked since he was seventeen. He now works as a painter, a job he likes. But he would prefer to work in an office, because he thinks it is a less demanding kind of job. Similar to

Kenan, Omar also dreams of being a manager, signing the odd paper and making a few phone calls. Omar has been fed up with school since ninth grade. However, in order to please his mother and because he has witnessed the limited options his elder brothers have had after not completing upper-secondary school, he is considering taking up school again.

In these two examples, we see that peers and neighbourhoods are factors that can pull individuals away from school and education, while crime and gangs are options for young men in certain neighbourhoods. The biographies of the two young men have a lot in common, but the social networks influencing their life course are different. Obtaining a job as a painter, like Omar has, may have served as a counter-factor to crime, but also the will to avoid ending up like his brother (or other peers in the neighbourhood). Kenan also wants to stay clear of criminal activities, but has not managed this equally well. Kenan states that he keeps his distance from gangs, but on the other hand, he seems to be very familiar with the codes of the criminal landscape of his peers and in many ways represents the kind of self-presentation that is prevalent in his neighbourhood and that pulls him in the opposite direction of education and work.

Difficult family background, but finding one's way
In the previous section we discussed two cases of young men growing up in a peer environment that was pulling them towards being street-wise, and away from school. In this section we will discuss a case from a better neighbourhood, but where the negative family atmosphere has made it difficult to achieve (Fangen and Lynnebakke, 2010). Fatima grew up in a neighbourhood in the southern part of Oslo, one of Oslo's first suburbs, where there is a mix between elderly ethnic Norwegians and immigrants and their descendants. Fatima liked it there, and from her comments it is clear that she prefers not to live in an immigrant dense neighbourhood, and especially not a place where many Pakistanis live. She particularly refers to a short period when she lived in a suburb dominated by Pakistanis.

Fatima's father came as a labour migrant from Pakistan to Norway in the early 1970s. Some years later, he married Fatima's mother, bringing her over from Pakistan. She had originally planned to study, but her plans were changed when she got married, moved to Norway, and gave birth to four children. The mother stayed at home and took care of the children, while Fatima's father worked to support them all. He built up his own shop, selling *Bollywood* movies, and he had to work long hours. Therefore, they normally did not eat dinner together as a whole family. Fatima sometimes skipped meals because she lost her appetite due to the atmosphere at home. Struggling economically in a three-room apartment with six people took its toll on the family.

Fatima's parents wanted to nourish their Pakistani background by visiting Pakistan occasionally. The cost of these trips added to the expenses, and the father had to work even more. It is quite painful and challenging when only one person can pay back the home loan and feed six persons at the same time, Fatima states. She reveals that: 'If you have too much debt, you get no help. You have to get rid of the entire loan to get help. Especially dark people struggle with this'. Fatima recounts that when her father came home in the evenings her parents often quarrelled in the living room. The children often found themselves in conflict with their father; they did not feel he had time for them, while the mother was always present. Fatima states that her father had retained the, 'traditional beliefs' that the position and decision-making role of the eldest male in the family should be much more respected than what his children were taught in Norway. Fatima refers (in third person) to the cultural and generational gap between their father and his children. Fatima attributes her father's remoteness to the fact that he immigrated without his closest family to Norway and lost his own father at a young age. Fatima's father wasn't comfortable with seeking social security benefits because: '... mostly foreigners, dark people who didn't have money came there. Felt like begging for money.'

The family's difficulties and her father's depression resulted in him leaving the family. Since the mother did not speak Norwegian, new challenges for looking after the children arose. Returning to Pakistan was not an option because after the divorce the relatives in Pakistan rejected her. According to Fatima, the turning point came when her elder sister explained to her mother about the possibilities Norway had to offer: '... This is Norway, not Pakistan; a woman has as much right as a man. A woman does not need to be dependent on her husband. She (...) will not let herself be treated unjustly.'

The struggles within the family clearly marked Fatima, and for a period of time, she was depressed too. According to herself, she was always at home, had few friends and was never together with friends after school. She struggled to finish high school and changed school several times. At the age of twenty-three she finished upper secondary school successfully, completing her final exam on the fifth attempt. But since then Fatima has gradually taken command of her own life, and many of the struggles of growing up are left behind. She found a job in a convenience store, her first job ever. She really enjoyed this job, both in terms of tasks and colleagues. Today, she only works there when they need extra help, and in the meantime she has an interim position as a schoolteacher. Fatima's dream is to become a teacher; even though she found school tiresome earlier. She has got a new mission to help children in a similar situation to cope better in school.

Fatima has gradually found her way, come out of depression and for the first time experienced inclusion, both at the convenience store where she now works part-time, at a course where she learned to make films and at the school where she has a temporary position. Fatima's case reveals how the feelings of inclusion and exclusion change over time and how they may relate to both the parent's migratory story and one's own sense of isolation or community. Fatima's case illustrates the importance of agency: by trying out different paths, she found her way and managed to free herself from the demotivating influence of her family situation.

Planful competence and self–efficacy: The will to succeed

The previous examples are a great contrast to several cases in our material that illustrate what we have termed *planful competence*. The statistical data indicates that educational success, or at least the absence of failure, correlates with certain background factors, but this does not mean that it is *determined* by social background. *Planfulness* is the orientation of those young persons who not only do whatever they can to overcome the barriers they face, but who strategically plan to work their way up the ladder in order to achieve their educational and professional goals.

Twenty-two-year-old Haile is an obvious example of this attitude (Paasche, 2010). He came to Norway from Ethiopia seven years ago. His entire family in Ethiopia had good sources of income since they had all pursued an education. Haile's mother was a teacher in Ethiopia, but after coming to Norway her rib broke, so she engaged in an adult learning programme. His step-father, who was a head teacher in Ethiopia, now works as a bus driver. The reason why Haile's step-father emigrated was that he was forced to join the government political party. Both Haile's stepfather, Haile's mother and for a short period Haile himself, were imprisoned. Haile's stepfather, however, managed to flee to Kenya, then to Norway as a quota refugee. Haile wanted to finish his education in auto-technology before emigrating through family reunion. He thought this education would give him competence in newer technologies. Initially, after arriving in Norway, Haile applied for a number of jobs in the field of automechanics without any luck. In his opinion this was partly due to his imperfect grasp of the Norwegian language, but also due to having a foreign name and being deemed untrustworthy by employers who favoured ethnic Norwegians.

It would take years of studying for the Norwegian authorities to verify his educational qualifications, so Haile preferred to start his education in Norway from scratch. After spending seven months in a reception class, he completed the Norwegian language test with 88 out of 100 points. He may have been lucky to have been enrolled in the school where he ended up, which he describes as *fantastic*, and which ranks among Oslo's best schools with a lot of very focused pupils. On the other hand, it was not easy for him being the only pupil in class who had recently immigrated to Norway. His lack of Norwegian language skills meant that none of the other pupils wanted to do group work with him or help him out in class, making it hard to practice his Norwegian and improve. Nor was anyone keen on conversing in English with him. 'Yeah it went on like that for a long time, really. But I don't care because if I don't understand I ask the teachers.'

His peers were not favourably inclined to what they saw as favouritism by the teachers towards Haile. He was bullied by one of the pupils. Once, this classmate called him 'negro,' leading him unwillingly into his first fight. He says he is not that kind of person. Over time his Norwegian improved spectacularly. In the interview he said that he used all his time on school-work, and even though he made several friends, he tried to spend as much time on school work as possible, minimising the time spent with friends.

In the end he was able to successfully complete upper secondary school with generally good grades within three years, the average amount of time. One of the teachers would prove crucial in his personal development, by offering support way beyond the parameters of professional involvement. This teacher was always willing to answer his questions and even met Haile after school hours, sometimes accompanied by family members. The teacher was a Christian, like Haile, and had travelled repeatedly to Ethiopia because of his fondness for the Ethiopian people. This may have partly formed the basis for their friendship, which also outlasted Haile's school days.

After having completed upper secondary school, a friend of Haile helped him get a job at a nursing home. When Haile's teacher heard that he had got a job as a nurse and was contemplating taking up nursing studies, the teacher continued to support him. 'My teacher called and asked several places, and he got in touch with a friend of his who had specialised as a nurse, to ask him for all kinds of information. Then he said, "Haile, you must choose nursing. It's a secure job and it's multicultural". This was confirmed by Haile's own enquiries at the nursing home where he worked. So he opted for this line of study. He did not take a gap year and has chosen not to work alongside his present studies at the nursing school, but instead dedicates himself fully to them. If his grades are good, he plans to continue with neurology. Some of his patients from the nursing home have neurological problems, and he thinks this is an interesting field of specialisation. This is another thing that he likes better about Norway, namely that you have different career options and possibilities. Here, Haile says, if you set goals for yourself you can make a good future.

Haile keeps in close contact with his own family in Norway, and attributes his relative success to his family. As for making a family of his own, that is not yet on the short-term agenda, as he first needs to establish himself professionally. He did have a girlfriend in school but found it stressful, as he did not have much time to spare. He believes he has spent maybe two to three times more time than his native peers on school-related work, and will need even more time during higher education.

His friends with immigrant background, some of whom come from Gambia and Somalia, are similarly hard-working and ambitious, and they sometimes study together. Still, Haile states, there is a special cultural disposition for education in Ethiopia. Exceedingly few do drugs, he says. This cultural trait is something Haile thinks emigrants bring with them.

> Yeah, you know, in the homeland, there's just one way. You have to study, finish your degree; like that you improve your economic situation and other things. That line of thought is still there with us here. Here there are jobs, you can earn money. But it doesn't matter, we still think like that. It helps a lot. One has to be strong, physically and mentally.

This example might serve to illustrate several aspects of how different mechanisms work together to produce a certain outcome. First, it must be pointed out that Haile's parents had much higher education than the parents of both Kenan and Omar when they arrived in Norway. Thus, part of the explanation of Haile's high ambitions and achievements can be traced back to his family background. Another important aspect is Haile's strong will to succeed. He has met several barriers since he came to Norway, including being bullied at school, applying for jobs without getting any answer and so forth, but he never gave up. He was willing not to spend too much time with friends and not have a girlfriend just in order to prioritise his school-work. Another explanatory factor was the support he received from some significant others, like the schoolteacher who followed up on Haile not only at school but also outside. Haile's life course also illustrates that environment is not static, environment changes with the actions of the subject; with a new job, a new social context appears.

Factual families; Family pressure and socio-economic background

In our sample there are also young migrants or descendants of migrants whose parents made a lot of effort guiding their children to pursue certain kinds of occupations, good school performance and to take élite educations. In particular, we see this among some of our informants with Indian origin. Take for example twenty-three year-old Mahan who says he never felt forced by his parents to take a higher education, but that he was always told the benefits of it. Since primary school his parents, especially his father, stressed that it is positive to have the opportunity to learn. Many family members have a higher education. His father thinks that when one has a different ethnicity to the majority population in a country one needs to, 'excel and show that one is just as good'. To have the same job opportunities it was necessary to do better than ethnic Norwegians, according to his father's view. Mahan himself always felt that if he did something—i.e. sports and school, he might as well do his best. Mahan internalised his father's view about the necessity to outperform others, but states that nowadays he doesn't feel his Indian background will be a disadvantage in the job market. However, later he says that he feels that in his profession he needs to work harder because he might not have the same network.

Mahan feels that his parents worked hard, 'to make sure that I and my little brother have all the opportunities in the world.' Mahan became a doctor because his family wanted him to. His father was explicit about this. The father found medical studies valuable because it is a highly esteemed profession all over the world. Mahan also believes his father is happy about his son's choice because he didn't follow this path himself when he had the opportunity twenty years ago, but instead decided to follow the IT boom. Initially, Mahan wanted to choose another line of study; he was interested in the social sciences and wanted to study international relations. Mahan's grades from upper secondary school were very good, and his father convinced him to give medicine a shot for a year since he had the opportunity. His father promised that if he didn't like it, he wouldn't, 'pester him any more'.

A similar example is Daiva, who is studying in her final year of dentistry. She was born and raised in Oslo. Daiva's parents, both from New Delhi, came to Norway thirty years ago. Her parents emigrated because they wanted to increase their opportunities and, 'get out of the misery' of high competition for few jobs. They had jobs, but wanted greater stability and to achieve more, Daiva says it was a bit like the American dream. Daiva's mother is educated as a nurse from India, whereas her father had some kind of engineering education from India. In Norway he pursued further education as a mechanical engineer and then did some further studies after that too. Ten years ago he was authorised as an accountant and now runs his own accounting firm. Daiva's father likes to learn new things and is now studying real estate and stocks. He invests in properties abroad, something Daiva would perhaps like to do herself because it will enable her to travel, which she loves. Daiva's mother worked as a nurse in Norway until she got partly disabled.

Similar to the previous case, Daiva's family also expects her to pursue higher education. She did not feel pushed; it was just an expectation of her. Her parents always *hinted* that because of the path they followed, they were in a better position now, rather than telling Daiva specifically what to do. She first considered medicine and later decided to go for dentistry in order to have more spare time and not work shifts. In addition to working with people she wanted to have a secure job. She enjoys her chosen field a lot.

Daiva says her parents used to brag about her studies, that this generated pride among Indians. But she told them not to take credit for her achievements. She says there is a lot of comparison of children's achievements among the Indian community, and that the kids that excel according to the ideals are pointed out as an example to follow for the other children. She laughs and says that, 'after a lot of war' her parents have accepted that she did not want to be compared with others.

When Daiva had an exam at school her parents went out of their way to ensure she was comfortable, for instance driving her to school, making sure it was quiet for her to study at home, and she was exempt from performing housework. She says they were more nervous than she was. But they were also supportive if she feared failing, telling her it is not the end of the world and that she will have more chances. Daiva explains Indians' focus on getting a high prestige education by the fact that they come from a country with fierce competition for jobs, even when one has a higher education. These attitudes carry over here, she explains.

Despite her parents' involvement in her pursuit of a higher education, Daiva says they don't know much about the Norwegian educational system. Daiva has one younger brother who studies economics at a private business school. Daiva's friends have different ethnic backgrounds, but most of them are ethnic Norwegians. Daiva states that she has not felt discriminated against for being dark-skinned and thinks this may be due to growing up in a multicultural environment on the east side of Oslo. From kindergarten to upper secondary school she had friends from various backgrounds and never felt discriminated against. She says she might be naïve and arrogant because she has never felt excluded for being different the way she has heard others have. Daiva thinks that generally speaking, ethnic Norwegians and those with a minority background have the same opportunities in the labour market.

In both these examples we see that family pressure is partly related to cultural background, at least according to these interviewees themselves, who highlight this kind of family pressure as typical of Indians. This factor is not fully equivalent to cultural capital, since it is not only about knowledge, mastery of the majority culture and qualifications. It is more about family pressure and expectations, what Lareau (2003) referred to as *concerted cultivation*. Although these young persons also have an internal drive to accumulate the *capital* necessary to succeed in their careers, this drive is also born out of the family culture, as well as by their expectations of what they need to do in order to be ranked high among other Indians.

Comparison and discussion of case stories

In the qualitative cases presented here we see actions that illustrate the aggregated patterns, but also a much more complex interplay of different factors than the quantitative data can reveal. Life stories can take unexpected paths, and the interplay between roots (background) and routes (the way one more or less consciously chooses) is not possible to unravel with general correlations.

In many of the cases presented here we see the importance of general social background factors, however, the influence of these factors is modified by values and expectations of the significant others that the individual has around him/her. Both the young men of Turkish descent grew up in a north eastern suburb of Oslo and have parents with low education and either peers or siblings who were involved in criminal acts. One of them dropped out of school after the mandatory nine years and got a manual labour job, whereas the other finished upper secondary school, but has no regular job, and earns his way by different kinds of work (including gambling). These young men both have a wish to stay away from gangs and criminality, but between the lines we understand that they have not succeeded one hundred per cent. They both have an urge to gain quick money and the perhaps unrealistic dream of becoming a boss of some big business. The neighbourhood influence pulls them away from education. However, Kenan's and Omar's relations to the environment differ somewhat; Omar has parents who struggle to keep him out of the criminal environment, whereas Kenan indicates that he is proud of being able to fight, and he knows the codes and styles of the street. Omar has a greater distance from the criminal masculine environment, partly because of strict parents who want him to behave better than his brothers.

In Fatima's case we see the importance of individual agency. Despite coming from a family haunted by severe conflicts and living in a small apartment with many siblings, Fatima managed to finish upper secondary school after the fifth attempt. Her background made her route through the school system a difficult one. Making friends and an income of her own for the first time made her job in the convenience store feel like a great achievement and made her feel included. Later on she got a job-with-benefits position as a schoolteacher, and she has become inspired to take up school again in order to become a teacher, helping other children who are equally tired of school as she once was. Previously it seemed that higher education was not a necessary factor for Fatima's life satisfaction, but as life improved, she started considering this. It was the gradual feeling of autonomy when making friends in the mixed-ethnic environment of the convenience store and at a film course arranged by a youth organisation that kicked off her transition from exclusion to inclusion. This illustrates that good peers and a welcoming environment are important to social inclusion, especially for someone who felt school was a struggle and who felt isolated during her school years. Life course events are related to deeper social structures and role patterns, but there are also crucial events than can open the way to future inclusion.

Haile, Mahan and Daiva have parents with higher education and they come from an environment where higher education is praised. Haile seems to have had a stronger internal drive to achieve, whereas Daiva and Mahan both explain their relative success partly by family pressure; as the family culture is strongly directed towards education. Pressure can be seen as one specific quality of social capital. The success of many Indian students in Europe (Fekjær, 2007; Fry et al., 2008) cannot be explained by the transmission of habitus, in Bourdieu's sense, but by parental pressure and a specific family culture.

For Haile, the most important factors seem to be his own strong will and the support of his teacher, rather than strong expectations from his parents. The teacher represents the significant other that incidentally comes into some young people's lives. Haile also sees himself as part of an educated culture, he expects himself to achieve a high level of education.

In the few cases we have presented here, we see that the different outcomes with regard to educational performance are related to factors such as the level of education of parents, environmental factors (both from the homeland and from the neighbourhood), and social capital in the form of the presence or the lack of support from family or others, but also to individual agency.

Conclusion: The dynamics of inclusion and exclusion

What can we learn from a combined analysis of qualitative and quantitative material? The factors that were identified by the statistical analysis are also found in the life courses depicted in the interviews. The relationship to schooling is critical for the future life course. The various cases illustrate how school achievements reflect broader processes of socialisation and resources available in families, schools and neighbourhoods, but they also illustrate the importance of individual agency. Failure at school may increase the likelihood of risky behaviour and being involved with crime. Social capital is important, but the qualitative data show that social capital takes many forms. For young immigrants, the encouragement and expectations of parents are particularly important, since the family is not part of the dominant cultural habitus. The young individuals' own *planfulness* may in fact be inherited as forms of cultural and social capital, but can also be a capacity that is gradually developed through the child's experiences with planning, choices, and success.

At the micro level we see that gangs and peer cultures that are attractive to some are not so to others. The gradients of attraction and distance are developed through processes of socialisation and influence from significant others. The environment represents a symbolic system of codes, as well as a system of resources. The local environments are partly conditioned by structural conditions, but accidental events, new contacts and changes of environment can be the necessary tools for a young individual to change his or her course. Significant others are not necessarily parents or class mates; teachers or peers from other contexts, such as temporary jobs and leisure activities can in some cases offer the encouragement an individual needs in order to find his or her way. The individual biographies illustrate that *planfulness* and agency are positively related to resources in the environment and not least in the family. But they also show that agency is developed by a set of factors and relations, and is not just a reflection of the general indexes of resources.

The statistical analyses provide information on general social patterns and directions for policy making, for instances, when failure in compulsory schooling influences the life course. But the mechanisms of this development have to be sought behind the data given in the tables. Grades are influenced by the social or cultural capital of the family, but children are also directly influenced by the intensity of the monitoring of the parents. Both our Indian cases have parents with higher education, but in her study of young Norwegian-Indians who pursue élite educations in Norway, Finne (2010) also had several informants whose parents only had lower education, but where the pressure on the children to go on to higher education was strong anyway. This seems to be explained by the fact that part of the reason why their parents migrated was to improve the educational opportunities for their children. The parents have sacrificed much, and the children are expected to repay this with their struggle to get themselves a good education.

The fact that having finalised upper secondary education correlates with a positive future life course does not imply that all children will profit from trying to complete the upper secondary level. Some young people can be qualified for jobs they like through other channels; Fatima's first step towards a trajectory of inclusion was a job at 7-Eleven. She is now interested in pursuing further education to become a teacher, but it took time for her to come to this conclusion. The upper secondary level may support her in realising other ambitions, but the positive consequences of her job illustrate something that is also indicated in other studies: a correlation between not completing the upper secondary level and future marginalisation does not mean that traditional upper secondary schooling provides all young people with inclusion; there are other routes to inclusion in the labour market.

The important information that can be gained from life stories is that even if major trajectories can be identified from the statistical material, paths are dynamic processes in which actions and sequences of actions influence the future life path. The development of *policies* requires knowledge about patterns, as well as about the heterogeneous dynamics behind the patterns.

References

Berlin, M., Vinnerljung, B., and Hjern, A., (2011) School performance in primary school and psychosocial problems in young adulthood among care leavers from long term foster care, *Children and Youth Services Review,* 33(12): 2489-2497.

Bourdieu, P., (1984) *Distinction: A social critique of the judgement of taste,* London: Routledge.

Clausen, J. S., (1991) Adolescent competence and the shaping of the life course, *American Journal of Sociology,* 96(4): 805-842.

Dinovitzer, R., J. Hagan, and Parker, P., (2003) Choice and circumstance: social capital and planful competence in the attainments of immigrant youth, *Canadian Journal of Sociology* 28: 463-488.

Fangen, K., (2010) Social exclusion and inclusion of young immigrants—presentation of an analytical framework, *Nordic Journal of Youth Research,* 18(2): 133-156.

Fangen, K. and Lynnebakke, B., (2010) *Born in Norway, Pakistani parents: Fatima's story, illustrative case,* EUMARGINS. Available at: www.sv.uio.no/iss/english/research/ projects/eumargins/illustrative-cases/norway/fatima.html, accessed on November 11, 2012.

Fekjær, S., (2007) New differences, old explanations can educational differences between ethnic groups in Norway be explained by social background?, *Ethnicities,* 7(3): 367-389.

Feliciano, C. and Rumbaut, R. G., (2005) Gendered paths: Educational and occupational expectations and outcomes among adult children of immigrants, *Ethnic and Racial Studies* 28(6): 87-118.

Finne, S. H., (2010) *Indiske etterkommere i eliteutdanninger: en kvalitativ studie av utdanningsvalg blant indiske etterkommere i eliteutdanninger. [Indian descendents in elite educations: a qualitative study of educational choice]* Master-thesis, Department of sociology and human geography, University of Oslo.

Fry, G., Hunter,S., Law, I., Osler, A., Swann, S., Tzanelli, R. and Williams, F., (2008) *Country Report on Education: United Kingdom,* EDUMIGROM Background Papers. Budapest: Central European University, Center for Policy Studies.

Frønes, I., (2010) Status zero youth in the welfare society, *Child Indicators Research.* 3(3).

Granovetter, M., (1973) The strength of weak ties, *American Journal of Sociology,* 78: 1360-1380.

Henriksen, K., (2007) *Fakta om 18 innvandrergrupper i Norge, [Facts about immigrant groups in Norway],* Statistics Norway report no. 29.

Kalter, F. and Kogan, I., (2006) Ethnic inequalities at the transition from school to work in Belgium and Spain: Discrimination or self-exclusion?, *Research in Social Stratification and Mobility,* 24: 259-74.

Kennely et al., (2009) Special issue introduction: Youth, cultural politics, and new social spaces in an era of globalization, *Review of Education, Pedagogy, and Cultural Studies,* 31:4, 255-269

Lareau, A. (2003) *Unequal Childhoods,* Berkeley: University of California Press.

Luthar, S. S. and Zigler, E., (1991) Vulnerability and competence: A review of research on resilience in childhood, *American Journal of Orthopsychiatry.* 61: 6-22.

MacDonald et al., (2005) Growing up in poor neighbourhoods: The significance of class and place in the extended transitions of 'socially excluded' young adults, *Sociology,* 39(5): 873-891.

McNally, S and Telhaj, S., (2007) The Cost of Exclusion: Counting the cost of youth disadvantage in the UK, London: Princes Trust, (Centre for Economic Performance, London School of Economics. Available at: www.princes-trust.org.uk/pdf/COE_full_report.pdf Accessed on October 24th, 2012.

OECD, (2012) *Equity and equality in education: Supporting disadvantaged students and schools.* OECD Publishing. Available at: www.oecd.org/edu/preschoolandschool/49478474.pdf Accessed on October 24th, 2012.

Olsen, B., (2009) *Unge innvandrere i arbeid og utdanning. Er innvandrerungdom en marginalisert gruppe? 4. Kvartal 2007 Hvor forskjellige er de i forhold til majoriteten?, [Young immigrants in work and education: Are immigrant youths a marginalised group?]*, Working Paper No. 41. Oslo: Statistics Norway. www.ssb.no/emner/06/01/rapp ung_innv/notat_200941/notat_200941.pdf

Pew Research Centre, (2012) *The rise of Asian Americans,* Available at: www.pewsocialtrends.org/files/2012/06/SDT-The-Rise-of-Asian-Americans-Full-Report.pdf Accessed on October 24th, 2012.

Paasche, E., (2010) *Adapting and integrating—Haile's story,* illustrative case, EUMARGINS. Available at www.sv.uio.no/iss/english/research/projects/eumargins/illustrative-cases/norway/haile.html Accessed on October 24th, 2012.

Raffo, C. and Reeves, M., (2000) Youth transitions and social exclusion: developments in social capital theory, *Journal of Youth Studies* 3(2): 147-166.

Schoon, I. and Bynner, J., (2003) 'Risk and resilience in the life course: implications for interventions and social policies', *Journal of Youth Studies* 6(1): 21-31.

White, R. and Wyn, J., (1998) Youth agency and social context, *Journal of Sociology,* 34(3): 314-327.

Chapter 2

Subculture, ethnicity and the politics of (post)modernity

Sune Qvotrup Jensen

Introduction

Contemporary academic debates about youth subculture often claim that we live in a time where the cultural articulations of young people are depoliticised—if indeed there was ever a moment when there was a political content. Therefore, it is argued, youth subcultures should be understood as arenas for the expression of individuality rather than as articulations which may contain implicit or explicit social criticism. Simultaneously social structures and inequality are often regarded as having little relevance for the study of youth subcultures, discarding by implication the notion that youth subcultures may sometimes be understood as creative collective *answers* to a shared social situation. Both claims are often framed within an understanding of contemporary society as post-modern. Yet, it seems that these claims are problematic for some of the most obvious and visible contemporary youth subcultures, for instance those revolving around the musical genres of hip-hop and rap and in particular young ethnic minority men's involvement herein.

The aim of this chapter is therefore to critically assess the claim that contemporary youth subcultures are postmodern and therefore depoliticised and that the relevance of social structures has lessened for understanding contemporary youth subculture. This assessment is informed by an analysis of musical material from a number of contemporary Danish hip-hop groups with male ethnic minority members. Methodologically I follow a modified version of what Layder (1998) refers to as *Adaptive Theory*. Consequently the aim is neither to test a theory in a narrow sense, nor to advance a purely empirical analysis, but to produce dialogue between data and theory, i.e. to advance a theoretical informed analysis that feeds back and informs theoretical debates. The analysis focuses on the relevance of social structures, the presence of political content as well as dimensions of modernity and post-modernity.

Theoretical starting points

The first wave of subcultural theory was coined by the Chicago School which had a particular interest in urban life and criminology. The first known use of the concept is by Chicago School author Vivien Marie Palmer in 1928. In the aftermath of the Chicago School the concept became central to American criminology in the late 1950s and 1960s. A central work was Albert K. Cohen's classic work on *Delinquent Boys* (1955). Later commentators have suggested that here Cohen outlined the first proper subcultural theory (Bay and Drotner, 1986). Cohen suggested that subcultures could be understood as a cultural solution to a shared problem among working class boys. These boys suffered from low status because of their class position, but the subculture could provide them with status based on alternative criteria (Cohen, 1955). The subculture therefore had a social function for those involved. Cohen thus combined a Weberian understanding of class as a stratified status system with a structural functionalist understanding of culture as functional solutions to problems.

The second wave of subcultural theory was coined at the University of Birmingham in the 1970s by the Centre of Contemporary Cultural Studies (CCCS) (Cohen, 1972; Cohen, 2002 [1972]; Hall and Jefferson, 1991 [1975]; Willis, 1978; Mungham and Pearson, 1978; Hebdige, 1979; for overviews see Brake, 1985; Gudmundsson, 1992; Muggleton, 2005). The CCCS produced a theoretical understanding of subcultures based on a Marxist analysis of British post war capitalist society. Although a broad and diverse strand of theory it can be argued that the CCCS had in common that subcultures of working class youth—such as punks, skinheads, mods and teddy boys—were understood as creative cultural *answers*—or attempts at solutions—to problems that were specific to both generation and class position and *at the same time* as forms of resistance against social dominance. The political or resistant dimension of subcultures was said to take a subtle or implicit form as opposed to explicitly political counter cultures. In this resistance the young people were furthermore said to draw upon a wide range of resources including, but not limited to, the classed culture of the parents. In their focus on power, class and politics the CCCS were thus quite unorthodox in their understanding of the political, which contemporary Marxist scholars tended to locate in 'traditional forms of union activism' and not in the youth cultural sphere (Griffin, 2011: 246).

The idea that subcultures could be understood as attempts at a solution to a shared situation did not necessarily imply an optimistic prognosis for such solutions. As the theoretical introduction to *Resistance to Rituals* explains the 'problematic of a subordinate class experience' can be *lived through*, negotiated or resisted' but not resolved on a subcultural level (Hall and Jefferson, 1975: 47). In fact Willis demonstrated that resistance against class dominance may sometimes be functional to the reproduction of the overall class system (1978). This does not mean that CCCS ruled out that subcultures can win space for their participants. As Brake points out they were seen to offer some kind of *magical* solution to structural problems, win space for young people, offer meaningful leisure activities and offer a viable identity on the individual as well the collective level (1985:24).

In addition to, and somewhat intertwined with, the political dimension another important contribution of the CCCS was the addition of a semiotic dimension to subcultural theory. Thus the CCCS devoted analytical attention to the analysis of style. This included focus on the ways subcultures appropriated already existing symbols and gave them new meaning, through processes which the CCCS conceptualised as *bricolage*—a term borrowed form classic French structuralist anthropologist Claude Levi-Strauss. The CCCS then argued that resistance was often expressed on the stylistic level, frequently unknowingly. Taken as a whole the CCCS continued to understand subcultures as a meeting point between the cultural and the social—an understanding already present in the first wave of subcultural theory—but added class conflict, politics and semiotic analysis of style.

The theoretical work of the CCCS has been criticised from numerous positions: Feminist scholars who were themselves a part of the CCCS argued that the theoretical work was male biased (McRobbie and Garber, 1975; McRobbie, 1980, 1990), and argued that the CCCS did not offer enough attention to misogyny and masculinism in subcultures (see also Brake, 1985; Frosh, Phoenix and Pattman, 2002: 53). The CCCS theorists were also criticised for an inadequate theorisation of race and ethnicity, and for legitimating racism among white working class youth (Gilroy, 1993a; Frosh, Phoenix and Pattman, 2002; Carrington and Wilson, 2004). Consequently, Bjurström has criticised the CCCS for neglecting how the forms of resistance of working class subcultures are intertwined in *complex chains* of resistance and dominance which can only be comprehended through a sensitive analysis of the relation between class, gender, ethnicity and race (1997: 108).

The end of the 1990s saw the rise of a third wave of subcultural theory which I will here refer to as Post-Subcultural Studies (Cohen, 1987; Thornton, 1995;

Muggleton, 2000; Bennett, 2000; Muggleton and Weinzierl, 2002; Bennett and Kahn-Harris, 2004). This broad group of scholars was to some extent inspired by the criticism of the CCCS discussed above. Consequently, Post-Subcultural Studies raised a number of critical questions about the work of CCCS including scepticism towards the emphasis on class, dominance and resistance. This scepticism was often framed in general sociological theories about post-modernity.

A defining moment of the Post-Subcultural Studies scholarship cannot be defined definitely, but Stanley Cohen's 1987 foreword to the CCCS classic *Folk Devils and Moral Panics* can be read as a stating point.[5] Herein Cohen pointed out that CCCS tended to see youth subcultures as a political battleground between classes' (1987: xlix). He argued that the political interpretations were tied too closely to a forced semiotic analysis with the result that 'the symbolic baggage the kids are being asked to carry is just too heavy (Cohen, 2002[1987]: lix).

A later representative of this scholarship, David Muggleton, has argued that today it can be necessary to ask who exactly is doing the resisting' (2000: 30). He furthermore argues that 'the break down of mass society has ensured that there is no longer a coherent dominant culture against which a subculture can express its resistance (2000:48). He argues that subcultures are not group solutions to collective problems related to class position and that the relation between structural position and cultural practice was never adequately demonstrated by the CCCS, who simply projected their own political and theoretical ideas onto the subjects they studied (Muggleton, 2000: 167). Furthermore Muggleton pointed out that rather than resisting majority culture, subcultures often radicalise tendencies of mainstream society (2000).

Parallel to this criticism Post-Subcultural Studies offered a number of theoretical alternatives to CCCS's understanding of subcultures. According to Post-Subcultural Studies young people today live their lives under social conditions of postmodern fluidity which, it is claimed, cannot be grasped by the conceptions of the CCCS. Alternatively Post-Subcultural Studies often interprets subcultures as self chosen manifestations of individual autonomy in a post-modern world, rather than collective or resistant answers to shared problems (Muggleton, 2000: 167). Bennett has suggested that the concept of subculture is rethought in conjunction with Maffesolis' (1996) concept of neo-tribalism (Bennett, 1999, 2000). This means that subcultures are conceived

---

5   Stanley Cohen was central both to the CCCS *and* to the criticism towards the CCCS.

as loosely defined collectivities, neo-tribes, which individuals can choose to participate in for a period of time.

The criticism of the CCCS theory carried out by the Post-Subcultural Studies and the turn towards post-modernity and fluidity as an overall theoretical frame did not go unnoticed. On the contrary, a criticism of the criticism of CCCS soon emerged, forming what I have earlier referred to as a neo-Birminghamian understanding of subculture (Jensen, 2010b). This chapter may read as a part of this current. The criticism of Post-Subcultural Studies from neo-Birminghamism has focused on the tendency to decouple structural conditions from the understanding of contemporary youth culture. Hence Carrrington and Wilson criticised the postmodern understanding of the Post-Subcultural Studies scholars for decoupling power and structural inequality from the analysis, and criticised de-politication of subcultures (2004). Other authors such as Blackman (2005) and Hesmondhalgh (2005) have argued against the voluntaristic individualism which they considered central to Bennett's application of neo-tribalism to subcultural theory.

Generally the neo-Birminghamian current has argued for the continued relevance of social structures for the study of youth subcultures, since young people and their cultures are framed within and to some extent conditioned by social hierarchies and inequalities. Some authors have pointed to the continued relevance of class, since it is not all young people who have access to the consumerism central to some subcultures (Shildrick and MacDonald, 2006; Jensen, 2006). Another argument for the continued relevance of class has been that youth cultures develop in local settings which are classed due to the classed divisions of cities (Shildrick, 2006). Other authors have pointed to the relevance of ethnicity and race. Carrington and Wilson for instance argue that many contemporary accounts of subcultural theory 'lack attention to 'racial formation, ethnic identity construction and the articulation of racism within and between subcultures (2004: 71). Generally the argument has been that there are differences between the subcultures' or taste-cultures of privileged young people and the subcultures produced by socially and economically underprivileged youth. These differences are related to the intersection between class, ethnicity and race. I concur with this argument, and as the analysis below will illustrate, find that Shildrick and MacDonald have a strong argument when they maintain that the Post-Subcultural Studies scholars have focused their attention towards taste-cultures of privileged youth, and therefore have no basis for assessing whether structural inequality plays a role for contemporary youth subcultures in general (2006).

Post-modernity, subculture and hip-hop

In addition to subcultural theory, the discussions in this chapter relate to an overall debate about post-modernity, subculture and hip-hop. As mentioned above Muggleton argues that contemporary subcultures should be understood in the light of post-modern society. However his empirical analysis of young subculturalists in Britain leads him to a complex conclusion. *On the one* hand contemporary subcultures are inscribed in the postmodern; they exist in a social world where many choices are possible, where simultaneous participation in several subcultures is possible and where boundaries between different subcultures blur. *On the other* hand Muggleton's interviewees do not subscribe to a decentered or anti-essentialist understanding of identity: they conceive of their participation in subcultures as an expression of their true selves—and thereby articulate an, essentialist, authenticist and quite modern understand of identity (Muggleton, 2000).

As Muggleton's analyses suggest there are different dimensions to the discussion of youth culture and post-modernity. Consequently there are different assessments of whether and in what sense hip-hop is a post-modern cultural phenomenon. On an abstract level it is possible to argue that most black diasporic cultures are post-modern because of their successive *reworking, recombination and redefinition of the cultural.* Hence according to Sewell black *bricolage* cultures provide empirical examples of 'a post modern exercise', which is otherwise often discussed in purely abstract terms (1997: 144). In this vein Walcott argues the 'continuous practices of parody, deferral, bricolage, pastiche, collage, indirection, reversal, and numerous other postmodern practices' (103) as well as the concrete practice of sampling prevailing in hip-hop disrupts the idea of authenticity and originality inherent in a modern understanding of music (1999).

It is however not the presence of hybridity and *bricolage* in itself which defines hip-hop as distinctively post-modern. These phenomena exist in all cultures. On the contrary, the post-modernity of hip-hop lies in its *constant* and *accelerated* transformation and hybridity. It is furthermore possible to argue that the *orientation towards style and surface* in hip-hop is a postmodern trait. In relation to these dimensions all hip-hop, including all the hip-hop groups analysed in this chapter, can meaningfully be described as postmodern in an aesthetic sense. It is however obsolete to operate with a clear binary distinction which aims at determining whether hip-hop is *really* an articulation of post-modern aesthetics or not. Rather we might think of the distinction between the modern and post-modern as a continuum—or rather a number of continua related to several dimensions which intersect, interact with and overlay each other.

Another dimension, central to sociological understandings of the post-modernity, is the decentering of identity. In relation to this dimension Pedersen has argued that hip-hop is postmodern in its aesthetic form, but often entirely modern in its celebration of stabile authentic subjects (Pedersen, 2008). Consequently, *keeping it real* is a central value in hip-hop culture implying 'that people should not present themselves for what they are not' (Cutler, 2003: 5). Pedersen grasps a central ambiguity of hip-hop, however we might benefit from thinking of these two dimensions as continua; on the aesthetic dimension hip-hop can be understood as close to the postmodern pole on the continuum between modernity and postmodernity, whereas on the identity dimension most hip-hop can be understood as close to the modern pole. One might even suggest that (some) hip-hop has found a post-modern way to articulate authentic identity. It is thus problematic to think of modernity and post-modernity as clear cut historical phases which replace each other. Instead we might think of the contemporary world in general and hip-hop culture in particular as spaces where modernity and post-modernity exist side by side in multidimensional, intertwined and overlapping ways (cf., Hall, 1986).

Such a way of thinking may get us some way, but there are further paradoxes involved. For instance, the constant performance of excess and pimping, central to some subgenres, may be difficult to combine with the demand of realness and authenticity. *Keeping it real* thus implies *both* authenticity *and* connectedness to street life (Cutler, 2003); dimensions that may not always be easy to combine. In some cases this may lead to demands of doing what one boasts, sometimes— although rarely—resulting in physical confrontations between rap rivals.[6] Furthermore hip-hop sometimes entails humour, parody and exaggeration adding further to the multidimensional complexity of hip-hop.

Subcultural and national context

The music analysed in this chapter is a public manifestation of a larger subculture. Hence the analyses advanced are related to a broader field of studies of ethnic minority male youth's engagement with hip-hop in Scandinavia. Despite variations in methodology a number of Scandinavian studies have identified a

6   Of the groups analysed here Pimp-A-Lot has been involved in such confrontations.

distinct subculture of marginalised ethnic minority men who live in the suburbs of the larger cities (Jensen, 2007; Andersen et al., 2001; Sernhede, 2001, 2002; Sandberg and Pedersen, 2006; Sandberg, 2008; Hviid, 2007; Jonsson, 2007; Hammarén, 2008; Klinker and Bilde, 2009). Several studies (Jensen, 2007, 2005, 2010b; Sernhede, 2002; Sandberg, 2008; Sernhede and Beach in this volume) document that this subculture draws heavily on elements of hip-hop, although it is not synonymous with hip-hop culture in a narrow sense.

The relation to hip-hop has been analysed differently, but generally research suggests that although elements of hip-hop are today part of mainstream youth culture there are specific dimensions in the way (male) ethnic minority youth relate to hip-hop: 1) Hip-hop offers a way to ascribe value to ethnic/racial minority status, i.e. it allows young marginalised ethnic minority young men to capitalise on being positioned at the ethnic/racial other and to stage themselves as attractive and masculine (Jensen, 2007, 2008, 2010a, 2011; Sandberg and Pedersen, 2006; Sandberg, 2008); 2) the engagement with hip-hop can sometimes be based on a conscious identification with the marginal position of urban black USA (Prieur, 1999; Mørck, 1999; Sernhede, 1999, 2001, 2002; Jensen, 2008; Jensen and Hviid, 2003; Sandberg and Pedersen, 2006; Sandberg, 2008); 3) hip-hop offers a repertoire to reflect and comment upon experienced marginality and ascribed otherness (Sernhede, 2002; Jensen, 2007, 2010b). The latter resonates with the more general finding that hip-hop has taken root in many national contexts where it has often 'become a vehicle for various forms of youth protest' used to 'make political statements about local racial, sexual, employment, and class issues' (Mitchell, 2001: 10). It also resonates with McLaren's claim that hip-hop is a cultural form that can be used in anti-racist discourse (1999).

The specific Danish context is central to understanding the analysis in this chapter. Generally Danish public debates about migration integration and multi-ethnicity have taken a turn towards nationalist or cultural conservative sentiments during at least the last two decades and it is now common to problematise the presence of ethnic minorities, to consider their alleged culture problematic and to pose demands for assimilation or sometimes expulsion (Horst, 1991; Schierup, 1993; Diken, 1998; Yilmaz, 1999; Røgilds, 1994, 2002; Hervik, 1999; 2004; Andreassen, 2005). Consequently, some commentators have characterised Danish discourses about *immigrants* as an example of *new racism* based on a logic of cultural difference (Schierup, 1993). It can thus be argued that the Danish welfare state, which did relatively well in ameliorating inequalities related to gender and class, is facing difficulties handling multi-ethnicity.

These currents are well documented in research: Karen Wren has argued that cultural racism has found fertile ground in Denmark, resulting in a widespread popular discourse constructing especially Muslims as not belonging (2001); Peter Hervik has described the popular discourses of many Danes as a 'Cultural World of Unbridgeable Differences' in which the assumed culture of so-called foreigners is constructed as radically different from and inferior to Danish culture (2004). He describes how the popular discourse of many Danes as characterised by a culturalist dichotomy between we and they implying that 'cultural difference is beyond questioning and regarded as insurmountable' (256); Rikke Andreassen (2005) has analysed Danish media coverage of visibly different ethnic minorities as preoccupied with crime, oppression of women, aggression and an assumed lack of integration.

Some of these discourses specifically address marginalised young *immigrant* men who mass media often construct as a threat to society. In the words of Andreassen such young men are often described as criminals and 'as members of gangs, as irredeemable, and as inhabitants of lawless areas' (2005, 122). These discourses influence life of young ethnic minority men living in Denmark (Jensen, 2007, 2010a) and therefore constitute a common problem which the subculture and its public manifestations could be understood against. It should however be emphasised that the shared situation of these young men cannot be reduced to the consequences of ethno-racial marginality. On the contrary they are marginalised both in terms of class and in terms of race/ethnicity. However, as I will return to below, class does not seem to offer the same repertoire of symbols and meanings as race or ethnicity does via its centrality to hip-hop.

Material and method

The empirical material consists of musical material from several hip-hop groups and individual artists in Denmark, with either minority or multi-ethnic background.[7] The selection of groups is inspired by frequent but informal screenings of the Danish hip-hop internet site rapspot.dk. The definition of hip-hop employed is broad. The groups are: Pimp-A-Lot, P4L (Perker4life), B.O.C. (Bombs over Copenhagen), Marwan, Skurken, Zaki, Outlandish, Ataf Khawaja, Ali Kazim, De Sorte Får, Albertslund Terror Korps, Lisbent and Kim Young Ill. Visual material accompanying the music (CD covers and videos) is included in

---

7   Two of the group include all-Danish members (B.O.C. and Pimp-A-Lot).

the analysis, which also draws on various internet sources (for instance *MySpace* has been used to track relations between groups).

As a secondary source I draw upon ethnographic research for my Pd. D. project, which focused on the subculture produced by marginalised ethnic minority men in reaction to othering (Jensen, 2007). The methods employed here included field work and interviews. A total of twenty-three young men aged from fifteen to twenty-five years-old were interviewed in eighteen taped semi-structured qualitative interviews, and a total of 126 observations were conducted in four Danish youth clubs, mainly at evenings. Furthermore, magazines and internet material was included (see Jensen, 2007, 2010a). The analysis focuses primarily on the texts of the groups analysed. Although text is almost by definition central to hip-hop there are methodological dangers involved in reducing music to text. In an attempt to strike a balance, the sound of the music is included in the analyses when particularly important.

Empirical Analysis

The empirical analysis below takes a tentative typology as its starting point. This typology clusters different rap artists in terms of style. The analysis focuses on 1) the relevance of social structures, 2) whether, to what extent and in which form political resistance is articulated, and 3) dimensions related to modernity and post-modernity, in particular the ways identity is articulated.

'Dangerous' young ethnic minority men as street politicians

The groups in this cluster (Pimp-A-Lot (including early Marwan), P4L, B.O.C. and Skurken) articulate a hard and explicit style of hip-hop. The groups can be said to both reflect and stage marginality. Two of the groups refer for themselves or are commonly referred to as *perker rap*—a subgenre of Danish hip-hop which accentuates ethnic minority background, as *perker* is a strongly derogatory Danish term for immigrant from North Africa or the Middle East. This genre is known for its explicit contents as well for routine use of heavy accent and alternative grammar.

Pimp-A-Lot, which is a loosely defined musical collective, emerged from the creative milieu of the underprivileged urban area Århus Vest.[8] The group's name is a reference to American rap label Rap-A-Lot known for distributing such groups as Geto Boys and Scarface; *gangsta* rappers famous for their ghetto centric explicit lyrics depicting guns, violence, drugs, sex and sometimes misogyny.

8   Århus with 250.000 inhabitants is the second largest city in Denmark.

The same is to some extent true for Pimp-A-Lot's lyrical universe. However, the lyrics are at the same time, sometimes within the same song, articulations of social criticism. In an interview in the Danish hip-hop internet site, rapper and producer Abu-Malek (also interviewed in Jensen, 2007) characterises the music as *street politics* and explains.[9]

> You know, life isn't pink flowers. No matter where you are. Maybe for those who live in Risskov[10] and by the beach, and then they can talk about that. But when we represent the shit down here ... then we need to rap about the truth. The reason I make music like that is that I want it to get into the brains of people. And gangster rap gets into your soul. And that is the purpose. *StreetPolitics*, that is also the name of our next record. So political, sure—in the streets [...] As I have said before, a guy like Anders Fjog,[11] right? They come and they talk [...] and he is on TV. It is the same with us—we are just on the street [...] telling it to you through music. So politics, maybe not so much about countries and stuff like that, but street politics—100 per cent.
> (Passage from the interview *Under Masken på 8210*, *www.hiphop.dk*,
> 28, Sept, 2006)

In the passage Abu-Malek explains that he considers the music political. According to Abu-Malek ganster-rap is chosen as a style because of its ability to get through to people. A broad definition of the political is employed in the sense that he distances himself from institutional politics.

One of the central artists in Pimp-A-Lot is SLP/Marwan. SLP—the moniker used in the earlier material—is an acronym for StateLess Palestinian (in Danish, *StatsLøs Palæstinenser*) implying that the very choice of pseudonym may entail social criticism.[12] Marwan has released two CDs under his own name, besides appearances on various Pimp-A-Lot material. The first CD is entitled *P.E.R.K.E.R.* One song from this CD is *selvgjort, velgjort*. The title is difficult to translate but refers to a Danish saying that implies that if you do things yourself you are sure they are done properly. In the chorus line of the song Marwan raps

---

9   All citations are translated from Danish to English by the author.
10   Risskov is a privileged neighbourhood in Århus.
11   Nickname for the Danish Prime Minister at the time of the interview, Anders Fogh. *Fjog* is Danish for fool.
12   Marwan's parents are Palestinian refugees.

Vote for the red,
Smoke the green,
Sell the white,
Work black, *selvgjort velgjort*

At first glance the text appears as a street smart description of marginal life: *Smoking the green* refers to use of cannabis, *selling the white* to dealing with amphetamine or cocaine and *black work* refers to tax evasion in everyday Danish. However the text is political in two ways: Manifestly as Marwan positions himself as left wing (vote for the red) and latently in the references to ethnicity and the Palestinian Diaspora: red, green, white and black are the colours of the Palestinians flag!

Another song, worth mentioning for its visual material, is *'no hope'* (Danish, *intet håb*). The semi-documentary video of the song—which shows among other things a person being stabbed and a young man overdosing from heroin use—visualises the differences between rich and poor and entails a strong social criticism of the social circumstances of life in the underprivileged suburbs.[13] The bleakness of the video is underpinned by melancholy of the piano sample central to the music Marwan raps over. At the same time there is a dimension of documenting a relation to street life in the video. This reference to street life can be understood as a way of *keeping it real* (Cutler, 2003).

The cover of the CD deserves mentioning. On the front cover Marwan is pictured in the same way as a criminal in a crime register—this genre of pictures is known from other rap covers and can be interpreted as an inter textual reference to the Houston based rap group Geto Boys. On the inner cover another picture depicts Marwan looking out the window in a pose which paraphrases Malcolm X in the well known 'By any means necessary' photograph. This may also, at the same time, be a reference to KRS—one's pose on the cover of the classic rap album *By all means necessary* (Jive Records, 1988). The inter textual references to Malcolm X on the one hand and Geto Boys on the other is illustrative of the double articulation of a *gangsta* position on the one hand and a militant but intellectual political anti-racist position on the other.

---

13 www.youtube.com/watch?v=Lrd_JQrD5KA

Another central group of the *perker rap* sub genre is P4L, an acronym for *Perker for Life*.[14] In a song entitled *I fear only Allah* (*Jeg Frygter kun Allah*), the P4L member Turco raps,[15]

> Of course we get stopped by some pigs
> Wholla, I'm telling you they are a fucked up joke
> They ask us where we have been, what the fuck we have been doing, which potatoes[16] we have smashed
> Only because of *BT* and *Ekstrabladet*[17]
> The Danish media are some fucking racists,
> The same is true for your ugly minister
> [...]
> You are only after some fucking *perkere*
> Turks, Arabs, Pakistanis and Serbs

The text criticises police harassment and racist media discourses. However in somewhat the same way as Marwan it does so from a position of the hard, dangerous and masculine young ethnic minority man.

The last group I will address in this cluster is B.O.C., an acronym for Bombs over Copenhagen. Contrary to Pimp-A-Lot and P4L B.O.C. is not referred to as *perker rap* but is considered to belong to the *grime* genre.

B.O.C. is not as street-political on the textual level as Pimp-A-Lot and P4L, however their music and the visual material accompanying it contains a dimension of social criticism. One example is the song *still the best* (in Danish, *stadig den bedste*).[18] The video accompanying the song documents the harsh reality of the concrete blocks of the underprivileged suburbs where many young ethnic minority persons live. It thus visualises the differences between rich and poor. At the same time the style of the music is important. *Grime* was developed in the UK. It is currently debated among hip-hoppers whether *grime* is subgenre of hip-hop or a distinctively different type of music. In a sense *grime* is oppositional and marginal, even within hip-hop. Contrary to most modern hip-hop, *grime* has an up-tempo, industrial, machine-like, disharmonic and dissonant sound, not unlike the musical material of such classic hip-hop groups

---

14 P4L/Perker for life is itself an intertextual reference to the Los Angeles-based rap group NWA (Niggaz With Attitude) which had commercial success with the album *Niggaz For Life* (Ruthless Records, 1991).

15 www.youtube.com/watch?v=yUottyrTVuo

16 Potato is slang for ethnic Dane

17 Danish tabloids.

18 www.youtube.com/watch?v=O8b4pw4l-fE, found 2/6 2011

as Public Enemy. The sound of *grime*, combined with the visual characteristic of the concrete suburbs depicted in the video confronts and disrupts normality, consensus and middle class whiteness, thereby constituting a form of latent or implicit street politics.

Summing up, the musical material analysed in this cluster articulates either implicit or explicit social criticism of the circumstances of life in the underprivileged suburbs. Masculinism and misogyny is, however, also articulated, for instance one song by B.O.C. is entitled *fissehul*—a derogatory slang word for vagina. This term is used to articulate disrespect towards other rappers (See Jensen, 2005, 2010a for a discussion of the gendered articulations in Pimp-A-Lot and P4L). This observation points towards misogyny as a dimension of claiming a masculinist position as a *dangerous young black man*, coming close to what Young refers to as 'a process of essentialising oneself' (2003: 406). The embracement of this position can be interpreted as a strategy for accruing social value in the face of social marginality. In a fashion not far from the processes the CCCS conceptualised as *bricolage*, the *sign* of the dangerous black man is appropriated and imbued with value (Sandberg, 2005).

In terms of the discussions about post-modernity, subculture and hip-hop raised above, one might argue that, at face value, the rappers included in this cluster articulate an understanding of (their own) identity which is closer to the modern pole on the modern—post-modern continuum in the sense that they insist on claiming authenticity. For instance Abu-Malek, producer and anchor man of Pimp-A-Lot, in an interview for my Ph. D. project explained that it is important to him that the rappers in his crew do not pretend to be something they are not. However, upon closer scrutiny further complexities can be unravelled. The musical material is thus highly hybrid and might be said to articulate complex and transnational identities which contrast the texts' insistence on a somewhat one-dimensional masculinity. Furthermore the use and reuse of musical material, including the widespread use of already existing instrumental hip-hop tracks breaks with notions of musical originality and authenticity. Pimp-A-Lot for instance on their first CD raps over a number of instrumentals of known rap artist. They refer to this practice as *jacked* tracks[19] on the back of their cover thereby re-inscribing musical *in*-authenticity in the *gangsta* ethos.

19 To jack is hip-hop slang for robbing.

Rappers as (modern) black intellectuals

The hip-hop artists in this cluster articulate a somewhat different form of hip-hop style than the *dangerous* young men. They appear as well formulated, peaceful, progressive young men, educated—if not formally then on the street. In this cluster I include Zaki, Outlandish, late Marwan, late Artaf Kwawaja, Ali Kazim and D.S.F./De Sorte Får (Danish for the black sheep). One example is the Danish-Egyptian rapper Zaki. In 2002 Zaki released his debut, which included the song *Tragic* (in Danish, *Tragisk*). Here he raps:

> You never wanted to house me / you don't need folks like me
> [...]
> When you see my colour you think the problem is in my genes
> I'm constantly told I'm just a problem
> In Denmark all people have the right to think what they think
> Except us, because we are Muslims.
> (Zaki, Musikmusiak, Ukendt Grammofon, 2001)

The anti-racist and social criticism in the text is articulated from a position which can most often be described as that of a modernist intellectual, i.e. someone who is rational, progressive, deliberate and willing and able to explain his cause. In that sense Zaki and the other artists in this cluster draw upon a tradition of rappers appearing as black intellectuals. Historically hip-hop artists such as KRS-one, X-clan, Paris, early Intelligent Hoodlum, Chuck D, Brand Nubian, Digable Planets and Talib Kveli have taken up this position. It can be argued that these rappers have been part of a wider historical tradition containing black intellectuals as Frantz Fanon, W. E. B. Du Bois and Malcolm X. Compared to the *dangerous black men* these artists thus articulate a different form of black masculinity with different class connotations.

Contrary to the musical material of the *dangerous young men* the texts of the rappers in this cluster don't contain sexism or misogyny.[20] In fact they sometimes appear as pro-feminist. For instance Ataf Khawaja's song *Butterfly* (in Danish, *Sommerfugl*), addresses gendered violence:

> the blow hits her cheek paralyses her mind
> cause she never though he would hit her again
> [...]
> she collects the fragments from the mug

---

20 Although this discussion falls outside the scope of this chapter it can be argued that the position of the steadfast and militant black intellectual is also a masculinist position (Hughey, 2009).

> he smashed on the way out of this house build on blues
> she sees the question marks in her boys eyes
> will she tell him the truth or fill him with lies
> she does the last, 'cause it is far the easiest
> convinced that the boy will forget it
> but in vain 'cause her face is way to swollen … .
> (Ataf Khawaja, Paraderne nede, ArtPeople, 2005).

In the last verse of the song Ataf depicts the main character as a strong woman who breaks out of the violent relationship. He then adds, 'I am her first-born. She is my mother'

The *black* intellectuals included in this cluster display a number of ambiguities concerning the modern—post-modern continua. In one sense they stage themselves as modern intellectual, almost modernist in their rationality. However as the *dangerous young men* the musical material is highly hybrid and might be said to articulate complex and transnational identities which are not reducible to the modern. Thus there is nothing essentialist, authenticist or modernist in inscribing oneself in the intellectual tradition of the transnational black diaspora. Furthermore these groups do not claim a one-dimensional masculinity as the *dangerous black* men, but neither do they seem to be involved in radical identity play. This latter is however a rule with exceptions: Outlandish recorded a new version of the classical Danish song *I Danmark er jeg født* (*I was born in Denmark*), originally written by the Danish national poet Hans Christian Andersen in 1850. This can hardly be considered anything else than a post-modern deconstruction of national and ethnic identities.

For further illustrations of the work of hip-hop artists of this type the reader may consult Beach and Sernhede's contribution to this volume.

Postmodern identity play and left radicalism

This cluster includes Albertslund Terrorkorps (Kid Kishore and VJ Cancer), Lisbent and Kim Young Ill. Here the focus is on DJ, producer and remixer Kid Kishore. The name Albertslund Terrorkorps in itself carries ambiguous meaning. Albertslund is an underprivileged suburb at the periphery of Copenhagen widely known as a lower working class area with a high proportion of ethnic minorities. The term Terrorkorps may be a mocking parody of contemporary discourses about ethnic minority young men as potential terrorists, and at the same time an intertextual reference to New York rap crew Terror Squad.

As a remixer and producer Kid Kishore does not limit himself to the hip-hop genre in the narrow sense. His music to a very high degree takes the form of an aesthetically postmodern *bricolage* of genres and styles, which are remixed, recombined and distorted. Illustrative of this is his usage of genres as different as Indian *bhangra* and *Bollywood*, Danish hip-hop, and popular Danish pop singers like Kim Larsen, John Mogensen and Nik and Jay. Such a *bricolage* itself can be understood as a postmodern musical practice that transcends what Gilroy calls ethnic absolutism (1993b) and it is therefore political in a deconstructive sense. The textual content of the music is also often political. One example is Kid Kishore's remix or the popular Danish R'n'B duo Nik and Jay's well known hit song *Hot*. Kid Kishore distorts and remixes the song and gives it a new title *Dannebro er hot* (*Dannebro is hot*)—but he also changes the context by inserting and exchanging words.[21] The line *burning gas on HC Andersens Buolevard* (Danish, *brænder benzin af på HC Andersens Boulevard*) is changed to *burning Dannebrog*[22] *on HC Andersens Boulevard* (Danish, *brænder Dannebrog på HC Andersens Boulevard*). The content of the song is hereby changed from a celebration of car consumerism to a comment on the rioting which has taken place in Copenhagen in connection to the so-called Cartoon Crisis. Kid Kishore similarly plays around with popular Danish 1970 singer John Mogensen's *Danish turf for the Danish* (*Danmarks jord for de danske*) from 1972—originally a left wing anti EU protest song. In Kid Kishore's hip-hop mashup version which is accompanied by a psychedelic animated video the song becomes an ironic comment to contemporary anti-immigrant discourses in Denmark.[23]

Kid Kishore has a direct relation to *perker rap* including P4L, Marwan and Pimp-A-Lot which were mentioned above. A considerable proportion of his music consists of remixed versions of *perker rap* songs. One modification is however central to the analysis in this chapter: sexist, homophobic and racist terms, including the term *perker*, are consequently cut out and replaced by distorted techno sounds. Kid Kishore is however not preoccupied with distancing himself from *perker rap* groups. On the contrary they are mutually present on each other's list of friends on social network internet sites and he is currently collaborating with artists involved in the genre.

As the artists analysed above, Kid Kishore comments on and questions Danish anti-immigrant discourses musically. For instance he started a performance

---

21 www.youtube.com/watch?v=2OhSXj-hiMI
22 The Danish flag.
23 www.youtube.com/watch?v=hAu2li6jbTs

on Danish Public Service TV by proclaiming that, 'this one goes out to the ones who decide for themselves how they want to be integrated'.[24] The political project is however not limited to anti-racism. Kid Kishore also actively advocates feminism/anti-sexist, anti-homophobia/queer, and anti-capitalism, just as he played a role in the formation of the organisation P4U—*Perkere for Ungdomshuset*[25] (note how the acronym style paraphrases P4L). He also appeared at a concert in support of controversial Muslim female candidate for the Danish parliament election, Asmaa Abdol-Hamid, who ran for parliament for *Enhedslisten*, the most left wing party with political representation in Denmark. Furthermore he has performed at several demonstrations in the radical left milieu. Kid Kishore is thus involved in explicitly political collective mobilisation.

Kid Kishore's musical practice can be considered radically postmodern. However he also articulates a postmodern position on the identity dimension. His public appearances are characterised by identity play. He is often depicted in police uniform and has appeared on television wearing a police shirt. At one point in time he took on the name *Trentemøller*—and created a profile under that name on the social internet site *MySpace*. That was an example *par excellence* of a postmodern subversion of stabile and authentic identity, since there was at the same time a highly popular ethnic Danish DJ by the name of *Anders* Trentemøller. Kid Kishore later commented that he specifically called himself Trentemøller and not *Anders* Trentemøller, and added that the use of this name was not a joke.[26] Another postmodern trait is the usage of a large number of pseudonyms: Trentemøller and Kid Kihsore are not the only two names adopted by the biological person behind Kid Kishore. He also has several other names, including DJ Hvad (DJ What). On this dimension Kid Kishore breaks with the idea of a real and authentic identity which otherwise prevails in hip-hop.

To sum up Kid Kishore as an artist is closer to the postmodern pole on several dimensions than any of the other artist analysed in this chapter. Importantly he is the artist who articulates an identity position closest to the postmodern understanding of identity as his public performances are to a very high degree characterised by identity play. He thus illustrates that postmodern identity play and political substance are not mutually exclusive. On the contrary it could be

---

24 In Danish, *Den her går ud til dem, der selv bestemmer hvordan de vil integrere sig.* DR 2, Den 11. time, 23, April, 2007.

25 *Ungdomshuset* was a culture house in Copenhagen primarily used by radical left wing youth.

26 In interview on DR 2, Den 11. time, 23, April, 2007.

argued that he is simultaneously the most post-modern, most collectivist and most explicitly political artist analysed here.

Discussion

The analysis above shows that the analysed groups vary to a very high degree in terms of style and in terms of dimensions of modernity/post-modernity. The groups in the first cluster stage themselves as almost stereotypical *dangerous* black men, the groups in position two articulate social criticism from the position of the black intellectual. Taken at face value these groups also articulate an understanding of identity which on the modern—post-modern continuum is closer to the modern pole in the sense that they stage themselves as stabile, authentic and *real* subjects. Further analysis however identifies complexities as these articulations of authenticity are expressed through a highly post-modern musical form; and one might speculate that the realness staged in the lyrics does not correspond neatly to the actual lives lived by these young men. Nevertheless the claiming of realness marks a difference to the identity play of the groups in the third cluster which display a postmodern decentering of identity almost par excellence. Here there is no staging of realness. Nevertheless, regardless of whether or not the musical material includes a postmodern articulation of identity *all* three positions articulate some form of political resistance.

The analysis calls for three discussions. *Firstly*, the analysis suggests that social structures are still relevant to understanding youth subcultures. The analysis thus illustrates the centrality of ethnicity as a social structure to the study of youth subcultures. Anti-immigrant discourses are being commented upon, criticised and answered in a variety of ways in the musical material. This suggests that the Post-Subcultural Studies scholars were indeed premature in their discarding of CCCS's understanding that youth subcultures may sometimes be understood as collective answers to a shared social situation. But it also illustrates the critiques that CCCS overstated the importance of class has some merit. In fact class is never mentioned directly in the musical material analysed, although the young men producing the music are affected by simultaneous classed and ethnic marginality. Explanations may be that hip-hop offers a discursive repertoire better suited for commenting on racism and/or that racism and ethnicism is experienced as more important than class by the young men. *Secondly*, the analysis points to the relevance of gender to contemporary discussions of subculture. All the artists mentioned above are *men*, mirroring the troublesome question of whether the hybridity and *bricolage* often celebrated in analyses of *new ethnicities* (Hall, 1991,1992) and post-modernity are in fact more accessible to young men than to young women (Prieur, 2002).

Female musicians thus make up a minority among ethnic minority hip-hop artists in Denmark. Gender is also relevant to a discussion of misogyny and masculinism in hip-hop. As illustrated above especially the first cluster of the typology routinely articulates sexism. There are different assessments of misogyny in hip-hop. Some pro-feminist scholars emphasise the problematic gender politics of hip-hop (Crenshaw, 1991; McDowell, 1997; Armstrong, 2001; Cole and Guy-Sheftall, 2003; Weitzer and Kubrin, 2009) while other— not necessarily anti-feminist—scholars consider it less of a problem (Hooks, 1994a, b; McLaren, 1999; Walcott, 1999; Baxter and Marina, 2008: 111; Møller, 2009).

The misogyny can be thought of as a dimension of constructing a public image as a dangerous young black man. *Thirdly*, the analysis questions the claim that contemporary postmodern youth cultures are depoliticised. The artists analysed are postmodern on different dimensions and to different extents. However even Kid Kishore, an artist whose public performances often takes the form of radically postmodern identity play, is explicitly political. This questions the very idea of depoliticised post-modern youth cultures as well as the more general idea that post-modernity implies de-politisation (Hall, 1986). In the words of Carrington and Wilson the conception of post-modernity employed by Post-Subcultural Studies is too narrow, because 'politics, if it remains at all, is shorn of its emancipatory potential' (2004: 74).

With a terminology borrowed from Peter McLaren, hip-hop and rap including *gangsta* rap, can be considered *an oppositional political practice* (1999: 23; also Baxter and Marina, 2008; Sernhede, 2002; Jensen, 2005, 2007). This point should not be confused with arguing that hip-hop is an *unproblematic* political practice. The resistance articulated in hip-hop is sometimes intertwined with misogyny (McLaren, 1999, 44) and/or with reproduction of the stereotype of the dangerous young black man (Jensen, 2010a). However these imperfections do not make hip-hop any less political. Problematic politics are not non-politics.

Conclusion and theoretical implications

The analysis in this chapter questions Post-Subcultural Studies' claims about youth culture on two dimensions: 1) It demonstrates that the production of hip-hop among ethnic minority men in contemporary Denmark can only be understood if the analysis is contextualised in overall social structures—in particular race, ethnicity, gender and class. It thus questions the claim made by Post-Subcultural Studies that structural forms of inequality have relatively little relevance to the study of contemporary youth subcultures. 2) It demonstrates that hip-hop among ethnic minority men in contemporary Denmark has explicit and implicit political dimensions. This is true regardless of where on the modern-postmodern continua the groups place themselves. This observation questions the idea that we live in a time where the cultural articulations of young people are postmodern and therefore depoliticised. Because the musical material analysed here is a public manifestation of a larger subculture the analysis illustrates that post-subcultural theory is inadequate for understanding substantial trends in contemporary youth culture. This does not mean that all contemporary youth subcultures are all about politics, nor does it mean that the wider subculture of ethnic minority young men whom these hip-hop groups are part of is political all the time. But it questions the grand claims by Post-Subcultural Studies scholars that youth subcultures of the present are generally depoliticised. However the analysis also supports the critique of class reductionism often raised against the CCCS, as it illustrates the centrality of gender and ethnicity.

This conclusion has further theoretical implications for what aspects of subcultural theory that might continue to be useful. It thus illustrates the relevance of a neo-Birminghamian conception of subculture. The core of such an understanding would be that insights can be gained from analysing youth subcultures as creative and open-ended collective *answers* to shared situations. Such an understanding insists that analysis of youth subcultures should be contextualised in terms of social structures. It also maintains an empirical openness towards political dimensions of contemporary youth subcultures although the explicit political content of some of the hip-hop groups analysed here challenges the distinction between sub-and counter-cultures. Furthermore such understanding breaks with the class reductionism inherent in the CCCS theory in favour of analyses of the interplay of class, gender, ethnicity and race (Carrington and Wilson, 2004). For that purpose much could be gained from the intersectionality perspective, which argues that social categories such as class, gender, ethnicity and race should be analysed as mutually constitutive (Crenshaw, 1991; Staunæs, 2003; McCall, 2005). In a sense the structural situations which young people answer and sometimes attempt to resist in their subcultures are by definition intersectional.

Acknowledgements

I would like to thank the two anonymous reviewers, the CASTOR research group at Aalborg University, my friend journalist and musician Rasmus Poulsen, and the Scandinavian Youth and Marginalisation Network, all of whom helped improve the analyses forwarded in this chapter.

References

Andersen, M. A., Mørck, R. V., Christensen, S. and Minke, L., (2001) Rodet ungdom—unge rødder, [Messy Youth—young roots], *Social Kritik*, 77: 18-47.

Andreassen, R., (2005) *The Mass Media's Construction of Gender, Race, Sexuality and Nationality*. Thesis (Ph. D.) University of Toronto.

Armstrong, E.g., (2001) Gangsta misogyny: A content analysis of the portrayals of violence against women in rap music, 1987-1993, *Journal of Criminal Justice and Popular Culture*, 8 (2): 96-126.

Baxter, K. and Marina, P., (2008) Cultural meaning and hip-hop fashion in the African-American male youth subculture of New Orleans, *Journal of Youth Studies*, 11 (2): 93-113.

Bay, J. and Drotner, K., (1986) *Ungdom: en stil, et liv*, [*Youth: a style, a life*], København: Tiderne skifter.

Bennett, A., (1999) Subcultures or neo-tribes? Rethinking the relationship between youth, style and musical taste, *Sociology*, 33(3): 599-617.

Bennett, A., (2000) *Popular Music and Youth Culture: Music, Identity and Place*, London: Macmillan.

Bennett, A. and Kahn-Harris, K. (eds.). (2004) *After Subculture—Critical Studies in Contemporary Youth Culture*, New York: Palgrave.

Bjurström, E., (1997) *Högt and lågt: Smak och stil i ungdomskulturen, [High and low: taste and style in youth culture]*, Umeå: Boréa.

Blackman, S., (2005) Youth Subcultural Theory: A Critical engagement with the Concept, its Origins and Politics, from the Chicago School to Postmodernism', *Journal of Youth Studies*, 8(1): 1-20.

Brake, M., (1985) *Comparative youth Culture*, London: Routledge.

Carrington, B. and Wilson, B., (2004) Dance Nations: Rethinking Youth Subcultural Theory, in Andy Bennett, A. and Kahn-Harris, K., (eds.) *After Subculture—Critical Studies in Contemporary Youth Culture*, New York: Palgrave.

Cohen, A. K., (1955) *Delinquent Boys*, New York: The Free Press.

Cohen, P. (1972) Subcultural Conflict and Working Class Community, *Working Papers in Cultural Studies* vol. 2.

Cohen, S. (2002 [1972]) Folk Devils and moral Panics, London: Routledge.

Cohen, S., (2002 [1987]) Symbols of trouble: Introduction to the Second Edition, in Cohen, S., (2002 [1972]) *Folk Devils and moral Panics*, London: Routledge.

Cole, J. B. and Guy-Sheftall, B., (2003) *Gender Talk: The Struggle for Women's Equality in African American Communities*, New York: Ballantine.

Crenshaw, K. W., (1991) Mapping the Margins—Intersectionality, Identity Politics and Violence Against Women of Colour, *Stanford Law Review*, 43 (6): 1241-1299.

Cutler, C., (2003) 'Keepin' it Real': White Hip-Hoppers Discourses of Language, Race and Authenticity, *Journal of Linguistic Anthropology*, 13(2): 1-23.

Diken, B., (1998) *Strangers, Ambivalence and Social Theory*, Aldershot: Ashgate.

Frosh, S., Phoenix, A. and Pattman, R., (2002) *Young Masculinities*, Basingstoke: Palgrave.

Gilroy, P. (1993a) Between Afro-centrism and Euro-centrism: Youth Culture and the Problem of Hybridity, *Young*, 1(2): 2-12.

Gilroy, P. (1993b) *The Black Atlantic—Modernity and Double Consciousness*; London: Verso.

Griffin, C. E., (2011) The trouble with class: researching youth, class and culture beyond the 'Birmingham School', *Journal of Youth Studies*, 14(3): 245-259.

Gudmundsson, G. (1992) *Ungdomskultur—som overgang til lønarbejde, [Youth culture as a transition to wage-labour]*, København: Forlaget. Sociologi.

Hall, S. (1986) On Postmodernism and Articulation: An Interview with Stuart Hall (interview edited by Lawrence Grossberg), *Journal of Communication Inquiry*, 10(2): 45-60.

Hall, S. (1991) Old and New Identitites, Old and New Ethinicties, in King, A. D.,(ed.) *Culture, Globalization and the World-system—Contemporary conditions for the representation of identity*, London: Macmillan.

Hall, S., (1992) New Ethnicities, in Donald, J. and Rattansi, A., (eds) *'Race', Culture and Difference*, London: Sage.

Hall, S. and Jefferson, T., (eds) (1991 [1975]). *Resistance through Rituals: Youth subcultures in post-war Britain*, London: Routledge.

Hammarén, N., (2008) *Förorten i huvudet: unga män om kön och sexualitet i det nya Sverige, [Suburbs in the head: young men on gender and sexuality in the new Sweden}*, Thesis (Ph. D.), University of Gothenburg.

Hebdige, D., (1979) *Subculture. The meaning of style*, London: Methuen

Hervik, P., (ed.). (1999) *Den generende forskellighed—danske svar på den stigende multikulturalisme, [The annoying difference – Danish answers to the increasing multiculturalism]*, København: Hans Reitzels Forlag.

Hervik, P., (2004) The Danish Cultural World of Unbridgeable Differences, *Ethnos*, 69(2), 247-267.

Hesmondhalgh, D., (2005) Subculutres, Scenes or Tribes? None of the Above, *Journal of Youth Studies*, 8(1): 21-40.

hooks, b., (1994a) Gangsta Culture—Sexism and Misogyny—Who Will Take the Rap, in hooks, b. *Outlaw Culture: Resisting Representations*; London: Routledge.

hooks, b., (1994b) Ice Cube Culture—A Shared Passion for Speaking Truth, in hooks, b., *Outlaw Culture: Resisting Representations*, London: Routledge.

Horst, C., (1991) Marginalisering og etnicisme, *Dansk Sociologi*, 2(4): 66-85.

Hughey, M. W., (2009) Black Aestethics and Panther Rhetoric: A critical Decoding of Black Masculinity in *The Black Panther*, 1967-80, *Critical Sociology*, 35(1): 29-56.

Hviid, K., (2007) *No life*, Thesis (Ph. D.), Aalborg University.

Jensen, S. Q. (2005) Subkulturelle hypermaskuliniteter i det offentlige rum, [Subcultural hyper masculinities in public space], *Grus*, 26 (75-76): 130-150.

Jensen, S. Q. (2006) Rethinking Subcultural Capital, *Young, Nordic Journal of Youth Research*, 3 (14): 257-276.

Jensen, S. Q. (2007) *Fremmed, farlig og fræk: Unge mænd og etnisk/racial andenhed— mellem modstand og stilisering, [Foreign, dangerous and sexy: young men and ethnic/racial otherness – between resistance and stylization]*, Thesis (Ph. D.), Aalborg University.

Jensen, S. Q. (2008). 8210-cent, Perker4livet og Thug-gangsta, [8210-cent, Perker4life and Thug-gangsta], in Krogh, M. and Stougaard, B. (eds) *Hiphop i Skandinavien*, Århus: Århus Universitetsforlag.

Jensen, S. Q. (2010a) Masculinity at the margins—othering, marginality and resistance among young marginalized ethnic minority men, *NORMA*, 5(1): 7-26

Jensen, S. Q. (2010b) Østerbro Outlaws'—om subkulturteori og marginaliserede unge mænd med indvandrerbaggrund, [Østerbro Outlaws – on subcultural theory and marginalised young men with immigrant background], *Tidsskrift for Ungdomsforskning*, 10(1): 3-21.

Jensen, S. Q., (2011) Othering, Identity Formation and Agency, *Qualitative Studies*, 2(2): 63-78.

Jensen, S. Q. and Hviid, K., (2003) *Perker rap, [Perker rap, ghetto Noise and Social work]*, Ghettostøj og socialt arbejde, *Social Kritik*, No. 89: 22-41.

Jonsson, R., (2007) *Blatte betyder Kompis, [Negro means friend]*, Stockholm: Ordfront.

Klinker, S. and Bilde, M. H., (2009) Gadens Koder i A-town—status og respekt blandt etniske minoritetsfyre, [Codes of the street in A-town—status and respect among young ethnic minority men], *Dansk Sociologi*, 20(4): 37-56.

Layder, D., (1998) *Sociological practice*, London: Sage.

Maffesoli, M., (1996) *The time of the Tribes: The decline of Individualism in Mass Society*, London: Sage.

McCall, L., (2005) Managing the complexity of intersectionality, *Signs: Journal of Women in Culture and Society*, 30(3): 1771-1800.

McDowell, D. E., (1997) Pecs and Reps: muscling in on Race and the Subject of Masculinities, in Stecopoulos, H. and Uebel, M., (eds) *Race and the subject of masculinities*, Durham, NC and London: Duke University Press.

McLaren, P., (1999) Gangsta Pedagogy and Ghettocentricity: The Hip Hop Nation as a Counterpublic Sphere', in McCarthy, C., Hudak, G, Miklaucic, S. and Saukko, P., (eds) *Sound Identities—Popular Music and the Cultural Politics of Education*, New York: Peter Lang.

McRobbie, A.,(1980) Settling accounts with subcultures: A Feminist Critique, *Screen Education*; 34(1): 37-49.

McRobbie, A., (1990) *Feminsim and Youth Culture*, Basingstoke: Macmillan.

McRobbie, A. and Garber, J.,(1975) Girls and Subcultures, in Hall, S. and Jefferson, Tony (eds) (1991 [1975]) *Resistance through Rituals: Youth subcultures in post-war Britain*, London: Routledge.

Mitchell, T., (ed.) (2001) *Global noise—Rap and Hip—Hop outside the USA*, Middletown: Weslyan University Press.

Muggleton, D., (2005) From Classlessness to clubculture—A genealogy of post-war British youth cultural analysis, *Young, Nordic Journal of Youth Research*, 13(2): 205-319.

Muggleton, D., (2000) *Inside Subculture—The Postmodern Meaning of Style*, Oxford: Berg.

Muggleton, D. and Weinzierl, R., (2003) What is 'Post-subcultural Studies' Anyway?, in Muggleton, D. and Weinzierl, R., (eds).*The Post-Subcultures Reader*, Oxford: Berg.

Mungham G. and Pearson G., (eds) (1978) *Working-Class Youth Culture*, London: Routledge and Kegan Paul.

Møller, R., (2009) Eminem: Flertydige maskulinitetsdannelser mellem gangsterrap og mainstream ungdomskultur,[Eminem: Competing interpretatiions of masculinity between gansta rap and mainstream youth culture], *Kvinder, Køn og Forskning*, 18(1): 20-29.

Mørck, Y.,. (1999) Faktisk er Blågårds Plads utrolig smuk—hårde drenge på Nørrebro, [Blågårds Plads is actually quite nice—the hard cases of Nørrebro], N *Social Kritik*, 65/66: 45-58.

Palmer, V. M., (1928) *Field studies in Sociology: A Student's Manual*, Chicago: University of Chicago Press.

Pedersen, B. S., (2008) Total glokal—En undersøgelse af sprogspil I dansk rap med stedet som markør, [Total glocal—an investigation of language games in Danish rap], in Krogh, M and Stougaard, B., (eds) *Hiphop i Skandinavien, [Hiphop in Scandinavia]* Århus: Århus Universitetsforlag.

Prieur, A., (1999) Maskulinitet, kriminalitet and etnicitet, [Maculinity, criminality and ethnicity], *Social Kritik*, No. 65/66: 33-43.

Prieur, A., (2002) Gender Remix, *Ethnicities*, 2(1): 53-77.

Røgilds, F., (1994) Avedøre—en forstad til Sarajevo?, [Avedøre—a suburb of Sarajevo?] in Madsen, A., Ejersbo, S. and Damkjær, S., (eds) *Den kultursociologiske omtanke, [Cultural sociological thoughtfulness]*, København: Akademisk Forlag.

Røgilds, F., (2002) Den nye racisme: Aktører. Forhistorie. Modstrategier, [New racism: actors, history, counter strategies], *Dansk Sociologi*, 13(3): 101-110.

Sandberg, S., (2005) Stereotypiens dilemma, [The dilemma of stereotypes], *Tidsskrift for Ungdomsforskning*, 5(2): 27-46.

Sandberg, S., (2008) 'Get rich or die tryin'—Hiphop og minoritetsgutter på gata, ['Get rich or die tryin'—Hiphop and minority lads on the streets], *Tidsskrift for Ungdomsforskning*, 8 (1): 67-83.

Sandberg, S. and Pedersen, W., (2006) *Gatekapital*, {Street capital], Oslo: Universitetsforlaget.

Schierup, C., (1993) *På kulturens slagmark, [On the battleground of culture]*, Esbjerg: Sydjysk Universitetsforlag.

Sernhede, O., (1999) Alienation is our Nation—Reality is my Nationality, in Amnå, E. (ed.) *Det unga folkstyret*, No. 93,.Stockholm.

Sernhede, O., (2001) Los Angered og forstadens krigere, [Los Angered and the warriers of the suburbs], *Social Kritik*, No. 74: 39-50.

Sernhede, O., (2002) *Alienation is My Nation*, Stockholm: Ordfront Förlag.

Sewell, T., (1997) *Black Masculinities and Schooling: How Black Boys Survive Modern Schooling,* Stoke on Trent: Trentham Books.

Shildrick, T., (2006) Youth culture, subculture and the importance of neighbourhood, *Young, Nordic Journal of Youth Research*, 14(1): 61-74.

Shildrick, T. and Macdonald, R., (2006) In defence of Subculture: Young People, Leisure and Social Divisions, *Journal of Youth Studies*, 9(2): 125-140.

Staunæs, D., (2003) Where have all the subjects gone? Bringing together the concepts of intersectionality and subjectification, *Nora*, 11(2): 101-110.

Thornton, S., (1995) *Club cultures*. Cambridge: Polity Press.

Walcott, R., (1999) Performing the (Black) Postmodern: Rap as incitement for Cultural Criticism, in McCarthy, C., Hudak, G., Miklaucic, S. and Saukko,. P., (eds) *Sound Identities—Popular Music and the Cultural Politics of Education*, New York: Peter Lang.

Weitzer, R. and Kubrin, C. E., (2009) Misogyny in Rap Music—A Content Analysis of Prevalence and Meanings, *Men and Masculinities*, 12 (3): 3-29.

Willis, P., (1978) *Learning to Labour*, Aldershot: Ashgate.

Wren, K., (2001) Cultural racism: Something rotten in the state of Denmark?, *Social and Cultural Geography*, 2(2): 141-163.

Yilmaz, F., (1999) Konstruktionen af de etniske minoriteter: Eliten, medierne og 'etnificeringen' af den danske debat, [The construction of ethnic minorities: the élite, the media and the 'ethnification' of the Danish debate], *Politica*, 31(2): 177-191.

Young, J.,(2003) Merton with energy, Katz with structure: The sociology of vindictiveness and the criminology of transgression, *Theoretical Criminology*, 7(3): 389-414.

Chapter 3

On creativity and resistance in Nordic youth culture on the margins

Dennis Beach and Ove Sernhede

Introduction

Over the last twenty-five years the urban music and dance style known as hip-hop has become a widespread form of communication carried out and enjoyed by people throughout the world. However it has grown from its original roots in rap music and break dancing in many different directions. On the one hand it represents a multi-billion dollar industry of big-time, best-selling artists who market songs that focus on wealth, possessions and crime, often with a misogynistic attitude. But on the other it is a way of life for many young people with a political awareness that is intricately woven into every aspect of their daily lives.

This chapter explores some dimensions of the creativity of hip-hop as expressed through the activities of one group of performers, a group who are known as the Filthy Dozen Incorporated: FD.Ink. They are a community-based underground group of rappers from a suburb on the outskirts of a large Swedish city who write and perform against the mass appeal and commercialisation of the *gangsta* genre of hip-hop. Their style of hip-hop valorises the qualities of their region, which we have called Olleryd, and uses regional news as lyrics on CDs, in performances and on YouTube, which they communicate in both local communities and with youth in places as far flung as London, Tokyo, Paris and New York. As one of the group said to us, 'we belong to a global community of rappers who are talking about their marginalisation using similar lyrics, similar music and similar dress ... You ask what hip-hop is to us ... That is what it is'. In addition to this group we have also developed data connected to an Arab-fusion hip-hop group from a suburb in another city about an hour from Olleryd. The present article deals mainly with FD.Ink.

Following the present short introduction the chapter starts with a fairly formal presentation of the concept of creativity as expressed in creativity research. It identifies important definitions of creativity and creativity learning and then links these to the performances and values of the Filthy Dozen. When making this analysis we note how the group use hip-hop styles and rap to talk through their lyrics about their stigmatisation, about police and media harassment and about the material poverty of their neighbourhood. They provide in this way a critical voice against an oppression and marginalisation which they feel they share with others from their neighbourhood and more broadly (Beach and Sernhede, 2012). They have what we call a resistant fervour that is expressed through their lyrics and teachings as a means for raising awareness on and talking back to mainstream society. We liken this resistance to resistance through art form representations such as the poetics of Brecht and the artistic style known as the German expressionist movement.

We have been involved in research with interests in creativity previously. Three projects can be cited specifically. These are a national project led by Ove Sernhede on suburban subcultures (see e.g. Sernhede, 2007), a European project called CLASP (Creativity Learning and Student Perspectives) and a VR HumSam project called *Researching creativity in education: New forms of expression, new responsibilities and new media in the development of creative and aesthetic learning* (VR Reg. no. 2004-11499-26389-27) (Beach, 2006, 2008).

These projects took different departures. They consider educational and life experiences for youths from one particular type of context—multicultural, multi-poverty, territorially stigmatised suburban areas—based on ethnographic research on young people's learning and creativity and the encounter between local cultural identities and schools as formal institutions (Sernhede, 2011). The research involving Beach focused on what seemed to support or obstruct creative teaching and learning and the development of creativity in formal education. The work led by Sernhede explored creativity outside of school. The symbolic and artistic creativity of the group of young adult-male hip-hoppers introduced above was in focus in particular (Sernhede, 2007; Beach and Sernhede, 2012). In the present context we have linked our work and also added some new data from two recent projects *Schools and their Surroundings* (VR Reg. no. 2005-3440) and *Stereotypes, naïve theories, cultural norms and their effects on school performance* (VR Reg. no. 721-2006-2554). Possibilities that the autonomous learning activities in a hip-hop collective may have a potential to break urban segregation patterns are considered in particular.

We have looked at the artistic productions of these individuals outside school and at cases of learning in school that have broken the otherwise predominant trends of social and cultural reproduction that tend to hold immigrant groups within the grip of a failing suburban subaltern identity (Sernhede, 2011; Beach and Sernhede, 2011; Beach et al., in press). Six different schools in four urban areas with sizeable intakes of pupils from multi-racial, multi-lingual and multi-ethnic catchments have been involved. Each of the areas is among the areas in Sweden that are formally identified as impoverished and territorially stigmatised suburbs on the edge of major cities. Roughly thirty-five different first languages are spoken in the schools there. The research in them involved over 3000 hours of participant observation and more than 200 interviews. Some of this research was done by us but most was done by research associates in projects that we coordinated or that we were involved in (see e.g. Beach, 2006, 2008; Beach and Dovemark, 2009, 2011; Sernhede, 2011; Schwartz, 2010; Möller, 2010; Borelius, 2010; Öhrn et al., 2011; Beach et al., in press).

In addition to this institutional ethnographic work, we and colleagues have also conducted research in some of the local communities surrounding these schools (see e.g. Beach and Dovemark, 2007, Sernhede, 2007; Beach et al., in press). As part of this work one of us lived in one of the researched areas for a six month period, in the same housing block as the housing association offices and laundrette, the social security office and the regional social club for one ethnic sports and one ethnic cultural organisation; and the other conducted long-term participant observation in a similar city district over a three year period. These participant observation experiences and the data they produced have broadened the basis of our analysis.

Perceptions of creativity and the present research

As Jeffrey and Woods (2003) and Craft (2001) have written, creativity began to be systematically investigated at the end of the nineteenth century, within psychology, where it was concentrated around aesthetic fields such as art and music. One of the first systematic studies was on the relationship between creativity and genius by Francis Galton (Craft, 2001). Four major traditions of enquiry developed from this work: the psychoanalytic, including Freud's discussion of creativity as the sublimation of drives and Winnicott's work on affective human nature; the cognitive, from Galton's and Guilford's explorations of divergent ideas; the behaviourist, from Skinner; and the humanistic.

The humanistic tradition is the one closest to ours. It emphasises self-actualisation and characteristics of the aesthetic self, such as being *problem focused* and having *autonomy* of attitude or self-responsibility. These ideas do not just relate to psychological concepts such as self-motivation, intellectual curiosity, holistic learning, desire for self-realisation, self-confidence, attraction towards complexity, capacity for emotional involvement in inquiry, they also relate to culture, history, ideology and social, material and discursive constraints.

We can relate here back to some of the CLASP project findings on how creativity learning occurred primarily when learners were able to valorise their class-cultural values and subjectivity products as formal educational capital without losing control over the learning process and opportunities to take ownership of their education. We found that co-participatory practices that drew on the whole environment and made use of space and participating pupils' individual skills was important, as was using external and community support in the development of positive discourses about the value of these experiences. There was talk of *third space* experiences that were neither only aesthetic nor purely cognitive based on the ability to recognise lived circumstances and reinterpret and re-articulate a critical view of existing social conditions and relations that challenged conventional understandings. Bertolt Brecht wrote on such things in *On the Critical Attitude*. He maintained the need to give criticism arms so that despotic States could be demolished by it and expressed that educating a person for transforming a State are instances not only of fruitful criticism but also of art.

This background to creativity and creativity research suggests something of the ways in which perceptions of creativity have changed across history, from the ancient Greek concept of freedom of action that separated art from craft, to modern conceptions of creativity as related to new products and divergent thought. This breadth of interest has meant that creativity has been investigated from many perspectives in different subject areas and that there is no finally accepted definition of what it is or how it is learned (Csikszentmihalyi, 1990, 1996; Eisner, 2002; Kim, 2006; Compton, 2007; Hunter et al., 2007; Hu et al., 2010; Althuizen et al., 2010).

Without trying to provide an all encompassing definition of creativity our chapter examines what we consider as a good example of it as it has developed in the informal learning community introduced above, who perform *back to* and against the commercialisation of big-time, best-selling artists and defy common restrictions for people from the places and backgrounds they come from. This creativity is dependent on shared social judgment and a capacity to produce original products that are not only commercially valuable but also valuable in other senses. That is, they have a genuine use-value as well as (or opposed to) only an economic exchange value (Willis, 1990). The Filthy Dozen are we suggest exceptional intellectually profound, symbolically gifted and productive exponents of this kind of production (see also Beach and Sernhede, 2012 and Qvotrup, this volume).

This description forms a very different label for this group of young people than youths of their background are used to from their contacts with the mainstream institutions of Swedish society, such as the media and the school (Beach and Sernhede, 2011; Beach et al., in press). Born of immigrant parents they have grown up in territorially stigmatised suburbs on the outskirts of one of our country's major cities and have lived in more cramped and inferior housing conditions to their white peers and appear to be given undeservedly low grades in relation to their educational performance in school. They are confronted by things such as media racism (Möller, 2010) and teachers in schools who may hold negative stereotypes about them and their abilities based on stereotypical ideological understandings of an assumed and passively accepted superiority of western culture (Schwartz, 2010).

As described also by Schwartz and Öhrn (2012) these things are visible in the ways the pupils from these areas are spoken of. They are reflected also in the transcription field-notes and interview extracts from our research and that of some of our close colleagues. The pupils in these areas are often described as, 'a special kind of pupil ... with special needs (that have) to be met by us' (John, Teacher, School X). They are said to come from, 'particularly difficult backgrounds (and to have had) many bad experiences from their neighbourhood' (Head-teacher, School X). They are often called, 'broken children ... with special educational requirements' (Carole, Teacher, School Y). They are exposed to special kinds of pedagogy in schools that adopt particular working doctrines connected to strong leadership and the development of discipline and motivation (Schwartz, 2010). As the youths from the areas in question have put it, 'people outside know nothing of this place but they treat us (as if) they did and in a special way because of what they think' (Mamoud). They point out that, 'such views follow us everywhere ... In stores, on the buses, in school ... everywhere' (Miriam).

Methods

We have used ethnography as the main methodological approach in our research. This approach is now quite common in Scandinavia, particularly in educational research, where it is used for developing theoretical and practical descriptions of education lives, identities and activities through detailed situated investigations that are anticipated to produce knowledge about the basic educational conditions and practices and the perspectives of the participants involved in them. The aim is to identify and develop previously unexplored dimensions of everyday life and learning without over-steering from purely personal ideas.

As our research has been conducted in multi-cultural, multi-racial suburban areas we have also made particular use of discussions about ethnographic research in Scandinavia in such areas (Beach and Lunneblad, 2011) and the written products developing from our projects have been analysed together with writing from other projects. Particularly important has been work in the Nordic NordForsk sponsored research network behind the present book, *Youth and Marginalisation* of course, but also work from a second Nordforsk network called *NordCrit* (e.g. Öhrn et al., 2011; Öhrn, 2012; Beach et al., in press).

The analysis in this *combined* and *multi-sited* part of the research has involved a kind of meta-analysis that has recently been called meta-ethnography (Weed, 2006; Savin Baden et al., 2008). It is a response from within ethnographic research to critiques from outside about ethnography being tied to individual cases and being unable to provide generalisations of data and analyses that are possible to apply more broadly. Parallel to other forms of meta-analysis it involves comparisons across different research projects that explicitly share something in common, in an attempt to synthesise key elements produce a broader more general account of the issues investigated (Beach, 2009, 2011; Beach et al., in press).

Meta-ethnography is not without criticism from within conventional ethnographic circles and can be judged to in fact defeat the very intentions of ethnography, to illustrate complex individual details from individual cases (Beach et al., in press). For this reason, as did the authors in Beach et al., (op. cit.), we have gone to some lengths to try to ensure that important basic ethnographic theories and principles such as ethnography's emphasis on an active and creative citizen and its generally accepted assumption that there is always a dialectical relationship between human social practices, human consciousness, social structures and material conditions, are respected in the reanalysis and that an attention to ethnographic details in the individual case studies is also reflected in this chapter, which also provides excerpts from field data in relation to the arguments and ideas developed.

Research in suburban subaltern cultures

Research on modern suburban regions in Scandinavia and several other countries often expresses these places as residential areas with high poverty levels that are usually located on the edge of large towns and cities (Dikec, 2007; Hill, 2009; Gannon, 2009; Beach and Sernhede, 2011). They often contain immigrant-dense territorially stigmatised housing areas that are separate (physically, racially, economically and psychologically) from the rest of society, with prominent patterns of marginalisation and discrimination that affect both the activities of schools and the communities established by young people outside them (also Gannon, 2009) and they are also often characterised by local historical divisions of race and class that are offered by the media and other institutions as explanation for current tensions in suburban communities (Dikec, 2007) and the shortcomings of their schools (Hill, 2009; Shim, 2012; Beach and Sernhede, 2012) with schools that share a set of common features that are characteristic for public-sector schools in multi-racial suburbs across the country, such as low grade-point averages, vandalism, stigma and staff-recruitment and retention difficulties, and the areas themselves are generally openly under-funded in relation to their needs (Sernhede, 2007). Researchers characterise the areas as socially vulnerable, low-income, high unemployment, high social insecurity regions with low levels of formal education and health standards (Borelius, 2010; Schwartz, 2010; Möller, 2010) and the suburbs we have been involved in are no exception to this.

As written in Beach and Sernhede (2012) the development of these suburbs in Sweden liken in several respects processes taking place during the 1980s and 1990s in large parts of Western Europe, through the structural economic transformation processes that have changed several important aspects of the Keynesian economic model that dominated the political climate in the decades after the second-world-war (Beach, 2009) towards a neoliberal set of economic policies that extends and disseminates market values to public institutions. A number of Swedish researchers and debaters are prepared to consider these changes as representing an epoch shift (Bengtsson and Wirtén, 1996; Beach and Sernhede, 2012).

For the young people in these areas schools no longer appear to be the obvious passageway into Swedish society and may instead constitute a barrier rather than a means for integration (Beach and Sernhede, 2011, Schwartz and Öhrn, 2012, Beach et al., in press). They are not spoken of as arenas where they can develop self-respect, knowledge and an understanding of the time in which they live (Sernhede, 2007) and they provide the youngsters attending them with educational grades far below national averages that add to their integration problems. Obtaining *standard* work or continuing to advance through the various levels of school and into higher education are not possible on the basis of the grades these pupils obtain (Schwartz, 2010; Beach and Sernhede, 2011).

This is highly significant. In an advanced knowledge society such as Sweden, higher education is increasingly becoming a main if not the key aspect of social integration (Stehr and Böhme, 1986). Schools in territorially stigmatised suburban areas risk adding to a massive democracy deficit in future society and this is a problem we are trying to address in the chapter by drawing attention to the creative capacities of youth there, who are otherwise often looked upon as a lost hope in education terms.

On the other hand we must not forget that the areas in question have a long history as materially under-resourced and stigmatised regions that reaches back over many years, as far as the beginnings of the so-called Golden Era of the Swedish Welfare State in the sixties and early seventies, where they formed part of the Social Democratic *Million Homes Project*. The aim of this project was to provide housing of good standard for the white working class, who up until then had lived in cramped, substandard accommodation, but this housing was unfortunately built predominantly as white working-class worker-ghettos. In them workers and their families were corralled within easy access of the major sites of economic production in the region in areas with their own public institutions, shops and services. They thus formed self-contained areas of the metropolitan region for white working-class people that were later used also by migrant labour and then, more recently, by other migrant groups when conventional economic production was transformed into its current post-industrial, post-modern forms of global capitalism (Beach and Sernhede, 2011; Beach et al., in press).

Thus, as also Shim (2012: 216) suggests, what we see today is not only a product of today. It also holds historically class coded roots that pass through the media and other institutions into both the present and the future to shape both the experiences and expectations of communities and the people in them and interpretations of their actions. For the areas in question this means, as also suggested in Beach et al., (in press), that the *ghetto-stigma* has remained (Beach and Sernhede, 2011, 2012), though now also together with a multi-cultural, multi-racial, multi-lingual immigrant population suffering extensive unemployment and increased economic poverty, social isolation in accommodation the has exhibited heightened levels of material decay in recent years (Borelius, 2010). Over seventy per cent of the families in these areas nationally live below the official national poverty level and unemployment amongst young adults between 20 and 25 years-old is more than five times higher than the national average for this age-group.

As noted by Sernhede (2007), young people don't passively accept and take the stigmatised definitions of place and space implied by *territorial stigmatisation* and similar processes as their own (also Shim, 2012). Rather, as is also suggested in the separate chapters by Möller, Qvotrup-Jensen and Mainsah in this volume, they often take a more creative response, and even create their own cultures and communities in a search for the respect, understanding, belonging, security, intimacy, meaning, identity and knowledge that Swedish society and its schools seem to have been unable to provide (Sernhede, 2007). These communities, sometimes criminal sometimes not, as suggested by for instance differential association and subcultural formation theories (Hall and Jefferson, 1976; Hebdige, 1979; Willis, 1990; Blackman, 1995; Dedman, 2011) become a means to provide cognitive maps to navigate the surrounding world by (Beach and Sernhede, 2011). One of our aims is to cast light on certain aspects of this by re-exploring data from research on a suburban youth subculture that developed around expressions of the experience of schooling and marginalisation and the expressivity of hip-hop, rap, break-dance and DJing practices by youths and young adults from these communities (Beach and Sernhede, 2012).

Learning creativity outside school: Creativity learning in a hip-hop community

As described also in the chapter by Qvotrup-Jensen, since its emergence on the North American east coast in the mid-1970s, hip-hop has been defined in terms of four well-known elements—rap, breakdance, DJing and graffiti. However, a fifth element has recently emerged from the need to keep the hip-hop movement together (Chang, 2005; Sernhede and Beach, 2012). This fifth element consists of *knowledge and teaching* in what is now the worldwide net-based movement known as *The Universal Zulu Nation*. Although not the initial starting point for the Filthy Dozen, the ideologies of this fifth element have recently become important to their self-concept and practices. One of our subjects spoke on this as follows:

> The *Universal Zulu Nation* is an international culture and a kind of consciousness that unites races and religions. There is entertainment but not at any cost. We are talking about multi-skilled, multi-cultural, multi-racial communication (that) speaks against injustice and for an

equal society and a more peaceful world that can heal divisions and address legitimate concerns.   (Diaz, interview)

A similarity between Diaz consciousness and the intentions behind the critical cultural theory of the CCCS group at Birmingham University in the nineteen-seventies and eighties could be suggested here. This is not far-fetched. Similar suggestions have been made in the past about activities and living consciousness on the part of individuals like Diaz and the sub-cultural formations they belong to (also Hall and Jefferson, 1976; Hebdige, 1979; Willis, 1990, 2004; Blackman, 1995; Dedman, 2011 and Qvotrup-Jensen, this volume). However, it is also obviously apparent in relation to the transformation of the Black-American DJ known as Afrika Bambaataa, broadly recognised as the founder of hip-hop and the *Zulu Nation*, from gang warlord to movement founder and leader when he began to re-hone some of the skills he had learnt from organising street-gang activities into something more positive to the black community. Bambaataa's intention was to build a youth movement out of the creativity of a new generation of outcast youths with an authentic, liberating worldview (Chang, 2005), which he did in a way that is recognisable amongst other creative artists across history.

There is a strongly critical perspective in expressionist art. This was premised on the idea that modern societies had turned into closed totalitarian systems that are heavily determined by stinting and dehabilitating post-colonial worldviews that limit individual autonomy and full subject possibilities for all human-kind. The intention was, as with Bambaataa later on, to get the intense emotional experiences invoked through participation in such circumstances into a communicative media in order to *give voice* to the subjective emotions that these experiences arouse (Chang, 2005) and speak out about the frustration, anxiety, disgust and discontent felt about contemporary situations and the contradictions of modern life (also Dedman, 2011).

This kind of recognition and commitment can also be sensed in the artistry of the Filthy Dozen and shadows many of the comments they have made. One example is provided by Enrico. Enrico came to Sweden from Latin America in the early 1980s. Similar to Bambaataa his parents were politically aware and they encouraged him to study, he said. However, again like Bambaataa, he never really found a home for his talents and interests in the formal school and felt he gained a more useful education outside of rather than inside it. He became a fairly average pupil in the formal school. He commented on his experiences there in ways similar to the following block of transcription field-notes prepared from comments on school experiences by low-performing vocational and independent programme pupils and used recently in an article by Beach and Dovemark (2011):

> School is boring ... I hate some of the lessons like hell ... The teachers nag at you and some even ... humiliate you ... It's an insulting place (and) we would rather die than be like (the swots) ... It's not what we want ... We (often) meet in the café, listen to music ... play pool or just hang out ... Lessons are (no) fun ... We all have our faults but school has thousands ... I don't know why I'm here ... I only come when I feel like it ... I used to try but it didn't help and I never had a real picture of the purpose of it all ... Some teachers made me feel stupid ... I truanted ... I couldn't care less now ... I don't have an interest or time to do school work (and) rarely read even for tests and examinations ... I go to lessons if I feel like it (but) usually do other things there than we are supposed to ...

However, Enrico didn't fully fit this mould. His father was involved in the mobilisation of the local immigrant population and often took part in meetings and rallies designed to raise local consciousness and Enrico became socialised into a kind of thinking through following his father to meetings, that he then linked to the youth culture of his own generation. He did this, not dissimilarly to Bambaataa, first in terms of style and then in terms of the recognition of a need and desire to change things:

> When I was like fourteen or so I became interested in hip-hop. There were a couple of guys doing it and talking about the ghetto and black culture. I liked everything about it. The style of clothing, the music, the dance and the way they talked. But I also felt that it was a way of continuing doing what my father had done. It was our way to carry on with politics even though we were not political then, in the same way as my father was back in Latin America. I felt that we were the blacks of this country. We were not really accepted and we had to do something that was similar to what black people in the US had done and that was basically the same thing that my father and his comrades did in Latin America, fighting to get the voices of the repressed heard. (Enrico, interview)

A kind of resistant ferment seems to characterise the message from this extract. Sometimes this leads to overt violence and vandalism. In other cases it leads towards a symbolic revolution, as in the case of Enrico, Bambaataa and the art-forms of the German Expressionist movement mentioned earlier. According to other research it can also be found in Brazilian *favelas*, American ghettos, African shantytowns, Middle Eastern Kasbahs and French *banlieus* (Dikec, 2007; Beach and Sernhede, 2012) and the core of music-and style-based sub-cultures such as *grime* (Dedman, 2011). It foregrounds an idea recognised by the CCCS in Birmingham about how resistance can be performed as an aesthetic class practice (Hall and Jefferson, 1976; Blackman, 1995) to form a source for an agency that is expressed through styles of clothing, deportment and a music culture that identifies cultural knowledge and creative engagement as significant factors in youth group affiliations and their commitments (Hebdige, 1979; Willis, 1990). This applies particularly for those who like Enrico are at the centre of their localised musical scenes (Dedman, 2011).

Enrico's commitment to (and through) hip-hop thus appears to develop as a reaction against the urbanisation of his respective time and place and a desire to forge representations that convey a concern for the contradictory truths embedded in those social situations. This forms a starting point for analyses and messages that problematise the social reality in which we live through a challenge that involves more than a mere symbolic or ritualised resistance against the prevailing order (Sernhede and Beach, 2012). It contains a political dimension that relates to future development and ways of thinking about and dealing with the social, economic and cultural devaluation and deprivation (Chang, 2005; Schwartz, 2010; Beach and Sernhede, 2011). It has become, as in one of the classifications of hip-hop culture in Denmark described by Qvotrup Jensen (this volume), political. It aims to be a transformative art of the suburban reach spoken with voices that are usually formed outside of schools through the symbolism and artistry offered by the collective structure of hip-hop. The ambition is to provide an identity-bearing subaltern message as a correction towards common experiences from and representations of suburban life (Sernhede, 2007; Shim, 2012). When describing the lyrics and meaning of one of a local production a core group member, Victor, said:

> The suburbs are like a reservation ... But when I'm in my own neighbourhood where I've grown up, everything feels okay ... It's another world. I know everybody and everybody's just like me ... When I leave I

come to Sweden, and when I'm in Sweden I feel discriminated. It doesn't feel like my country and it never will ... I have a theory that the world is where you want to live. If a place feels good, you should live there. But Sweden doesn't feel like my country. When I look around ... I really don't want to be part of it ... I don't feel at home ... This is what our lyrics are about ... hip-hop helps us construct a message about this ... and we work around it together ... communicating and learning ... (Victor)

Enrico put things similarly when he said, 'what we're doing is a kind of adult education for our time'. He went on,

We try to get people we meet to develop ... and begin to think intellectually ... What we do is give belonging ... You know you can't just be an immigrant kid because then you're a nobody and that's what the gangs build on ... We give opportunities for another kind of belonging ... The schools and the ordinary ways of becoming members of society ... seemed to be closed to us. But when we make music and perform, we get in through the back door ... Our performances become a way of meeting all parts of the city to spread a message at youth recreation centres, to participate in debates, and to arrange lectures and workshops in libraries and so on. (Enrico)

The hip-hop community we have researched thus seems to clearly share a common passion that is expressed by people who interact regularly within a particular domain with the goal of gaining knowledge through sharing information and experiences. There is a process of recognition of the character of and of actively reflecting over the conditions of the surrounding world. Similar to Bambaataa, they then try to encourage people with similar experiences from similarly structured circumstances similarly sutured to the rest of society to think more politically about this. They are encouraging and forming a culturally critical community of practice with a commitment, earnestness and an agency that they lacked or were possibly denied without their art as individual pupils in the schools they went to. This is abundantly clear when comments by the group are compared to similar groups' comments and commitments in relation to their learning outside and inside school.

Rewriting creativity, resistance and learning

In the Marxist sense, in the common media representation and in schools, according to our analyses suburban youth are in a sense generally to be viewed as a class-in-itself: objectified, exploitable and often vilified, downtrodden and symbolically exploited in the mainstream media and common understanding (Sernhede, 2007; Beach and Sernhede, 2011). This is not an environment for developing a positive subject identity. The hip-hop collective on the other hand seems to be such an arena and may therefore also be, as suggested above, an arena (or a community in its resistant anti-commercialist forms) that is able to raise the consciousness of marginalised groups and others, by developing an aspect of the subaltern, in the senses meant also by Bambaataa, as a class-for-itself: aware, subjective, motivated and acting for change. This means of course that the collective and the school are obviously two very different arenas for learning. Regarding the latter we can observe that it is oriented towards *the outer world* the young people are part of and the need to accept this external social reality and a subjected and downtrodden part in it (Beach et al., in press).

What we are suggesting is that, much in the same way as Willis suggested was the case regarding the white working class urban youth of earlier periods and generations (2004), the world-view of the school is vertically imposed upon the subjective lived-world view of the youth themselves, and with some similar kinds of resistance (Willis, 2004; Beach and Sernhede, 2011). In Willis's example (and in the *ghettoisation* of working-class cultural forms of the *Million Homes Projects*) what was created was the possibility of a resistance that could be galvanised from forces emanating from the collective value assumed by an organised labour and common racial and ethnic heritage. But in the, '(post-)modern' suburban (anti-ghetto) the possibilities are different (Beach and Sernhede, 2011, 2012). There are still possibilities for the recognition of an inherent value in one's own area, but it is not found in the same common associations of a common cultural form (Beach et al., in press). The culture and messages of the hip-hop practiced by the Filthy Dozen give some clues. Their music is a way for others to find out what is going on in their regions with the ethnicity, poverty, unemployment and subjected experience (Dedman, 2011). But there is also, 'a value ... of place' (Enrico) expressed through the lyrics, 'of where I live' (Victor) as well as a desire to talk back and proclaim the virtues of this culture and place (Öhrn, 2011, 2012).

A good example is in the song *363 Dyrello* that pays homage to Olleryd, the suburb that the group comes from, and to two rappers who were killed in a tragic accident there. The song's references to the local city neighbourhood appear in a subtle and encoded way through portions of old local rap songs, allusions to specific events that are important to the initiated and the use of symbolism. The song has also become a short film on *YouTube* where it is one of the most frequently downloaded music videos produced by amateur musicians in Sweden. It has become an underground hit in many suburban areas as well as in other hip-hop communities around the country (Beach and Sernhede, 2012). The number 363 is Olleryd's postcode, and Dyrello is Olleryd written backwards.

It is through this kind of activity that the hip-hop collective offers opportunities to find an oppositional positive identity and consciousness from that they obtained in the formal school. In the formal school success is not brought about through oppositional recoding (Schwartz, 2010) but by pupils finding out and exploiting ways to consume time and other resources for personal gain (i.e. by them developing an aggressively competitive investment logic: Beach and Dovemark, 2009) through competitive practices then become transformed in everyday interaction and above all teacher talk, where they are described and acted towards as something more palatable: i.e. 'as showing intelligence (and) ability (and) performing at a level that less gifted pupils cannot reach' and as aspects of maturity, interest and giftedness (Beach and Dovemark, 2011). Desires to be competitive and acquire status have in this way become, if not confused with hard-work, interest, individual development and an inner-ability, certainly conflated with these issues.

The importance of mis-recognition also plays back on the ascribed identities of, 'under-performing' suburban youth in school contexts who are often, as already suggested above not judged as subjects in their own right, but more in terms of their lack of middle-class ascribed positive characteristics (Beach and Dovemark, 2011; Beach and Sernhede, 2011). They become, 'dull or slow' pupils (Brian, teacher) who are, 'troublesome and restless in class ... and often un-concentrated' (Gunnar, teacher). They are described as, 'lacking the qualities good pupils have' (Carole, teacher). They are said, as suggested earlier, to have, 'a weak (troubled and troublesome) background' (Carole) and to show a, 'lack of effort ... ability ... interest, or all three together' (Siv, teacher). None of these labels are communicated by what the pupils themselves say however (Öhrn, 2011, 2012):

I didn't see the meaning in it (and) didn't want to stick out too much from my friends ... A pass is enough ... It's not that I was

never interested ... I was ... But I didn't do well ... It just didn't
work out as well for me (so) I stopped really trying and was happy
enough to just pass ... A pass is enough (for) most of us ... I haven't
always ... got the grades (but) I don't like to take up too much of
the teacher's time and I have other interests ... School's not where I
try to be somebody ... I just never felt comfortable or at home there
           (Transcription field-notes: also in Beach and Dovemark, 2011)

Recognising the meaning of these comments for what they are about
(discomfort, alienation and resistance) instead of how they are normally
inscribed (deviance, deficiency and learning difficulty) is important. For what
the comments actually suggest is that the economic thinking and competition
that otherwise characterises school success at the individual level and that hinges
on 'working for naked self-interest, status attainment and private return' (i.e. an
investment logic and competitive consumerism) are absent, and that the group
in question lacks success not because of their background or where their parents
come from or their lack of intellectual abilities and motivation—as commonly
suggested by mainstream discourse (Beach et al., in press), but because of a sense
of solidarity and an absence of 'exaggerated self-interest and exaggerated personal
demands for private return' at any (or anyone's) cost (Beach and Dovemark,
2009, 2011). The hip-hop collective and its educational activities offer in this
sense a safe haven from which to develop a critical reflective identity and practice
protected from the stigmatisations of mainstream society and its school system
(Beach and Sernhede, 2012) and this may be why it is successful in ways that
the formal school system is not (Beach and Sernhede, 2011). However, it also
offers other learning opportunities as well (Beach and Sernhede, 2012), in terms
of skills such as, 'handling DJing programmes on the computer ... booking and
arranging a rehearsal hall or studio ... using film cameras or creating an internet
homepage and furnishing a meeting place' (Enrico).

These skills and also certain *administrative capabilities* are essential to the
creative artistic work of the group and they provide foundation-stones for
income-generating career-type activities. Moreover, communication skills
are also creatively developed to spread their counter-hegemonic voice in a
pedagogical fashion. As Enrico points out the members learn how to, 'run
study circles and how to manage and develop their economy' by arranging
and conducting meetings and, 'attending to the advertising of various activities'
(also Laslo). These things develop on the top of and off the back of an initial

recognition and an *experienced desire* to speak back and get inner needs and feelings across. As one of the young men in the group and one other informant said:

> When you feel bad it can be hard to talk about it ... It's not always so easy to know why you're down. Then it can feel real good to write some lyrics. To start to sing or just do some free styling to a fat beat. It feels like it's coming out. You feel relief somehow. (Noussam, 19 years, interview)

> But you can't live off feelings ... They can be a great driving force and source of motivation but to live ... you need much more ... Recognition is important, and respect, but you need to be able to sustain yourself, materially as well as spiritually. (Ali)

Questions raised and answered

In the collective's artistic productions—in rap texts, plays and films—it seems that questions are raised that have not been answered in the schools (Beach and Sernhede, 2012). These are questions like: why are our neighbourhoods stigmatised? How should the increasing class divisions between different parts of the urban landscape be understood? Does society have to consist of winners and losers? Why did we, of all people, end up in these poor areas? The young people's search for answers to these questions is intertwined with and communicated through their aesthetic practices (Dedman, 2011; Qvotrup-Jensen, this volume). They rarely form part of the formal school curriculum.

Schools fail to engage with the possibilities of real learning for groups like the Filthy Dozen and their sisters, brothers, cousins, friends and neighbours and kindred souls in far off places with similar capabilities, living situations, experiences, commitments, skills and knowledge (Sernhede, 2007). It fails to engage with such groups and to help them elevate their status and respectability as a class for itself and it marginalises them, through its competitive consumerism, curriculum content, performativity and mimetic learning practices. The knowledge of such groups and the consciousness that can develop from it is given little if any place in school (Möller, this volume).

Schools that are *for* rather than only *in* marginalised suburban areas can and must come to terms with these institutional shortcomings (Möller, 2010) if they are to develop opportunities for improving the situation and educational experiences and possibilities of and for marginalised youth (Schwartz, 2010;

Sernhede and Beach, 2012). They need to open up to their pupils and recognise the world they inhabit in their terms in order to be able to help them to identify, name, describe and respond appropriately to their feelings about their present situation (Schwartz, 2010). A disparate set of economic, cultural and cognitive variables impact on educational attainment and many urban geographers have highlighted how these variables intersect (Shim, 2012). They are, as we suggest in Beach and Sernhede (2011), spatially concentrated (Öhrn, 2011, 2012). What provides a commonality of focus is the spatial concentration and intersectionality of these factors (Shim, 2012).

Some schools have recognised and taken up this challenge. As some teachers in an adult education context put it in Beach (2006):

> The aim is to instil change and development ... by building on the pupil's own understandings and knowledge ... Their way of knowing the word has to be our starting point ... Education often reverses this and makes our starting point theirs. (Sandra)

Through expressions like these and an education practice that reflects them teachers like Sandra take a position where, 'good learning (is seen to develop) the learner's ideas and ... knowledge ... on the basis of reflexive thinking' (Sharon) where lived embodied experiences, 'help create personal orientations to the world ... that are useful' (Ingrid) and, 'must be used as the essential building blocks of learning' (Sandra). They want their pupils to feel, 'respect ... from the teachers' (Beiha) as well as, 'reward from the education' (Mamud) and they are evidently successful in this; at least some of the time. In Beach (2006) this was put as follows.

> (Several) things may be noted about ... the social order of (this) education. In line with also Jeffrey and Woods (2003) these are negotiation, thoughtfulness, reflection, authenticity and reciprocity. They are visible in negotiations of relevance in the curriculum that teachers 'allow to grow (naturally) out of their everyday engagement ... with students' (Sally), 'whose own first hand ... experiences, knowledge, values and practices are given sufficient space to influence the work' (Sue).

What these teachers seem able to recognise is that a more equitable education system, an education for all, is not possible without understanding how the interpenetration of economic distribution and cultural recognition act for and are experienced by different groups (Børhaug-Brossard, this volume). However, teachers do not always recognise this, not the least due to the characteristics of modern school curricula (Børhaug-Brossard, this volume). They can become coerced to commit to other things, particularly it seems when performativity requirements are high (Möller, 2010). Examination times and inspection periods were often quoted in this respect in all of the projects we have engaged in and are reporting from. Having to meet external demands through examinations creates conditions that, 'oppose (more) authentic practices' (Sandra). Performativity requirements take over, such as passing a course and, 'acting on direct orders' (Annie), 'delivering a curriculum' (Kath) or, 'taking it upon yourself to ... select and lift in a specific content' (Sharon). This, 'imposes a curriculum rather than encouraging learning' (Kevin). Reciprocity of interest and negotiation of meanings are suspended and the extent to which students are creative co-determiners of their education raising their own questions and consciousness is questionable (Beach, 2008). Learners become knowledge recipients in these circumstances who are subjected to principles of meaning-making and tasks of internalisation and recall that they do not control. A field-note extract used in Beach (2006) can illuminate what we mean by this.

> Teachers have responsibilities to teach about Law and order, social institutions, civic rights ... But there are problems ... For instance ... today (content) about the Muslim shawl and violence towards women (was introduced) as, 'current events focused in newspapers (and) sensitive issues (that) are meaningful for the immigrant community' related to cultural issues (and) male domination. (This) may be the case (and) the selections promoted avid discussion (both) in Swedish and also Arabic ... But there was some tension ... Tones ran high ... Moreover (other) issues could equally well have been used ... As one informant, Mohan, pointed out, 'the Muslim shawl, arranged marriages and crimes of honour' are all things Swedish culture looks down on 'without trying to understand' ... and they are 'forced into the curriculum ... whilst things students look down on (such as bodily exposure commercial advertising) aren't even considered as problems ... We are simply expected to accept them'.

What is suggested here is something that researchers such as for instance Eilard (2004) have taken up. It is that iconic symbols like, 'the Muslim shawl, arranged marriages and crimes of honour' (Beiha) are often made part of subjects like civic studies in formal education for migrant pupils in school (Möller, 2010; Schwartz, 2010) or adult education (Beach, 2006) but that their use may stretch into the affective domains with negative consequences for classroom relations (Beach, 2006).

As Eilard (2004) and Möller (this volume) have both suggested, practices such as these can lead to the cultural experiences of a dominant group becoming a universal and unremarkable norm that constructs others in terms of a lack or negation of what is good, right or proper. However, these authors add that if education really is to be a way out of a marginalised position, another important point is what, in the words and actions of education subjects, actually undergirds success in the competitive education context today's pupils are made part of. Success is usually expressed as founded on things like intelligence, application and hard work. But as suggested already earlier, some of our recent research allows us to question this normative idea (Beach and Dovemark, 2009, 2011; Beach and Sernhede, 2011).[27]

This is extremely important. It describes part of the workings of a kind of hegemony that operates by reaching into and reshaping attitudes and behaviour through associations of overt practices with values and ideologies which, whilst they do not rob subordinate groups of their true culture and its values, they do reshuffle values on a specific ideological terrain. This doesn't happen in learning communities who own the content rights of their own education. Recognising the value of such learning in the mainstream is still a problem. But it is a problem then that can be more easily recognised for what it is, that is, a problem of power and hegemony not a problem of the religious content, cultural practices or skin-colour of other people.

---

27 As suggested earlier two things are important, first ability from students to recognise, appropriate and convert available resources into education capital in one's own interest by responding to the demand for *competitiveness and status accumulation* as well as the ability to successfully promote *a good image* of oneself as a committed learner (Beach and Dovemark, 2009). These are processes of conversion and selfish accumulation in the interests of status and advantage over others. But they are misrepresented and relabelled as other things (Beach and Dovemark, 2011). This is fairly obvious when we think in terms such as those employed by Rancière (1991), as it is only by not seeing the performances of pupils as examples of a crass resource exploitation, investment thinking and status accumulation, but instead as examples of intelligence, enterprise and creativity, or similar, that teachers are (emotionally, ethically and professionally) able to support successful pupils in their activities (Beach, 2003). As Rancière's work suggests, teachers have to be ignorant of processes of exploitation such as these in order to lend them even passive support.

Conclusions

The chapter has explored some aspects of creativity in relation to the activities of a particular group outside school, the collective called the Filthy Dozen and has discussed them in relation to the performative, ideological routinisation of school practices and the experiences of these routinisations for pupils from territorially stigmatised suburbs on the outskirts of one of Sweden's major cities. It raises some important points about educational equity and integration, not the least with regard to the need and existence of alternative contexts for these youth in which to valorise their class cultural capital and values as socially important and educationally significant. What is suggested is that schools and the teachers in them need some help in seeing through, past or beyond currently dominant educational ideology to accomplish this and that they may need to begin to rethink the basis of educational success for pupils in a classed, segregated and racialising, racist society in more, 'real(istic)' ways, rather than as at present, in highly ideologically distorted terms. Teachers, curriculum planners and education leaders (including politicians in particular) may have to begin to think counter-hegemonically in other words (Børhaug-Brossard, this volume), in order to disconfirm and disbelieve common understandings and what we have suggested to be false beliefs (Beach and Dovemark, 2011). This is necessary if they are to be able to change the patterns of education production and its outcomes (Beach and Sernhede, 2012). Part of this involves learning to think of resistance to school not as an insult, threat or sign of some kind of intellectual weakness, but as a demand for respect and a desire to bite back at dominant ideology and its effects on one's status, self-respect and life prospects. The creativity of the youth researched in this chapter shows both of these commitments. School teachers, school leaders and perhaps above all today just particularly school politicians could perhaps learn something very important from them.

Earlier in the chapter we discussed briefly the ability of critical artists such as the German Expressionists and the poet Bertolt Brecht have to recognise lived circumstances and reinterpret and re-articulate a critical view of their conditions and relations in a manner that can challenged conventional understandings. This is what we feel groups like FD.Ink are able to do. The task of art for Brecht, such as in the play St Joan of the Stockyards, is to create a distance and enhance sensitivity to replace common perceptions of life (Beach, 2008). Brecht's *Tale* involves an upper-class girl who joins the Salvation Army but becomes disenchanted on discovering that the Army is involved in the contradictions of the capitalist system. It is a kind of public pedagogy of the kind recently attributed to hip-hop music and culture with intrinsic educational value by amongst others Marcella Runell Hall (2009). Thus is, we feel, the essential creativity of groups like FD.Ink (Beach and Sernhede, 2011, 2012).

References

Althuizen, N., Berend Wierenga, B. and Rossiter, J., (2010) The Validity of Two Brief Measures of Creative Ability, *Creativity Research Journal,* 22(1): 53-61.

Beach, D., (2006) Humanism and Creativity in Restructured Adult Education in Sweden, *Ethnography and Education,* 1(2): 143-54.

Beach, D., (2008) The Paradoxes of Student Learning Preferences in School Classrooms, *Ethnography and Education,* 3(3): 145-160.

Beach, D., (2009) The socialisation and commercialisation of health professions in Europe, in J. Houtsonen and G-B Warvik (eds) *European Nurses' Life and Work under Restructuring.* Rotterdam: Sense Publishers.

Beach, D., (2011) Restructuring in Education and Health-Care Professions: Some General Developments in Seven European Countries, in I. F-Goodson and S. Lindblad (eds) *Professional Knowledge and Educational Restructuring in Europe*:25-41: Rotterdam: Sense Publishers.

Beach, D and Dovemark, M., (2009) Making Right Choices: An Ethnographic Investigation of Creativity in Swedish Schools, *Oxford Review of Education,* 35(6): 689-704.

Beach, D. and Dovemark, M., (2011) Twelve Years of Upper-Secondary Education in Sweden: The Beginnings of a Neo-liberal Policy hegemony? *Educational Review,* 64(4): 313-327.

Beach, D., Dovemark, M., Schwartz, A., and Öhrn, E., (in press) Complications and contradictions of educational inclusion in economically depressed suburbs: Results from a meta-ethnographic analysis, *Nordic Studies in Education* (accepted 2013-01-29)

Beach, D. and Lunneblad, J., (2011) Ethnographic Investigations of Issues of Race in Scandinavian Education Research, *Ethnography and Education,* 6(1): 29-44.

Beach, D. and Sernhede, S., (2011) From Learning to Labour to Learning for Marginality: School Segregation and Marginalisation in Swedish Suburbs, *British Journal of Sociology of Education,* 32(2): 257-274.

Beach, D and Sernhede, O., (2012) Learning Processes and Social Mobilization in a Swedish Metropolitan Hip-Hop Collective, *Urban Education,* 47(5): 939-958.

Bengtsson, H. A., and Wirtén, P., (1996) *Epokskifte. En antologi om förtryckets nya ansikten, [Epoch shift. An anthology about the new face of repression],* Stockholm: Prisma.

Blackman, S., (1995) *Youth: positions and oppositions—style, sexuality and schooling,* Aldershot: Avebury Press.

Borelius, U., (2010) Två förorter, [Two suburbs.] *Ubildning and Demokrati,* 18(1): 11-23.

Chang, J., (2005) *Can't stop, Won't stop. hip-hop-generationens historia.* Göteborg: Reverb.

Compton, A., (2007) What does creativity mean? *Education,* 35(1): 109-116.

Craft, A., (2001). Little c creativity, in: Craft, A., Jeffrey, B. and Leibling, M. (eds), *Creativity in education,* London: Continuum.

Csikszentmihalyi, M., (1990) The domain of creativity, in M. Runco, M. A. and Albert, R. S., (eds) *Theories of creativity*: 190-211, London: Sage.

Csikszentmihalyi, M., (1996) *Creativity: Flow and the psychology of discovery,* New York: Harper.

Dedman, T., (2011) Agency in UK hip-hop and grime youth subcultures — peripherals and purists, *Journal of Youth Studies,* 14(4): 507-522.

Dikec, M., (2007) *Badlands of the Republic,* Oxford: Blackwell.

Eilard, A., (2004) Genus och etnicitet i en läsebok i den svenska mångetniska skolan. *Pedagogisk Forskning i Sverige,* 9(4): 241-263.

Eisner, E., (2002) *The arts and the creation of mind,* Newhaven: Yale University Press.

Gannon, S., (2009) Rewriting 'the Road to Nowhere': Place Pedagogies in Western Sydney. *Urban Education,* 44(4): 608-624.

Hall, S., and Jefferson, T., (1976) *Resistance through Rituals.* London: Hutchinson.

Hebdige, D., (1979) *Subculture, the meaning of style.* London: Serpentine.

Hill, D. K., (2009) A Historical Analysis of Desegregation and Racism in a Racially Polarized Region: Implications for the Historical Construct, a Diversity Problem, and Transforming Teacher Education. *Urban Education,* 44(1): 106-139

Hu, W., Shi, Q. Z., Han, Q., Wang, X. and Adey, P., (2010) Creative Scientific Problem Finding and Its Developmental Trend, *Creativity Research Journal,* 22: 46-52.

Hunter, S. T., Bedell, K. E., and Mumford, M. D., (2007) Climate for creativity: A quantitative review, *Creativity Research Journal,* 19(1): 69-90.

Jeffrey, B. and Woods, P., (2003) *The Creative School.* London: Routledge Falmer.

Kim, K. H., (2006) Is Creativity Unidimensional or Multidimensional? Analyses of the Torrance Tests of Creative Thinking, *Creativity Research Journal,* 18(2): 251-259.

Möller, Å., (2010) Den 'goda' mångfalden. Fabrikation av mångfald i skolans policy och praktik, [The 'good' diversity: The fabrication of diversity in school policy.], *Utbildning and Demokrati,* 18(1): 85-106.

Rancière, J. (1991) *The Ignorant Schoolmaster. Five Lessons in Intellectual Emancipation.* Transl. Kristin Ross. Stanford: Stanford University Press.

Runell Hall, M., (2009) Hip-Hop Education Resources, *Equity and Excellence in Education,* 42(1): 86-94.

Savin Baden, M., McFarlaine, L. and Saven Baden, J., (2008) Learning spaces, agency and notions of improvement: what influences thinking and practices about teaching and learning in higher education? Interpretive meta ethnography, *London Review of Education,* 6(1): 11-27.

Schwartz, A., (2010) Att 'nollställa bakgrunder' för en effektiv skola, [Ignoring background for an effective schooling.] *Utbildning and Demokrati,* 19(1): 45-62.

Schwartz, A. and Öhrn, E., (2012) Fellowship and solidarity? Secondary students' responses to strong classification and framing in education, in Pink, W. (ed.), *Schools and marginalized youth: an international perspective.* Cresshill, NJ: Hampton Press.

Sernhede, O., (2007) *AlieNation is My Nation. Om hip-hop och unga mäns utanförskap i det Nya Sverige, [AlieNation is My Nation. On hip-hop and the marginalisation of young men in the New Sweden],* Stockholm: Ordfront.

Sernhede, O., (2011) Varför uppfattar så många unga i storstädernas 'utsatta' förorter inte skolan som en väg i samhället? [Why do so many young people in multi-cultural urban suburbs not perceive shool as a way into society?] *Forskning om undervisning och lärande,* 6(1): 64-73.

Shim, J. M., (2012) Pierre Bourdieu and intercultural education: it is not just about lack of knowledge about others, *Intercultural Education,* 23(3): 209-220.

Stehr, N. and Böhme, G., (1986) *Knowledge Society*. Dordrecht: *D. Reidel Publishing*.

Weed, J., (2006) Interpretive qualitative synthesis in the sport and exercise sciences: The meta-interpretation approach, *European Journal of Sport Science*, 6(2): 127-139.

Willis, P., (1990) *Common Culture*, Milton Keynes: Open University Press.

Willis, P., (2004) Old Books, New Times, in Dolby, N. and Dimitradis, G. (eds) *Learning to Labour in New Times* (pp. 165-197), London: Routledge.

Öhrn, E., Lundahl, L., and Beach, D., (eds) (2011) *Young people's influence and democratic education. Ethnographic studies in upper secondary schools*, London: the Tufnell Press.

Öhrn, E., (2011) Class and ethnicity at work. Segregation and conflict in a Swedish secondary school, *Education Inquiry*, 2(2): 345-357.

Öhrn, E., (2012) Urban education and segregation: the responses from young people, *European Educational Research Journal*, 11(1): 45-57.

Chapter 4

Transnational literacy and identity in digitally mediated contexts: The case of youth in Norway

Henry Mainsah

Introduction

Today, it is not hard to find an adolescent immigrant sitting in a bedroom or on a school computer somewhere in Oslo doing some homework or project while simultaneously uploading pictures into a *MySpace* profile, reading an online gossip magazine, chatting on *Facebook*, and so on with other young people living in different geographical spaces and time zones. In these concurrent time spaces, the adolescent computer user may be presenting herself as an immigrant on a Norwegian website, but when she moves to another online context, say a global community of diasporic youth, she might switch to identify herself as a diasporic Pakistani, or Turkish, or Nigerian. Furthermore, the status of a Nigerian adolescent immigrant as a Norwegian-as-second-language learner, for example, might get translated into the linguistic mainstream once she enters an online fan community of Japanese pop culture whose members are located in parts of the world where English is mostly spoken as a second or foreign language. Such new mediascapes, changing scopes of space and time, modes of representation, symbolic materials, and ways of using language compel us to ask critical questions about identity, creativity, and literacy.

The aim of this chapter is to examine what role identity plays in the shaping literacy practices in digitally mediated contexts (specifically social networking websites in this case). I examine how the identifications and affiliations of a group of youth in Norway affect their literacy development and knowledge making on social networking sites. I analyse how the youth participate in online social networking communities particularly how they learn to negotiate identities, participate in debates, and share knowledge about international issues.

The study draws on ethnographic fieldwork carried out on a group of Norwegian youth whose parents are of African, Latin American and Asian origin. The participants in this study are confronted by a multitude of discourses that attempt to homogenise them into disempowering and marginal subjectivities *vis-à-vis* the Norwegian society. Categorisations such as *immigrant, refugee,*

Muslim, fremmedkulturelle (of foreign cultural origin) and *black* are in the Norwegian context culturalised terminology that are often used to rationalise their alienation and their status as the *Other* in Norwegian society. The mass media is a central arena where this marginalising discourse on immigrants and ethnic minorities in Norway is produced (see for example, Eide, 2003). In this media discourse, they are mostly portrayed as threats (criminal, violent) or as problems (economic, social and cultural burden to society), and often as being of lesser value (Eide, 2003). Studies show though that youth in these contexts sometimes use their condition as a resource for cultural creativity and agency (Back, 1996; Mørch, 1998; Vestel, 2009; Wulff, 1995). These studies focus on the boundary-transgressing aspects of multi-ethnic youth cultures and view the diasporic condition as opening for more flexible, situated and process-oriented approaches to identity. Other authors show digital online media environments as central arenas where diaspora youth negotiate identity (Mainsah, 2011; Parker and Song, 2009) and develop literacies (Lam, 2009).

Some researchers have stressed the need to examine literacy practices within intersecting local and global contexts and especially in relation to new communication technologies that are part of these intersecting contexts (Pahl and Rowsell, 2006; Lam, 2009). An approach to examining literacy across time and geography is particularly important when examining the practices of youth with multicultural backgrounds when they develop transnational relationships. This study extends research on literacy development in multicultural contexts, diaspora social networks, and ethnicity and race in digital environments.

Background

Literacy and identity

I view the processes through which the participants in this study produce and consume texts, and the mechanisms through which they interact on social networking sites as social. This is to say that these practices are contextually informed and that these participants bring to these texts and contexts meanings drawn from their own experiences, cultures and social position. This implies that 'social aspects are irrefutably part of literacy practices, and meaning is not just mediated straightforward by textual codes ... but is shaped by socio-cultural matters.' (Davies, 2008: 231). This approach draws on the paradigm of the *New Literacy Studies* (NLS) (Barton, 1994; Street, 1993). *New Literacy Studies* consists of research that examines the ways in which literacy practices are situated in social, cultural, and political contexts (McCarthey and Moje, 2002).

This is representative of a social turn in literacy theory and research (Gee, 2004) which has generated interest on the literacy practices of actual people and 'the roles of texts and literacy practices as tools or media for constructing, narrating, mediating, enacting, performing, enlisting, or exploring identities' (Moje and Luke, 2009: 416). Viewing literacy practices as social implies recognising the fact that people's identities mediate and are mediated by the texts they read, write, and talk about. Learning, from this socio-cultural point of view, implies that the way people participate, interact, and form relationships, is contextual. Furthermore, this has implications for how people make sense of themselves and others, and how they identify and are identified (Moje and Luke, 2009).

In an analysis of Latina/o youths' literacy practices across multiple spaces, Moje (2004: 30) argued the following:

> The access the youth had to particular kinds of space—most often to their ethnic community space—shaped the texts they consumed and produced, which in turn shaped the ways they chose to identify and were identified. The multiple spaces of their lives conjured up or enabled multiple ways of being, multiple tools—identity kits ... Whereas mall walking gave lessons in how to be mainstream, walking Virnot Street—one of the central neighbourhood streets—provided the youth with ways of being Latino/a, and Mexican, in particular.

Moje's study, as several others, illustrates how differently positioned the youth are both in terms of language and literacy skill and in terms of identities in the different spaces they inhabited, be it in the classroom, at home or in the online world (Chandler-Olcott and Mahar, 2003; Guerra, 2004; Lam, 2009; Mainsah, 2011; Sánchez, 2007). Literacy practices allow these youth to work through tensions and conflicts in a multiply situated consciousness. In each case, the subject gains agency in some spaces and not others, and literacy practices play a role in that agency. However, the ways that youth are called upon by others in power and the way they respond to these calls depends partly on the space and context they inhabit. In all these studies, there is an implicit conceptualisation of identity as *position* and as *consciousness* (Moje and Luke, 2009). Holland and Leander frames this in the following way:

The social positioning of persons and groups, whether through everyday discourse, spatial arrangement, text, film, or other media, is now considered a primary means by which subjects are produced and subjectivity forms. Power relations, in particular, are thought to shape a person's self (or a group's identity) through acts that distinguish and treat the person as gendered, raced, classed, or other sort of subject....

(2004: 127).

Drawing from all this, it will be interesting thus to explore how the youth in this study position and are positioned, how they identify and are identified, and how these constitute the baggage that they bring to their literacy practices in digital online spaces.

Digitally mediated literacies

With the changing technological landscape the boundaries between information and other media has become increasingly blurred. The internet, computer games, digital video, mobile phones, blogs, wikis, and social networking sites are much more than media for information retrieval.

Buckingham (2006) argues that these media cannot be seen just as a matter of machines and techniques, as 'hardware and software' or as 'information or technology'. These media provide new ways of mediating, communicating and representing the world. They convey images and fantasies, provide opportunities for creative self-expression, and serve as a medium through which intimate personal relationships and group networks can be formed. Buckingham argues that young people are engaging with these media not only as technologies but more importantly as *cultural forms*. This implies that we cannot confine our attention to the isolated encounter between the user and the web interface. We need to also take into account the interpersonal context in which this encounter takes place (where the text is created and read, with whom, how, and why), and the broader social and economic processes that determine how texts are produced and circulated.

Digital literacy as a concept is not new. Over the past couple of decades many attempts have been made to extend the notion of literacy beyond its original application to the medium of writing (see Buckingham, 2006). Notions such as *emergent literacies* (Spencer, 1986), *visual literacy* (Moore and Dwyer, 1994), *television literacy* (Buckingham, 1993), *cine-literacy* (British Film Institute, 2000), and *informational literacy* (Bruce, 1997) have been employed in previous contexts.

Some scholars challenge the extension of literacy to digital media, arguing that the term should be confined to the realm of writing (Barton, 1994; Kress, 1997). Others dispute the idea that visual media require a process of cultural learning that is similar to the learning of written language (Messaris, 1994).

However, Buckingham (2006) argues that while the analogy between writing and audio-visual or digital online media may be useful at a general level, such analogies often do not hold under close scrutiny. While it is possible to analyse broad categories such as narrative and representation across all these media, it is hard to compare, for example, the film shot and the word or the online game sequence and the sentence. In addition, other authors argue that using different media makes possible new ways of interacting with print and image (Kress, 2003).

These different media create new ways of interacting that change learning possibilities (Spiro, Collins and Ramchandran, 2007). They create new ways of interacting with others and with the self (Coiro, Knobel, Lankshear, and Leu, 2008). Furthermore, Lankshear and Knobel (2006) explain that literacies within the context of digital online media are produced in ways that are more collaborative, *less individuated*, more distributed and participatory. This has been highlighted in recent studies around the notion *affinity space* (Gee, 2007)—a supportive social structure for people coalescing around a common interest, passion, or proclivity. These studies have explored youth practices in online affinity spaces devoted to web page making (Chandler-Olcott and Mahar, 2003; Lam, 2006), fan fiction and fan art (Chandler-Olcott and Mahar; 2003; Thomas, 2007; Black, 2006), video gaming (Squire, 2007; Steinkuehler, 2008), and online journaling (Guzzetti and Gamboa, 2005). Buckingham (2006) identified some key conceptual aspects that are generally regarded as essential components of digital media literacy—representation, language, and production. First, all diverse forms of digital media do not just reflect the world as it is but are *representations* of particular selections of reality that implicitly embody particular values and ideologies. Thus informed users ought to be able to evaluate the implicit values and ideologies behind the material they create, distribute and consume and the discourses that these materials employ. This also means addressing issues about whose voices are heard and whose viewpoints are represented and whose are not. Second, truly literate users need to understand the *language* or *grammar* of particular forms of communication. They also need to be aware of broader codes and conventions of particular genres and within particular contexts.

Digital literacy thus among other things involves awareness of the unique *rhetoric* of online interaction. It involves knowledge of the use of visual and verbal *rhetoric* in the design of online content. It also involves among other things the codes and conventions and etiquette within different online communities. Third, Buckingham identifies *production* as one of the key areas of digital literacy. This involves not only the skills of producing digital content, but more importantly an awareness of how different social and interest groups use the web as a means of persuasion and influence. It involves technology and software that are used to generate and disseminate material on the web and the practice of web 'authors.'

These components of digital literacy, as identified by Buckingham provide a useful lens through which to analyse the literacy practices of the participants in this study on social networking sites. Social networking sites comprise a communication medium where youth can publicly express their ideas through symbols, moving images, photographs, and print text created by them or downloaded from other internet sites. Thus on these sites, youth are engaging in more than written commentary on their lives, they are also using a wide range of modes and medium to create and convey meaning.

The data

Since my study had to do with the internet, my field involved a crisscross of different virtual and physical contexts where I located my group of informants. I took an approach similar to that of Nicola Green (1999), who argues that to best study internet technologies one needs to employ a flexible method where the researcher follows people and objects and the stories about them simultaneously. Therefore, my approach consisted of following the participants back and forth through different online contexts joining and participating in the online communities they were part of while all along taking into account the wider socio-cultural context in which participants were immersed. The participants in my research were sixteen twenty year-olds. During the course of my research I interviewed twenty-six participants (seventeen female and nine male), but I had twelve key informants (eight female and four male) whom I observed and interacted closely with online for a year. All of these key informants were recruited on social networking sites and were from different parts of Norway.

The data for this study consisted of in-depth interviews; the content of the profiles of the participants on social networking sites (i.e. texts, videos, pictures, etc.); and participant observation on these sites. The in-depth interviews were conducted online through *Instant Messaging* (IM). The interviews covered subjects such as online experiences, identity and everyday life. The interviews combined with the participant observation helped provide a contextualised understanding of the participants' online networks, linguistic and meditational practices. In the analysis I will make use of interview excerpts and description of the content of the participants' profiles. The in-depth interviews were aimed at encouraging the participants to reflect on their experiences as actors within online social networks. The analysis of online texts aimed at examining the ideological constructions embedded in what the participants produced online. The participant observation, meanwhile, helped provide insight into the different micro networks the participants were a part of and how these contexts shaped the meanings that were produced in them.

Representations of self

There is large volume of research that shows that digital online environments are becoming important arenas where young people construct and negotiate ethnic, gender, religious, and sexual identities (see for example Leurs et al., 2012; Mainsah, 2011; Parker and Song, 2009). Many argue that these arenas offer new possibilities for self-representation and open up space for marginal voices to resist dominant discourses of race, ethnicity, and gender within European societies. Digital online media facilitate a blending of media genres, and forms of experimentation, modification, and reiteration. Weber and Mitchell (2008: 27) label the online productions of young people *identities in action*. They argue that these can serve as an ideal starting point for studying identity, since it is partly through the process of interacting with technologies that identities are tested, experienced and deconstructed.

On many social networking sites one of the sections that users have to complete on their personal profiles is the 'about me' section. This often provides an opportunity for some users to articulate identity and affiliation. The excerpt below is the message that greets the visitor to the 'about me' section of eighteen-year-old Jonathan's profile on a Norwegian social networking site.

> I am half-Norwegian, I was born and raised in Norway and I feel more Norwegian actually, but I haven't forgotten that I am Iranian though. I don't drink or smoke. I am Christian and proud of it. But I am not boring though because some of us Christians enjoy living live ... my humour is based on the fact that I can look at different cultures of the world with irony, without necessarily being mean. If there is anyone out there that

is racist for one reason or the other, please don't talk to me. However I think it is a pity that foreigners do not have any self-irony.

By describing himself in terms of his bi-national origins he engages a form of identification that is often associated within research and in public discourse in relation to youth of mixed origins. Some literature on young people in Britain, for example, suggests that people have the idea of living between cultures might constitute a 'cultural conflict' (CRC, 1976; Watson, 1977). According to this view there might be a conflict between say *Scandinavian* and *Persian* ways of life, where these are seen both as fixed and bounded categories. A lot of feminist and cultural studies work has critiqued the treatment of people in *essentialist* ways. By announcing that he can be *Norwegian* and *Iranian*, *Christian* and 'not boring' at the same time, Jonathan seems to articulate a notion of identity that contrasts with the fixed or static notion of identity evoked in public discourse in European countries today. As some have argued, it is possible to be 'between two cultures' or 'neither of one colour nor the other' and that it is possible to have identities, which are 'both/and' rather than 'either/or' (see Sreberny, 2005; Phoenix and Owen, 2000).

The way Jonathan represents himself and his identity is reflective of the discourse of many other Norwegian youth with multiple affiliations in everyday contexts outside of the web. This was brought to light during conversations with the participants. Here is what eighteen-year-old Lisa, one of the participants, said during our interview:

> … Mom and dad are from Turkey but had you asked me if I was Turkish or where I was from, I don't know what I would have answered. I am not Turkish and I am not Norwegian. I would say I am something in-between a Norwegian and a Turk. I sort of have a foot in both cultures … the Turkish culture is kind of the religion and the fact that we fast, how I look at things and the fact that, for example I don't go out to town every weekend. I might have got all these from my Turkish side … I do go out sometimes though, but not as much as my (ethnic Norwegian) friends. I am more attached to my family and I often stay at home and help my parents because of my upbringing … When you are Norwegian you are kind of like more free … you can see my Norwegian side through the way I look at some things and the fact that I am not so conservative. Turks

are more conservative than Norwegians. I am more in favour of gender equality and kind of have the Norwegian mentality. (Lisa, 18—female)

This statement is an illustration that because these youth are simultaneously members of multiple worlds and multiple layers of identities, they have to position themselves in terms of histories, culture, and social relations. By positioning herself as being 'something in-between a Norwegian and a Turk', Lisa tries to negotiate a 'third space' that is connected to, but at the same time, distinguishable from either Turkish or Norwegian identity. The quote also shows that having 'a foot in both cultures' for Lisa means negotiating between several and sometimes conflicting moral codes and gender roles. The sentiment Lisa describes here is similar to Vertovec's (1999; 2001) notion of transnationalism as a form of consciousness. This refers to a state of mind marked by dual or multiple identifications. As Hall (1990) has stated, this condition is comprised of ever changing representations that provide an 'imaginary coherence' for a set of malleable identities.

Besides such straightforward descriptions of self, I found evidence on the personal profiles of the participants of a series of other more creative linguistic practices of self-representation. The profile of an eighteen-year-old participant screen-named *Sugardaddy*, for example, is saturated with textual references to hip-hop. He begins the 'about me' section of his personal profile with a statement written in typical hip-hop slang, 'What's really good ya'll? It's ur boy Suga so holla if you wanna'. This is typical of hip-hop slang whose syntax includes alternative expressions (e.g. *holla* – call), alternative spellings (e.g. *suga*-sugar), alternative pronunciation, and conjoined words (e.g. *wanna*-want to). On the next line he writes in bold capital letters 'ERITREA'. The writing of Eritrea in bold letters here is similar to an informal literacy practice that Bruna (2007) refers to as 'shouting out'. In African-American derived popular culture, a 'shout out' is read as a special form of public recognition. Bruna identifies 'shouting out' as a literacy practice that newcomer Mexican youth in the USA employed to give special public recognition to their particular hometowns in Mexico. In the same way *Sugardaddy*'s writing of Eritrea on his profile can be seen as a kind of 'shout out', or public recognition of his country of origin. The use of capital letters in ERITREA is a rhetoric textual device to indicate emphasis.

Another type of literacy practice identified on the participants' profiles was that of code switching. Code switching involves the use of more than one language in the same conversation, usually in the same sentence. Evidence of this can be seen on sixteen-year old screen-named *Brown Sugar's* profile.

Hallais folkens ♥

her e det ... aka ... ☺, straight from AFRIKA ♥

for ya all who doesn't know me, i'm sweet as brownsuggh: that is just because mammy ain't raisin a fool ...

peace out folkenzzz 😸 ;)

'hip-hop for life'

Fo' shizzle my nizzle ...

Here we see *Brown Sugar* switching from Norwegian to English slang. We also see how she switches between two languages within the same sentence. By using emoticons juxtaposed with text, she employs a widely popular aspect of the oral language of the internet to signal emphasis on humour and endearment. Code-switching here is not just about language but it is also literally and metaphorically about the juxtaposition of different subjectivities.

All these examples eloquently demonstrate the point made in different studies of multicultural youth (Chandler-Olcott and Mahar, 2003; Guerra, 2004; Moje, 2004b; Lam, 2009; Mainsah, 2011) that show the relationship between identity and literacy.

These studies show how youth position themselves differently in terms of language, literacy, and identity in different spaces. What I found out in my study was that these youth represented themselves differently in different sites. All the examples of self-presentations from my participants above are taken from Norwegian social networking sites. While they often used racial and ethnic references to represent the self on Norwegian sites, they would use other references from popular culture in the design of their profiles on other international sites such as *Facebook* or *MySpace*. I would argue that the articulate ethnic discourse on Norwegian sites partly because they are *positioned* as the *Other* on these sites as well as in everyday life. This is eloquently illustrated on the self-introductory message of one of the participants on her profile: 'I could well have said I was Norwegian but nobody would believe me ... because I am totally *Chilena'.*

'Remix' practices

Besides print text, the participants made use of other multimodal features of social networking sites to signal affiliations as well. Upon entering twenty-year-old Anne's page, African music from a popular Ivorian group blasts on the air. Her music interests are further made evident by the virtual music play list she has embedded on her profile which includes soul, reggae, hip-hop R&B, African, house, and Latin music. The background of her page is wallpapered with little black panthers with crowns on their heads carrying a flag with Rastafarian colours.

The Rastafarian colours (green, red, and yellow) are used to decorate all other areas of her page. The Rastafarian theme continues on her page with a poster of the portrait of reggae icon Bob Marley with the Rastafarian colours painted on the face. Other embedded images on her profile include that of the face of a Buddha, an African sunset, and that of an ancient black man and a woman carrying a baby with animals in the background. All these different signs on the personal site described above can be interpreted as the articulation of a transnational identity, which fluidly draws on references from afro-Caribbean, Afro-American, and mainstream popular cultures. Indeed, Chandler and Roberts-Young (1998) have characterised homepages as spaces used by individuals to exhibit statements of identity through carefully selecting and putting together themes, designs, images, and colours. They show how teenagers draw selectively on cultural materials and imagery from consumer culture, popular music and the mass media to construct self-portraits on their personal sites.

Another example of the creative manipulation of images can be seen on the profile of the sixteen-year-old screen-named *Sissy Palestinian*. Most of what the user learns about the owner of the profile is through the images and graphics she has placed on her page. In one of the images, she has not only copied graphic signs but has re-fabricated them to give it a personal touch. In the image in question she copies media objects from another website (a pink heart and animal footprints) and incorporates them into a blank image frame where she had pasted pictures of herself together with two of her friends. She subtitles the image thus: 'Princesses of Arab—ha ha my work of art'. In another picture, which she embeds on her profile, the user gets a hint of her political views. In this picture there is a hand with two fingers raised in a sign of peace with a Palestinian flag in the background, with the caption 'Free Palestine'.

More importantly we see that these youth, in order to articulate their multiple group affiliations make use of forms of *bricolage* (Hebdige, 1979; Levi-Strauss, 1966) or *remix* practices (Knobel and Lankshear, 2008). The concept of *bricolage* refers to the process of taking the materials at hand and using them in an improvisatorial fashion to a construction or creation (for example, of a work of art or a craft project) that is improvised, using whatever materials are at hand. Through the process of writing, presenting and adapting materials (text, graphics, images, sounds, links to other websites), users like *Sissy Palestinian* shape their self-presentations in relation to the different identities she wishes to allude to. This is an example of a form of digital remix that Knobel and Lankshear (2008) call *photoshopping* remix, where users add text to images, creating photomontages that mix elements from two or more images together, or changing the image content in some way, and changing image properties.

I will argue that through these types of literacy practices, the youth gain a certain form of eloquence that facilitates the articulation of their voices. The practices of 'shouting out', code switching, and image *bricolage* described in this section can be understood as what Hamilton (2000: 20) terms 'literacies of display' of the transnational identities of these youth. In these 'literacies of display' the youth take elements of the Norwegian context, elements of the 'home nation', combined with global popular culture to both articulate a transcultural identity and inscribe themselves into a transnational imagined community.

Rhetoric of the image

McGinnis et al., argue that 'online spaces provide youth with venues to have a voice, to engage in important identity work, and to create texts around local, national, and global issues that are important to them', (2007: 289). However, although in theory social networking sites provide a multitude of tools that permit users to reach out to a wide public, not everyone possesses the skills to capture the attention and response of the audience. There was evidence in this study of the way in which some of the participants creatively employ the multimodal features of social networking sites to capture an audience and provoke discussion.

This could be observed on seventeen year-old Afran's profile page. The photos in her photo gallery are distinctly different from the personal photos usually found on the pages of other teenagers. Above her photo gallery she addresses a sort of invitation to other Kurdish youth inviting them to look at the photos by saying: 'Kurdish youth call themselves *Peshmerga*! Support one party over the other! But do you, fucking know what you are getting into? Why hate PKK, PUK, or PDK? Don't they all work for a free Kurdistan?! ... Take a look on the pics before u decide to call urself *peshmerge* again!' The first three photos on her gallery are of the late Pakistani leader, Benazir Bhutto, one where she was alone, and the other were old photos of her besides the her father Ali Bhutto and the former Indian prime minister Indira Gandhi. The next photo is that of the dead remains of a female suicide bomber with half of her body blown to pieces lying on a morgue table. The rest of the pictures are of dead soldiers slain in battle.

Most importantly Afran uses these graphic photos of dead soldiers and suicide bomber as a rhetoric device to *shock* her audience into a discussion. Through these images Afran attempts to initiate a conversation about the political situation of the Kurds. The presence of numerous comments written by other users on some of these photos is evidence of the fact that her call was answered. On the photo of the dead and mutilated female suicide bomber, she received fourteen comments, some of which were quite virulent:

> Solsiden said, 12, March: Seriously speaking? Do you believe this is the way to go to get your own country … ? I know I can't understand how it can feel not to have your own country, but do you think you ever will be able to get it this way … ?
>
> Afran said, 11, March: … Kurdistan has never been a country on its own, so far as I know. What do you suggest? Oral communication? Pssst
>
> Oldebo said, 10, March: Is this not simply nasty? P respect (;
>
> Afran said, 09, March: This is a Kurdish martyr, all respect to her—that I agree on. I am just trying to show people how far Kurds have gone to get their own country. Of course this provokes reactions. It is the whole point … I am a Kurd myself and I just want people out there to understand what it means to be a martyr and to know more about the Kurdish people's burning desire for their country
>
> Maren said, 08, March: ****
>
> Nasty Res said, 08, Mar: Wtf (what the fuck)? Æsj (yuck)
>
> (translated from Norwegian)

Afran uses photographs and comments as an eloquent means of articulating and exploring her identity as a diasporic Kurd living in Norway with significant political and emotional ties to Kurdistan. By initiating discussion on a Norwegian social networking site about an issue related to a far away country not often talked about, she also succeeds in creating a transnational space connecting Norway with Asia and the Middle East.

Understanding your networked public

The youths' accounts in this study show that they sometimes have to navigate through questions of identity and belonging in the local and transnational spaces they inhabit through social networking sites. Using several social networking sites and interacting with different publics simultaneously often requires an understanding of a wide set of gendered, raced, and ethicised discourses that vary from context to context. This stresses the importance of having a certain level of cultural fluency or cultural flexibility, which proved somewhat challenging for these youth.

Eighteen year old Norwegian-Iranian Jonathan posted this blog entry to his public profile on a Norwegian social networking site. This site is designed in such a way that every blog entry is automatically linked to a main blog menu section of the website visible to all users. On this blog entry he writes the following about international women's day:

> *Women's day*
> Women's day is the most unserious and screwed up day in the whole world. Who the hell gave these women women's day anyway? Traitor. Women go around complaining about how bad they have it, and being all self-important ... Just go on and have your women's day but remember the rest of the 364 days are ours.

This blog entry, it was revealed, was a playful attempt to provoke the audience. Here he parodies himself by posturing in the text as a male chauvinist. On one level his rhetoric strategy seems to have a desired effect because the comments section was flooded with comments. These are some of the comments from visitors of his blog in response to his blog entry:

> Falcone, eighteen year-old female,
> No! It is not in all sectors that we have equality between men and women. This is precisely why we have a women's day. Besides it's always nice for us to have a day where everyone can congratulate us and be nice to us.

Kari, eighteen year-old female,
Are you joking? … just because you have a father that beats up his children and spits on his wife, this does not mean that is how things are in Norway …

Tomas, twenty year-old male,
I agree totally!! They complain about earning less, meanwhile in cases when women have a better salary than men, men do not complain.

Monica sixteen year-old female,
Are you sick in the head or what? This is gender discrimination! If we had a 'men's day', I would also have written then 'Men Suck'!! Moron!

Mika, eighteen year-old female,
My goodness! Why are you making such a big deal out of this? Can't you just say congratulations? You know that all over the world it is men who have power. If this day means a lot for girls why can't you stand by their side…it is one fucking day of the year!

However Jonathan's reaction shows that he did not fully understand the implications of what he had written. He was frustrated by the fact that not all the audience 'got his drift', or understood that he was trying to be playful. He finds some of the comments hurtful and out of place. He explains this incident during the interview thus:

> I wrote the piece about women's day and I got a lot of crap for it. Actually I wrote it JUST to provoke so that we could start a debate. But people just focused on denigrating my *sexist* views. Take Kari for example. I had expected that people would disprove me with arguments. Some people did that but Kari just wrote a long comment about how I should stop beating up my wives and children and that I should get out of this country and things like that. I tried to write a friendly reply but she just continued with her rant.

This incident is a demonstration of the fact that in digital online contexts, identities are always embodied. Although we may forget our bodies when cruising in cyberspace all our actions are taken through them. Jonathan is most certainly made aware of the fact that identities, in online context, are always embodied. The comments made by Kari show that his blog entry is *read together* with his profile picture, which shows a middle-eastern appearance. Because of his appearance, Jonathan's discourse is read through the prism of Orientalist stereotypes where masculinity is linked with violence and misogyny.

Jonathan's example illustrates how the choices and processes young people make when navigating different online environments reveal and identify them in ways they might not even realise. In this way, this process might facilitate a certain level of reflexivity among youth.

Conclusion

In this article I have examined the role played by identity in the shaping of literacy practices among youth of diverse origins and affiliations on social networking sites. The study has demonstrated how the participants in this study use social networking sites both as technologies and as cultural forms. In the design of their personal profiles we see evidence of *photoshopping, bricolage,* or *remix* literacies where they use of digital tools to create new meanings by taking different media extracts and putting them together in new ways. Through these literacy practices they are designing their online identities and generating information and discussion around issues they care about. Through their self-presentations and online interactions they are showing a certain consciousness of how they are seen and positioned as subjects within the Norwegian context. We can see an example of this on Jonathan's discussion thread. By articulating racial, ethnic, and national belongings they are positioning themselves in relation to dominant identity discourses within the Norwegian public realm.

I will argue that the participants' practices reveal to some extent signs of the core digital literacy practices enumerated by Buckingham (2006)— representation, language, and production. Their engagement in *remix, photoshopping* and *code-switching* practices shows some knowledge of the *grammar* and *rhetoric* of communication on these sites. They are also experiencing how identities are articulated within these spaces. I will further argue that by engaging in different forms of *authorship* they are exploring different ways of using the web as a means of persuasion and influence. We see this through Afran's use of provocative images.

As Sernhede and Beach (in this volume) argue, educators need to consider how the role of artistic cultural production of youth can be integrated in learning. They need to look for ways to bridge their digital and academic worlds so as to provide 'space for youth to express and share their concerns and challenges related to local, national, and global issues and politics; and to encourage and build on such transnational literacy practices ... and view students as knowledgeable and active members of this fast-changing global culture' (McGinnis et al., 2007: 302).

References

Back, L., (1996) *New ethnicities and urban culture: Racisms and multiculture in young lives*, London: UCL Press. London: Duke University Press.

Black, R. W., (2006) Language, culture, and identity in online fanfiction, *E-Learning*, 3(2): 170-184.

Barton, D., (1994) *Literacy: An introduction to the ecology of written language*, London: Blackwell.

British Film Institute, (2000) *Moving images in the classroom: A secondary teacher's guide to using film and television*, London: British Film Institute.

Bruce, C., (1997) *The seven faces of information literacy*, Adelaide: Auslib Press.

Bruna, K. R., (2007) Travelling tags: The informal literacies of Mexican newcomers in and out of classroom, *Linguistics and Education*, 18(3): 232-257.

Buckingham, D., (1993) *Children talking television: The making of television literacy*, London: Falmer Press.

Buckingham, D., (2006) Defining digital literacy: What do young people need to know about digital media? *Nordic Journal of Digital Literacy*, 4(1): 263-276.

Chandler, D. and Roberts-Young, D., (1998) *The construction of identity in the personal homepages of adolescents*, URL (Accessed 4 February, 2012): www.aber.ac.uk/media/Documents/short/Strasbourg.html

Chandler-Olcott, K. and Mahar, D., (2003) 'Tech-savviness' meets multiliteracies: Exploring adolescent girls' technology-mediated literacy practices, *Reading Research Quarterly*, 38(3): 356-385.

Coiro, J. Knobel M. Lankshear C. and Leu D., (2008) Central issues in new literacies and new literacies research, in Coiro, J., Knobel, M., Lankshear, C., and Leu, D. (eds.) *Handbook of research on new literacies*, Lawrence Erlbaum: New York).

Community Relations Commission (CRC), (1976) *Between two cultures: A study of relationships between generations in the Asian community in Britain today*, London: CRC.

Davies, J., (2008) Pay and display: The digital literacies of online shoppers, in Lankshear, C. and Knobel, M., (eds.) *Digital literacies: concepts, policies and practices*, New York: Peter Lang.

Eide, E., (2003) The long distance runner and discourses on Europe's others: Ethnic minority representation in feature stories, in Tufte, T., (ed.) *Medierne, minoriteterne og det multikulturelle samfund: Skandinaviske perspektiver*, Göteborg: Nordicom.

Gee, J. P., (2004) *Situated Language and Learning: A critique of traditional schooling*, London: Routledge.

Gee, J. P., (2007) *Good video games + good learning: Collected essays on video games, learning and literacy*. New York: Peter Lang.

Green, N., (1999) Disrupting the field: virtual reality technologies and 'multisited' ethnographic methods, *American Behavioral Scientist*, 43 (3): 409-421.

Guerra, J. C., (2004) Putting literacy in its place: Nomadic consciousness and the practice of transcultural repositioning, in Gutierrez-Jones, C. (ed.) *Rebellious reading: The dynamics of Chicana/o literacy*, Center for Chicana/o Studies: University of California at Santa Barbara.

Guzzetti, B. and Gamboa, M., (2005) Online journaling: The informal writing of two adolescent girls, *Research in the Teaching of English* 40(2): 168-206.

Hall, S., (1990) Cultural identity and diaspora, in Rutherford, J. (ed.) *Identity: community, culture, difference*, London: Lawrence and Wishart.

Hamilton, M., (2000) Expanding new literacies: Using photographs to explore literacy as a social practice, in Barton, D., Hamilton, M., and Ivanic R. (eds.) *Situated literacies: Reading and writing in context*, London: Routledge.

Hebdige, D., (1979) *Subculture: the meaning of style*, London: Methuen.

Holland, D. and Leander, K. M., (2004) Ethnographic studies of positioning and subjectivity: an introduction, *Ethos*, 32 (2): 127-139.

Knobel, M. and Lankshear, C., (2008) Remix: The art and craft of endless hybridization, *Journal of Adolescent and Adult Literacy*, 52 (1): 22-33

Kress, G., (1997) *Before writing: Rethinking the paths to literacy*, London: Routledge.

Kress, G., (2003) *Literacy in the new media age*, London: Routledge.

Lam, W. S. E., (2006) Culture and learning in the context of globalization: Research directions, *Review of Research in Education,* 30(1): 213-237.

Lam, W. S. E., (2009) Multiliteracies on instant messaging in negotiating local, translocal, and transnational affiliations: A case of an adolescent immigrant, *Reading Research Quarterly*, 44(4): 377-397.

Lankshear, C. and Knobel, M., (2006) *Everyday practices and classroom learning*, 2nd ed., Maidenhead: Open University Press.

Leurs, K. Midden, E. and Ponzanesi, S., (2012) Bottom-up multiculturalism: Young Dutch-Moroccans' religious, ethnic and gender position acquisition through digital media, *Religion and Gender*, 1(2): 150-175.

Lévi-Strauss, C., (1966) *The savage mind*, Chicago: University of Chicago Press.

Mainsah, H., (2011) 'I could well have said I was Norwegian but nobody would believe me': Ethnic minority youths' self-presentation on social networks sites, *European Journal of Cultural Studies*, 14(2): 179-193.

McCarthey, S. J. and Moje, E. B., (2002) Identity matters, *Reading Research Quarterly*, 37(2): 228-238.

McGinnis, T. Goodstein-Stolzenberg, A. *and* Costa Saliani, E., (2007) 'indnpride': Online spaces of transnational youth as sites of creative and sophisticated literacy and identity work, *Linguistics and Education*, 18(3-4): 283-304.

Messaris, P., (1994) *Visual 'literacy': Image, mind and reality*, Boulder, Colorado: Westview.

Moje, E. B., (2004a) Powerful spaces: Tracing the out-of-school literacy spaces of Latino/a youth, in Leander, K., and Sheehy M., (eds.), *Spatializing Literacy Research and Practice*, New York: Peter Lang.

Moje, E. B., (2004b) Doing identity: On the complexities of researching social identities with urban youth, paper presented at the *Society for Research on Adolescence Biennial Conference*, 11-14 March, 2004, Baltimore, Maryland.

Moje, E. and Luke, A., (2009) Literacy and identity: Examining metaphors in history and contemporary research. *Reading Research Quarterly*, 44(4): 415-437.

Moore, D. and Dwyer, F., (1994) *Visual literacy: A spectrum of visual learning*, Englewood Cliffs, NJ: Educational Technology Publications.

Mørch, Y., (1998) *Bindestregs-Danskere: Fortællinger om køn, generationer og etnicitet [Hyphenated Danes: Narratives on gender, generations and ethnicity]*, Copenhagen: Forlaget Sociologi.

Pahl, K. and Rowsell, J., (eds.) (2006) *Travel notes from New Literacy Studies: instances of practice*, Clevedon: Multilingual Matters.

Parker, D. and Song, M., (2009) New ethnicities and the Internet: Belonging and the negotiation of difference in multicultural Britain, *Cultural studies*, 23(4): 583-604.

Phoenix, A. and Owen, C., (2000) From miscegenation to hybridity: Mixed relationships and mixed parentage in profile, in Brah A., and Coombes A. E. (eds.), *Hybridity and its discontents: Politics, science, culture*, London: Sage.

Sánchez P., (2007) Cultural authenticity and transnational Latina youth: Constructing a metanarrative across borders, *Linguistics and Education*, 18(3-4), 258-282.

Spencer, M., (1986) Emergent literacies: A site for analysis, *Language Arts*, 63(5): 442-453.

Spiro, R. J. Collins, B. P. and Ramchandran, A. R., (2007) Modes of openness and flexibility, in Khan, B., (ed.), *Flexible learning*, Englewood Cliffs, New Jersey: Educational Technology Publications.

Squire, K. (2007) Video game literacy: A literacy of expertise, in Coiro, J., Knobel, M., Lankshear, C., and Leu, D. (eds.), *Handbook of research on new literacies*, Mahwah: Erlbaum.

Sreberny, A., (2005) 'Not only, but also': Mixedness and media, *Journal of Ethnic and Migration Studies*, 31(3): 443-459.

Steinkuehler, C. A., (2008) Cognition and literacy in Massively Multiplayer Online Games, in Coiro, J., Knobel, M., Lankshear, C., and Leu, D. (eds.), *Handbook of research on new literacies*, Mahwah: Erlbaum.

Street, B. (ed.), (1993) *Cross-cultural approaches to literacy*, Cambridge: Cambridge University Press.

Thomas, A., (2007) Blurring and breaking through the boundaries of narrative, literacy and, identity in adolescent fan fiction, in Knobel, M., and Lankshear, C. (eds.), *A new literacies sampler*, New York: Peter Lang.

Vertovec, S., (1999) *Conceiving and researching transnationalism*, 22(2):447-462.

Vertovec, S., (2001) Transnationalism and identity, *Journal of Ethnic and Migration Studies*, 27(4): 573-582.

Vestel, V., (2009) The process of hybridization: Cognition, emotion and experience among multicultural youngsters in 'Rudenga', East side Oslo, in Alghasi, S., Eriksen, T. H. and Gorashi, H. (eds.), *The Paradoxes of cultural recognition*, London: Ashgate.

Watson, J., (1977) *Between two cultures: Migrants and minorities in Britain*, Oxford: Basil Blackwell.

Weber, S. and Mitchell, C., (2008) Imaging, keyboarding and posting identities: Young people and new media technologies, in Buckingham, D. (ed.), *Youth, identity and digital media*, Cambridge, MA: MIT Press.

Wulff, H., (1995) Introducing youth culture in its own right: The state of the art and new possibilities, in Veered, A., and Wulff, H. (eds.) *Youth Cultures: A cross-cultural perspective*, London: Routledge.

Chapter 5

Conflicting anti-racist values in Norwegian and French civic education: To what extent can the curriculum discourses empower minority youth?

Frédérique Brossard Børhaug

Introduction

This chapter is based on my Ph. D. thesis (2008) where I analysed the anti-racist discourse of two types of documents in the French curriculum for civic education in upper secondary school: the documents that provide the main objectives of this specific subject called *Éducation civique, juridique et sociale* (2003) and the explanatory documents relative to civic education in the use of the main curriculum (Ibid., 2000 and 2001). In this study I analysed the former version of the French curriculum in civic education and the current Norwegian curriculum discourse of the Core Curriculum, the Quality Framework, and the social science curriculum subject at upper secondary school. A theoretical framework combining separate theories: Lévinas (1982, 1993), Taguieff (2001) and Wieviorka (2001, 2003) have been used. Taguieff's theory serves as scaffolding in this framework as he seeks to analyse the main forms of anti-racism. However, his theoretical configuration is supplemented by Wieviorka's socialising model in order to discuss the different roles of the public school. Finally, the category of culture is deconstructed by making use of Lévinas' ethics. To analyse both countries' curricula, I used Laclau's and Mouffe's discourse analysis (2002) aiming to explore hegemonic concepts—their definitions, interconnections with other concepts and how they gained their dominant position-within the school discourse.

The school, the curriculum and integration

Integrating citizens has always been a major challenge in every community but today's global society acutely highlights the unfulfilled task of inclusion where much of the equality order we try to establish is *unequal*. Gert Biesta (2006) illustrates well this fundamental tension in democracy between including and excluding citizens stating that:

> But the history of democracy is not only a history of inclusion; it is at the very same time a history of exclusion. [...] The overriding argument here focuses on those who are deemed not to be *fit* for democracy, either because they lack certain qualities that are considered to be fundamental for democratic participation—such as rationality or reasonableness [...]—or because they do not subscribe to the ideal of democracy itself. (2006: 3)

Much of the civic educational project in school rests on a strong epistemological project. By providing good conditions for the development of comprehensive democratic knowledge and skills, we firmly believe that individuals will be able to participate actively as citizens in the democratic society. It sounds reasonable, but what if it also contributed to the further exclusion of the marginalised ones? In other words, could it be possible to understand the inclusion project not as a specific centre expanding towards the outside including progressively the less privileged—mainly through the acquisition of universalist knowledge and skills—but by establishing a new centre radically transforming the equality order? Quoting Gert Biesta again,

> Those who make the claim do not simply want to be included in the existing order; they want to *redefine* the order in such a way that *new* identities, new ways of doing and being become possible and can be *counted*.   (Ibid.: 14)

How then to redefine civic education in such ways that better prevent exclusion mechanisms that are particularly destructive for the less advantaged? How can school contribute to promote new beings and doings that can enlarge choices and real freedoms for all citizens within the multicultural community? And how to prevent monocultural school discourses that leave the multicultural school insufficiently prepared within its daily practice to support a democratic citizenship that can include non-dominant ethnocultural groups?

In order to discuss such fundamental educational issues, I propose to focus on anti-racist education. Indeed, in my view and because of the main position of racism in public debate, it is important not to dismiss this concept. Traditionally, anti-racist education aims to analyse and counteract negative asymmetric power relations, racial attitudes and discriminatory practices, and much of this content has been incorporated in intercultural and multicultural education (May, 2009,

Hauge, 2007). Still, within the blurred research field of intercultural and multicultural education (Allemann-Ghionda, 2009; Banks, 2009a; Bleszynska, 2008; Coulby, 2006; Gorski, 2008; Hauge, 2007; May, 1999; Portera, 2008) it is important to reflect on how bringing together equality and difference in society towards more social justice.

Based on this approach I first construct a theoretical framework analysing the main anti-racist values in the Norwegian and French curricula for civic education, and look at how they specifically combine the aporia of equality and difference. The interest in studying both countries' school discourses lies on the fact that France is often regarded at first sight as more assimilative compared to more progressive Nordic countries. In contrast with Norway, the concept of minority/majority and communities are controversial in French public debate and the colonial past is still a troublesome factor when establishing less conflicting social relations among citizens with diverse cultural background. However, we will later see many striking parallels between Norwegian and French educational discourses. In the second part of this chapter I will discuss the extent to which both curricula might contribute to empowering minority youth. Using the capability approach as a theoretical frame, I will consider the space for identity construction and participation possibilities for minority pupils within Norwegian and French school discourses in civic education and reflect on the possible dangers if curricula rest on excluding conditions. Eventually, I will question an exclusive culturalist approach reducing human beings to affiliation to particular ethnic groups; based on Lévinas' understanding of strangeness and responsibility, I will attempt to redefine the educational project by including ethical thinking about how to become a subject of action and responsibility.

How then to combine equality and difference in anti-racist education: Towards a theoretical framework highlighting the grounds of anti-racism?

In order to analyse the discourse of civic education in French and Norwegian curricula, I will shortly present a theoretical framework bringing together three distinct theories (Lévinas, 1982, 1993; Taguieff, 2001; Wieviorka, 2001, 2003).

Anti-racism as an ideological configuration
Pierre-André Taguieff's configuration model is made of two axes: one horizontal and one vertical. The horizontal axis is axiological, providing various values and meanings of human existence with two opposite values: universalism and

communitarianism. The former, universalism, states that human beings are part of the same humanity grounded on modern individual and universal values; the latter, communitarianism is founded on holistic values where human beings belong above all to distinct cultural communities (2001: 260). The vertical axis is ontological and provides two opposite modes of cognition: spiritualism and materialism. Where reason, rationality and progress are considered as the primary and legitimate source of authority, materialism emphasises the biological nature of human beings. Given the two axes and its four poles, Taguieff defines four different types of anti-racism: AR1s (*Universalist/spiritualist anti-racism*), AR1m (*Bioevolutionist anti-racism*), AR2s (*Communitarianist/spiritualist anti-racism*) and AR2m (*Materialist/zoological anti-racism*) (Ibid: 277). I will only sketch here some central features of AR1s and AR2s, because of their significance to the analysis of the French and Norwegian curriculum discourses.

Universalist/spiritualist anti-racism AR1s states that each citizen has the same rights and duties, and shall have the same opportunities to have a decent life. There is no fatalism in inequality; every person and group should be supported in order to reach a good level of development. Strong belief in human potential founded on reason and progress are central to the anti-racist AR1s project, but this may also ultimately imply paternalistic Western ideals and lead to assimilative strategies.

On the contrary, *Communitarianist/spiritualist anti-racism* AR2s states that everything is relative. It argues that the communities' distinct ways of living should remain different because they enrich humanity. AR2s denounce both global capitalism leading to uniformisation and assimilationist nation-state projects provoking the decline of minority groups. In its extreme form, however, AR2s may lead to separate communities.

Various societal models

The profound tension between equality and difference is being reinforced by various socialisation models in society. Michel Wieviorka defines four main societal strategies made to deal with cultural differences, conferring various tasks to public and private spheres (2001, 2003). These are (harsh) assimilation, tolerance, multiculturalism (also called recognition) and communitarianism. Here, we will only look at tolerance and multiculturalism strategies as only these are relevant to both countries' integration policies.

On the one hand, *tolerance* argues on individual rights and duties, but group identities are partially accepted if generally kept within the private sphere.

Visible cultural differences in the public room can be allowed as long as they do not destabilise the majority group's hegemony (2001: 18; 2003: 30). Therefore, the school discourse will not conceal the fact that pupils have different cultural backgrounds and may, to some extent, welcome this cultural diversity but without real recognition. The current French Republican integration model is often considered within the tolerance pole. Each pupil, beyond its cultural ties, is a becoming citizen within the political community and the French nation shall provide equal treatment to everyone. Still, this integration model is challenged by deep social inequalities, ethnocultural and social claims.

On the other hand, *multiculturalism* requires that the state seeks to reach a greater combination of universalism and differentialism. Full recognition within the public space is provided in an attempt to avoid assimilation and segregation (2001: 18; 2003: 31). Better equality in terms of outcomes for citizens with various backgrounds implies both cultural recognition and power redistribution. This strategy is defined in Wieviorka's term as 'integrated multiculturalism' aiming 'at reinforcing the nation by setting the recognition of cultural diversity and the struggle against social injustice in the context of national unity' (2004: 295). It corresponds to the establishment of multicultural states (Kymlicka, 2007), by enabling minority groups to act in political life just as majority members without denying them their specific ethnocultural identity. Contemporary minority rights for Sámi people reflect the Norwegian state's stronger multiculturalist policy towards this specific group.

Ethics as a necessary 'backlight'
Still, racism cannot be considered solely as a societal problem but as an ethical one too, for it jeopardises the society's moral norms and laws, as well as good human relations. Thus, it is necessary to support the anti-racist educational project by also developing an ethical reflection on the essence of man and the finality of his socialisation.

Emmanuel Lévinas raises a strong critic of any attempt to know the *Other* as oneself. He sees the I inextricably bounded to the *Other* in the act of responsibility, but still a stranger to himself (Poirié, 1996). In parallel to *Ricœur's understanding of recognition* (2005), and to Derrida's work on forgiveness (2000), Lévinas contributes to weakening a strong cultural discourse which confines human beings within culture and religion (Brossard Børhaug, 1999, 2008). Regardless of specific backgrounds, Lévinas argues that the ethical responsibility is the matter of the I, and not of the *Other* (1993). This responsibility is not only understood as formal rights and duties but also as a fundamental act of love, leading to peace and fraternity. The human community has therefore a double structure grounded in the relation to the *Other* and the Third, and the philosophy of Lévinas questions justice and its legitimate practices. By doing so, Lévinas reintroduces ethical difference within the political community. In other words, how the community can remain a place for unity and at the same time be open, respectful of difference and resistant to closure within 'a politics of ethical difference', (Critchley, 1999: 219-239; Lévinas, 1982: 74-75). Identity construction as an explanatory concept becomes therefore not sufficient to discuss the plurality of human existence and Lévinas' contradictory voice—at the end of this chapter—will be a necessary ethical *backlight* in an educational debate traditionally concerned with the emergence of the becoming citizen's autonomy and rationality.

Based on my theoretical framework, I will now provide a short overview of some of the main anti-racist values in French and Norwegian curricula for civic education. Non-dominant antagonist discourses exist but, because of the chapter's limited space, I will mainly focus on the major features of the hegemonic anti-racist one, AR1s.

Some main conclusions from my study of the Norwegian and French curricula

The school curriculum is an ideological key document for school practice and is aimed to provide, along with other legislative texts, regulations and main value priorities given to the education of the upcoming generation in a particular society.

The Norwegian curriculum discourse is divided within three parts: the Core Curriculum, the Quality Framework and the various subject curricula.[28] The Norwegian Directorate for Education and Training as the executive agency for the Ministry of Education and Research states that: 'The Quality Framework summarises and elaborates on the provisions in the Education Act and its regulations, including the National Curriculum, and must be considered in light of the legislation and regulations'.[29] Regarding the aim of the Core Curriculum it is stated that: 'The Core Curriculum shall elaborate the objects clause of the

28 www.udir.no/Stottemeny/English/Curriculum-in-English/ Core-Curriculum-in-five-languages [accessed 1.3.2013].

29 www.udir.no/Upload/larerplaner/Fastsatte_lareplaner_for_Kunnskapsloeftet/5/ prinsipper_lk06_Eng.pdf?epslanguage=no [accessed 1.3.2013].

Education Act, set major aims for education and training and include the value, cultural and knowledge foundations for primary and secondary education.[30] Likewise, the French Ministry of Education and Research gives a central place to the curriculum along with other legislative regulations such as *Le Bulletin Officiel de l'éducation nationale* and *Le code de l'éducation*. It states for the lower secondary school that: 'School programmes define the central knowledge and methods that must be acquired during the cycle by students. They constitute the national framework within which teachers organise their teaching taking into account the pace of learning of each student.'[31] It follows the same line of thought for the curriculum at upper secondary school, but includes a gradual specialisation of students in order to prepare them for higher education and working life.[32]

The school discourse in Norwegian and French curricula is explicit regarding racism and it openly states that the school shall fight any form of racism and discrimination in school and society by promoting democratic values. Still, it is essential to analyse how each anti-racist project is justified within its particular national context and its potential contradictions with regard to the need for preserving national unity *and* cultural diversity (Brossard Børhaug, 2008).

Society's diversity within the tolerance strategy

The Norwegian curriculum makes visible, to a larger extent than its French counterpart, the different minority groups' existence in the domestic society. It reproduces the established hierarchy of group minorities: 'indigenous population' (the Sámi); 'national minorities' such as people of Finnish origins (*Kvener*) with a longstanding residence in Norway; and 'newer minorities' composed of immigrants born abroad or who have parents or grand-parents born abroad. These three different groups are not always clearly defined in the curriculum which also promotes an uncritical picture of Norwegian culture (Ibid.: 151-154). The consecutive use of idealistic pictures from the national Norwegian heritage reinforces this pattern.[33] We can explain the distinction between groups by the

---

30 My own translation, www.udir.no/Lareplaner/Kunnskapsloftet/Generell-del-av-lareplanen/ [accessed 1.3.2013].
31 My own translation of the following article: Article L311-3 in Le code de l'éducation and www.education.gouv.fr/cid81/les-programmes.html [accessed 1.3.2013].
32 My own translation, www.education.gouv.fr/pid24239/les-programmes-du-lycee.html [accessed 1.3.2013].
33 www.udir.no/Upload/larerplaner/generell_del/5/Core_Curriculum_English.pdf?epslanguage=no: 1-44 [accessed 1.3.2013].

fact that the Norwegian discourse uses the category of ethnic background, which is somewhat unacceptable in the French universalist discourse. In France, the civic education discourse implies a strong rhetoric about the nation which is defined as an abstract political community. When the topic of cultural diversity is addressed, the French discourse often prefers to refer to particularity (as a contradictory pole to universalism) than to culture, immigrants and foreigners (Ibid.: 284-289).

Even the notion of community is equivocal: community is used both in the singular and the plural.[34] When the singular form is employed, it refers to the abstract citizen fellowship; when the plural form is used, it refers to distinct groups but always in a subordinate position. It is also important to mention that the notion of community is highly controversial in the French public discourse, as it is frequently associated with the notions of segregation and communitarianism (Ibid.: 328-330). Therefore, we can conclude that the Norwegian curriculum is apparently more willing to include elements focusing on minority background than the French one, which in actual fact mostly advocates for the common good of the republic, *Res publica*. Other universalist notions such as citizenship, representation, nation, equality and democracy reinforce the idea of the abstract political community (Brossard Børhaug, 2012).

We may consider the French school anti-racist discourse to be positioned within the tolerance strategy. At first, the curriculum distinguishes between public and private spheres and states that cultural differences can be cultivated within the family as long as they are not in contradiction with the exercise of individual rights. Secondly, the school discourse states that the republic respects cultural and religious diversity along with the principle of secularity and equal rights. Nevertheless, the alleged respect is not precisely defined when the curriculum comes to discuss the various types of human rights, the several forms of citizenship at local, national and global level (Brossard Børhaug, 2008: 317-324; 353) and when it avoids discussing in depth the actual dilemmas about social justice and cultural integration (Ibid.: 330-339). Particularly striking is the specific discourse on cultural differences always seen as subordinate to the common good of the republic. Concepts dealing with multicultural thinking such as discrimination, affirmative action and multiculturalism are either rarely mentioned or understood within a traditional French context where they are

---

34 For example the curriculum discourse uses the terms of *communauté de citoyens* and *communautés concrètes* (Brossard Børhaug, 2008: 328; www2.cndp.fr/archivage/valid/14966/14966-8206-9262.pdf: 46 [accessed 1.3.2013]

considered to weaken the shared foundations of the republic (Ibid.: 306-309). *Differentialist citizenship*[35] is understood as a potential threat to the universalist ground of the Republic. In many ways, one can see a parallel between the school discourse and the French public discourse showing scepticism and/or a negative answer to cultural differences (Bénichou, 2006).

A differentialist thinking, AR2s, is more prominent in the Norwegian anti-racist school discourse. Still, the Norwegian discourse cannot be considered as multicultural. One reason for this is the overstated importance given to the Norwegian culture. This heritage founded on Western humanistic and Christian values is presented as the shared body of references. Little attention is paid to minority cultures, even to the Sámi, and neither is there a great awareness of the dilemmas and specific needs of minority pupils (Brossard Børhaug, 2008: 198-201; 2012). The notion of multicultural society is neither used in the Core Curriculum nor in the Quality Framework, and the same stands for the expressions *multicultural school* and *multicultural nation*. Nevertheless, cultural diversity is mentioned in the three documents but often in an imprecise manner. Regarding the rights given to various minority groups, these do not provide equal treatment. While the Sámi gained formal group rights, the newer minority groups only are granted formal individual rights. This means no real recognition of their own culture, religion and language within the public sphere, and no or strictly limited support from the authorities such as in the national literacy policy (Engen, 2010). We can therefore conclude that the anti-racist school discourse follows the same pattern as the discourse of immigration in including elements such as the aim of integration and in excluding elements characterised by the limited, and often controversial, place given to minority cultures in the public space (Pihl, 2001; 2010).

As mentioned before, the tolerance strategy only gives restricted possibilities for minority cultures to further develop in the public sphere. That way, they are only tolerated and not really accepted. This situation therefore entails an asymmetric power relation when minority cultures are continuously subject to the evaluation of the majority group; evaluations which may from time to time decide that specific cultural traditions are no longer considered acceptable. Today, the symbolic use of the veil in both countries is a concrete example of the tolerance—or not—of a specific religious claim. After a long and ideological debate starting openly in 1989, France passed in 2004 a law forbidding any

---

35 *Citoyenneté différenciée* (Brossard Børhaug, 2008: 306; www2.cndp.fr/archivage/ valid/14966/14966-8206-9262.pdf: 31 [accessed 1.3.2013].

ostentatious sign or dress showing religious affiliation in public school, accepting only discrete signs.[36] However, one may wonder how to consider that a religious sign is ostentatious or discrete. Even though the law shall include all religions, it has also been heavily criticised for being mainly directed towards the use of the Muslim headscarf. Furthermore, many concrete problems arise in daily life, for example how to provide further education to girls wanting to use hijab but not able to attend public school, and include Muslim mothers using hijab and wanting to help in school trips outside school.

Thus, tolerance is not an unproblematic concept and the study of both curricula's anti-racist discourses, which are based mainly on tolerance justifications and strategies, shows a current bias of interest in favour of the stronger part, that is to say the majority groups.

An AR1s hegemonic discourse in both curricula

Based on the use of discourse analysis we might also consider the Norwegian and French anti-racist curricula as greatly influenced by the AR1s discourse, which can eventually be considered as hegemonic.

This statement is supported by the use of complex arguments in the curricula stating the over-importance of universal values. The necessity to educate pupils in democratic thinking and practice is a constant concern in both curricula. The Norwegian school document exemplifies this aim with a comprehensive presentation of the Norwegian culture founded on Christian and humanistic values (Brossard Børhaug, 2008: 143-158; 164-174). The French curriculum discusses respect for rights and duties and how becoming citizens have to learn loyalty to the shared values of the republic (Ibid.: 302). However, this universalist approach is not neutral, being based again on the interests of both majority groups.

Both anti-racist curriculum discourses also strongly stress the need of knowledge. The Core Curriculum states that: 'Our Christian and humanistic tradition places equality, human rights and rationality at the fore. Social progress is sought in reason and enlightenment, and in man's ability to create, appreciate and communicate.'[37] One main task in French civic education is to develop the individual's ability to use abstract and rational concepts; by using transdisciplinary knowledge when the pupils learn to construct their scientific

36 www.education.gouv.fr/bo/2004/21/MENG0401138C.htm [accessed 1.3.2013]
37 www.udir.no/Upload/larerplaner/generell_del/5/Core_Curriculum_English. pdf?epslanguage=no: 9 [accessed 1.3.2013]

argumentation, they are expected to be able to discern irrational feelings and prejudices from reasoned arguments.[38] The epistemological project therefore lays on the belief that rationality and reason will bring autonomy to the pupils, greater possibilities to make reasonable choices and consequently progress for the whole society. This faith in knowledge, which can be dated back to the Enlightenment period, is also concretised by the need of technological development in which Western ways of life are implicitly presented as desirable societal models. It is even reinforced by the use of pictures in the Core Curriculum of the Norwegian discourse showing implicitly an evolutional thinking where Western knowledge and practices are presented as modern and innovative while African and Asian art represent traditional and out-of-date customs.[39]

Finally, the strong value of equality is the core argument of the hegemonic AR1s anti-racist discourse in both curricula. The principle that all humans are equal before law and shall have the same opportunities to have a decent life implies for school to help pupils to become independent and well-educated, ensuring, that way, their further progress in society. This can be illustrated by the Core Curriculum stating that: 'Education should be based on the view that all persons are created equal and that human dignity is inviolable. It should confirm the belief that everyone is unique; that each can nourish his own growth and that individual distinctions enrich and enliven our world. Education should foster equality between the sexes and solidarity among groups and across borders. It should portray and prove knowledge as a creative and versatile force, vigorous both for personal development and for humane social relations'[40]. Still, equality as an ideal represents a problematic value if its pitfalls are not further considered (Brossard Børhaug, 2012). Equality appears to be a binding value embedded in formal rights, but it can conceal a lack of equal outcomes for minority members (Øzerk, 1993); such a critical reflection on redistribution and recognition is not expressed in either curricula.

We can therefore note many parallels between Norwegian and French anti-racist curriculum discourses. Still, I argue that the French school discourse is located on a higher level within spiritualism than the Norwegian one because of its high degree of abstract thinking. The French curriculum gives a rather

38 Brossard Børhaug, 2008: 263-265; www2.cndp.fr/archivage/ valid/41098/41098-6083-18145.pdf: 10 [accessed 1.3.2013].
39 www.udir.no/Upload/larerplaner/generell_del/5/Core_Curriculum_English. pdf?epslanguage=no [accessed 1.3.2013]
40 www.udir.no/Upload/larerplaner/generell_del/5/Core_Curriculum_English. pdf?epslanguage=no: 9-10 [accessed 1.3.2013]

difficult presentation of theories about citizenship and justice, quite far from daily school practice. Many difficult concepts are combined together, such as the notions of nation, state, democracy and law (Brossard Børhaug, 2008: 340; 358-359). One may wonder to what extent an abstract curriculum discourse is able to deal with *concrete* challenges in an unequal French society based on meritocracy and elitism. How then to avoid the exclusion of the community's own members? Many riots took place and are still occurring in French poor urban territories revealing a chaotic integration process of young citizens (Avenel, 2010; Dubet, 2008, 2010). The same question is also important for the Norwegian society which is trying to prevent the establishment of a lower class composed of citizens with immigrant and/or low educational background (Alghasi, Eide and Hylland Eriksen, 2012; Kjedstadli, 2008).

In conclusion, the school discourse for civic education implies too narrow an understanding of citizenship, excluding, to various extents, non-dominant ethnocultural groups. We may question to what extent anti-racist values in French and Norwegian curricula, defined within traditional nation-state discourse, may leave the school unprepared to deal with the current dilemmas of multicultural democracy. In order to take this issue further I will now present some main theoretical claims from the capability approach and will discuss how the curriculum as a social conversion factor may contribute in providing genuine opportunities for minority pupils to become agents in their own life as participative citizens.

Redistributive effects of education by expanding individuals' substantive freedoms

Often, the main focus is put on the economic value of schooling, on school performances and resource inputs. By looking at how the school can contribute to economic growth and boost the country's competition (well supported by the human capital theory), the main concern is less primarily the quality of life that people may enjoy. The capability approach, on the contrary, states that income and wealth are of limited value if they do not promote human development, understood here as a widening of all human choices. Human development therefore entails a careful analysis of the quality and distribution of economic growth, which is not an end in itself, but rather a means to achieve sustainable living conditions and human flourishing (Alkire and Deneulin, 2009). The capability approach seeks to assess the well-being of individuals, social arrangements, and policies designed through a multi-dimensional metric of justice (Robeyns, 2009). In this process, we need to pay attention to the school's own function because education is supposed to be empowering and transformative (Walker and Unterhalter, 2007: 11).

According to Amartya Sen, one of the two founders of the capability approach, education can expand people's freedoms, but in different ways. *Educated individuals will become able to participate* in public debate about social and political arrangements. They will also be capable to participate more in decision-making within the household, local community and at national level. And finally, they will be more competent in organising themselves politically which is fundamental for disadvantaged people. Sen therefore refers to education having an 'instrumental social role, an instrumental process role and an empowering and distributive role' (Unterhalter, 2009). *The redistributive* effects between groups at local and wider levels through education would enhance people's ability 'to use the benefits of education to help others as well as themselves and [it] can therefore contribute to democratic freedoms and the overall good of society as a whole' (Ibid.: 214). Lack of agency and constrained choices can in other words be seen as disadvantages reducing the individuals' ability to self-help and to influence the world (Walker and Unterhalter, 2007: 245). Still, the notion of disadvantaged is complex, and it is important to discuss what is disadvantage and how disadvantage is shaped through multifaceted dimensions. We need to look at how government policy affects the lives of individuals diminishing—or not—the risks and vulnerability they face in daily life (Wolff and De-Shalit, 2007: 4-6). Do such policies yield further disadvantages—what is called *corrosive disadvantages*—or on the contrary *de-cluster disadvantages* (Ibid: 10, 14)? School policy in this respect, is important to analyse in order to assess to what extent school (re)produces social inequality.

To use a human development and capability approach in anti-racist education provides an alternative evaluation frame which can help assessing the factors which can enlarge pupils' choices and substantive freedoms in an enabling school environment. Three notions are central: functionings, capabilities and agency. The notion of functionings is understood as the set of particular doings and beings that the person values and has reason to value. The notion of capabilities includes the person's real freedom to choose various beings and doings. As for agency, it represents the person's ability to realise valuable goals (Alkire and Deneulin, 2009: 22-26). Education as a site of symbolic control may be as oppressive as it is transformative. In critically considering the curriculum as a resource for minority pupils, I will discuss the kind of opportunities the two anti-racist discourses may provide minority pupils with, to enable them to choose what to do and be. In order to deepen the individual's ability to combine his/her own substantive freedoms within his/her specific living settings, I will focus on the social conversion factors understood as hegemonic norms and practices within society; in particular, I will look at the discourse about discriminatory practices and at the epistemological project in the curricula of civic education.

To what extent are the French and Norwegian curricula a powerful social conversion factor that helps minority youth reflect on discrimination?

How can schooling contribute to a more equal distribution of resources and opportunities, and to the recognition and equal valuing of human diversity (Walker and Unterhalter, 2007: 251)? The school discourse is included in a broader societal discourse and much of the anti-racist debate has lately dealt with the issue of discriminatory practices.

The minority victims' testimonies have been given more space in the French public room since the 1990s but they are only welcome provided they don't destabilise the public interest's hegemony. Furthermore, if racism is raised in the public debate, it is traditionally combined with the highly controversial issue of the lawless suburbs and minority youth. The image of victims in the media becomes distorted and overshadowed by the *deviant* youth of the suburbs. Integration becomes therefore a matter of politics solely based on social criteria—and not on cultural integration—where victims' experiences are included within an anti-racist discourse aiming at better social conditions. In other words, little space is given to positive connotations on minority background (Iteanu, 2005). French curriculum in civic education follows the same pattern because of its lack of positive connotations on cultural differences reaffirming the *Res publica* (Brossard Børhaug, 2008: 287). But the curriculum discourse shows even less attention being given to the issue of discrimination than within the public space: the lack of integration of citizens is not explained by discriminatory experiences of minority group members but is included in the universalistic explanation based on formal rights. Positive affirmation is not a concrete issue. Social integration thus is the main focus in establishing the political community (Ibid.: 333-336).

There is much indication that these majority-orientated learning goals and minority pupils' experiences of racism in daily life can create distortions in the classroom. This pattern might be lately reinforced by a chaotic use of the concept of racism in the current public debate. In 2012 one main politician from the right-wing party UMP, Jean-François Copé, described racism as anti-white racism (racism against white people) as a main problem in society and Laurence Parisot, the leader of MEDEF, the leading national movement for entrepreneurs, talked about 'racism against firms' describing a systematic stigmatisation of business owners by politicians and due to large fiscal reforms.[41] In a wider context, where deadly attacks against Jews occurred in Southern France in March 2012, anti-Semite aggression in the city of Sarcelles in September 2012, along with the prominent role of the *Front National* right-wing political party, the present public debate mixes complex issues of anti-Semitism, terrorism and the fear of the Muslim takeover (islamisation) of French society. To what extent can curriculum contribute to reflect critically on identity construction in such a sensitive context? Given the hegemonic value of formal rights and social integration embedded in the school discourse, there is much indication that classroom discussions might enhance the goals of social cohesion and unity based on the necessity to better integrate minority members into the whole community, indirectly implying no positive recognition of religious ethnicity.

In spite of a greater focus on minority groups and different cultures, the Norwegian school discourse is also very ambivalent. Cultural differences are expressed in the curriculum but in loose and idealistic terms. In the Core Curriculum for example it is stated that we need '[t]o teach and tend our national heritage and local traditions in order to preserve variety and uniqueness—*and* to meet other cultures openly in order to find pleasure in the diversity of human expression and to learn from contrast'.[42] This leaves little space for discussing the harsh reality of discrimination that minority pupils may experience. Another issue is the national tragedy that occurred on the 22 July 2011. The killing of seventy-seven people, mostly young people, by an ethnic Norwegian zealot, Anders Behring Breivik, shows the inner vulnerability of all democracies unable to prevent religious fear, animosity and hate towards fellow citizens, even in a rich country such as Norway. Much attention in the public debate has been directed lately towards the lack of safekeeping routines and social arrangements for ensuring an adequate protection of citizens. Though, one remaining fundamental discussion would be the need to discuss a civic educational ethics based on moral virtues in the multicultural society and the distinctive role of pedagogues.

41 www.lefigaro.fr/politique/2012/09/26/01002-20120926ARTFIG00428-cope-denonce-l-existence-d-un-racisme-anti-blanc.php [accessed 1.3.2013]
42 www.liberation.fr/economie/2012/10/03/parisot-craint-le-racisme-anti-entreprises_850650 [accessed 1.3.2013]

In such a context, one may eventually question the distinction between majority and minorities. It presents a taken for granted contingent construction of belonging where the affiliation to one's initial group is re-established without offering nuanced identity choices for individuals. You may belong to the group of *ethnic Norwegians*, or to the group of *Sámi*, or to the group of *national minorities* or to the group of *newer minorities*. However, such identity categories provide poor opportunities to construct more flexible identities that might be described as *dash-identities* or *creole identities* (Hylland Eriksen, 1997). And if the *dash-identities* are used in public debate one may notice the persistent excluding pattern using the alien ethnic background as the key marker. Why are second/third generation of individuals with Pakistani background described in the societal debate as 'Norwegian-Pakistanis'? Why not the other way around: 'Pakistani-Norwegians'? Such issues cannot be easily dealt within the classroom if the Norwegian curriculum applies the ethnic hierarchy as a main category of affiliation.

The concept of discrimination is however considered to be contradictory to democratic values in society and in the comprehensive school (Brossard Børhaug, 2008: 109-112). The core curriculum openly states it by saying: 'Education should counteract prejudice and discrimination, and foster mutual respect and tolerance between groups with differing modes of life'.[43] Still, the concept is not used in the social study subject where pupils are expected to discuss racism, prejudices, and xenophobia (Ibid.: 149). To what extent can pupils reflect on concrete terms of redistribution and recognition by challenging asymmetrical social relations, if discriminatory practices are not part of the explicit competency goals expressed in the social study subject?

The epistemological curriculum discourses: An emancipatory factor for minority youth?

As mentioned before, both curricula present an epistemological project where rationality, reasonable choices, autonomy and technology are highly valued. Thus, emancipation in the civic educational project rests on a strong faith in knowledge founded on Western views on reason and progress based on the understanding of a specific centre expanding towards the outside. But what if the pupils reject it because they cannot cope with the demanding requirements of the curriculum and/or because they reject it on various intolerant claims?

43 www.utdanningsdirektoratet.no/upload/larerplaner/generell_del/Core_Curriculum_English.pdf: 40 [accessed 1.3.2013]

More concretely, how can the rather abstract French curriculum deal with poorly educated pupils from segregated suburbs? How does one also deal with pupils who reject the evolution theory because of religious views? Carole Diamant, a French philosophy teacher, experienced it, becoming helpless before a silent opposition or insistent questions[44] from pupils as they were discussing different forms of human equality (2005: 37). How then to counteract religious fear and hate promoting islamophobia, anti-Semitism and racism? The killing on the 22 July, 2011 shows the limitations of an exclusive epistemological project, not including 'a systematic cultivation of the 'inner eye', the imaginative capacity that makes it possible for us to see how the world looks from the point of view of a person different in religion or ethnicity' (Nussbaum, 2012: 3).

If we consider that this is 'the margin that holds the page',[45] a well-known citation of the French-Swiss film director Jean-Luc Godard, how then to deal with the pedagogy's inner contradictions of socialisation/adaptation AND emancipation; of transmitting particular knowledge AND allowing the upcoming generation to go beyond it and subvert it if necessary; how then to combine the pupils' own interests AND open up new horizons; how then to teach youth to respect AND contest a legitimate authority? (Meirieu, 2007:68-69). The key issue in every pedagogical action is to conciliate the irreconcilable; the claim of that everyone is able to learn and access freedom AND the claim that no one can force the other to learn and implement her/his own liberty (Ibid.: 79). That is why it is highly problematic to use uncritically categorisations that may enclose human beings into predefined notions blocking their individual and collective trajectories (Ibid: 111). On the contrary, could we reverse our thinking and presuppose that it is the outskirts that make the centre progress? (Meirieu, 2012: 40). How to then redefine the unequal equality centre in order to be counted in civic education? Biesta (2011) argues for a subjectification conception of civic learning fostering democratic agency. It requires a shift from teaching citizenship to learning democracy where young people learn democracy through their experiences from every-day life. Such shift reveals that learning 'is situated in the unfolding lives of young people and how these lives, in turn, are implicated in wider cultural, social, political and economic orders. It

---

44 www.utdanningsdirektoratet.no/upload/larerplaner/generell_del/Core_Curriculum_ English.pdf: 12 [accessed 1.3.2013]

45 Some pupils may ask teachers if they are Jewish or Christian, challenging the school's norm of *laïcité*. New curricula subjects from 2012 also require teachers to address the topic of conflicts in the Middle East. Many teachers are expressing the sentiment of anxiety, solitude and lack of training facing complex issues and unruly pupils.

ultimately is this wider context which provides opportunities for young people to be democratic citizens—that is to enact their citizenship—and to learn from this' (Ibid.: 6). Therefore, we need to focus on 'individuals-in-interaction and individuals-in-context and on [...] peoples' actual condition of citizenship [...] highlight[ing] the importance of plurality and difference in understanding and enacting democratic citizenship' (Ibid.: 2).

In conclusion, the discourse about societal discrimination and the epistemological project show that the curriculum is clearly insufficient when dealing with pupils' experiences of the unfair multicultural society. The strong discourse about unity and cohesion establishing an abstract community of sameness blurs the harsh reality of discrimination and shows an ambiguous visibility of the minority groups within society. The lack of *positive* focus on their capabilities can harm the development of valuable identities. In a polarised and often populist public debate, flexible identities are not privileged. In order to give more genuine opportunities to individuals, public policy, here concretised in the curriculum discourse, could focus on how to develop more *fertile functionings*, i.e. functionings likely to secure further functionings (Wolff and De-Shalit, 2007: 10). Otherwise, it might result in a greater risk for the individuals already in a vulnerable position, to experience corrosive disadvantages such as a lack of positive affiliations, which yield further disadvantages (Ibid.: 185). The need for more valuable identity construction thus is a main concern.

Othering in the curriculum and 'the excluded from the inside'

Sen refers to the widespread view of considering people as being solely characterised by religious and cultural identities, but a more viable understanding would be to emphasise the fact that 'we are diversely different' (2007: xvi). The individual's freedom to determine his/her loyalties and priorities between different groups is fundamental but it is sometimes extremely limited because of the illusion of a singular choiceless identity (Ibid.: 5-8). To counteract such a divisive illusion we need to promote reasoned and strongly plural identity choices; this entails the substantive freedom for the individuals to choose relevant belongings and the relative strengths of their respective claims (Ibid.: 24; 29). Because life is not mere destiny, the issue is therefore not the fact of having the choice to whatever identity, but individuals' reasoned choices over alternative identities and priorities to the various chosen forms of belonging (Ibid.: 38-39).

How then to help pupils understand the plurality of identity differences in a constructive way? Democracy, which lies at the heart of any truly civic education, is an important issue to consider in order to reduce identity confinement. But instead of making democracy a quintessentially Western idea, pupils need to understand the global roots of democracy and the fact that democracy does not only belong to ancient Greece and enlightened Europe but has to be seen as a global process (Sen, 2005; 2007). Greece had indeed strong links with other ancient civilisations. The sharing of knowledge from many scholarly fields was carried out in Chinese, Arabic and Sanskrit for millennia and it shows that the dominance of Western science is a recent phenomenon in the world (Skuttnabb-Kangas et al., 2009: 324-325). In other words, the history of public participation and reasoning is a worldwide phenomenon, as opposed to a culture-specific idea (Sen, 2007: 55). To consider Western Europe as the cradle of democracy would therefore entail ethnocentrism, civilisational confinement and a reproduction of the colonised mind (Ibid.: 88-93). Such critical approaches are missing from the discourses of civic education and we could therefore see their position as a reproduction of the AR1s Western predominance of ideals and practices. This is why it is important to put in place a more multiculturalist curriculum which celebrates global cultural diversity and democratic innovation. 'If the roots of so-called Western science or culture draw inter alia on, say Chinese innovations, Indian and Arabic mathematics, or West Asian preservation of the Greco-Roman heritage [...], should there not be a fuller reflection of that robust interactive past that can be found, at this time, in the school curriculum of multi-ethnic Britain?' (Ibid.: 162). Such curriculum would question the hegemonic school practice based on AR1s argumentation by AR2s thinking but not without the need to emphasise the individual's freedom to choose complex identity affiliations. It should be based on meaningful insight both in the present time experiences and in the multicultural past of humanity.

However, focusing on individualism in identity work might not result as expected. André Iteanu (2005) identifies a relational vacuum in French suburbs characterised by the absence of local reliable relations over time and shows how some young troublemakers are not only passive victims but also actively contributing to social disorder themselves. In doing so, they reduce their own chances of successful integration and intensify the problems already found in the suburbs (Ibid.: 120). He explains this phenomenon as being the result of a social and cultural deprivation over a long period of time leading to extreme and destructive individualism and cut off from any viable social community. If there is however an attempt to establish a community between peers, it is based on local and territorial violence and constitutes radical forms of social actions

(Ibid.: 121-129). In other words, they participate in their further exclusion from society. This reality also significant in 2012 was already identified by Abdelmalek Sayad in 1985 as 'the excluded from the inside';[46] i.e. a desperate attempt to obtain existential visibility caught between a massive assimilation pressure from the majority group, poor employment opportunities and a negative self-confinement in own ethnic group (Brossard Børhaug, 2008: 186-187). The transformation of the democratisation order, through the establishment of a new centre of identities with valuable beings and doings from the outside, gets its full strength (Biesta, 2006). Considering the curriculum as one possible conversion factor does not allow providing an overview on the complex dynamics of identity construction. Still, this present analysis of French and Norwegian curricula in civic education attempts to critically reflect on the extent to which the school discourse could provide fairer grounds for the development of minority youth's capacity to aspiration.

A fairer curriculum fostering greater capabilities to express and act

Culture does matter, but the real question is how to avoid too narrow a view of cultural attributes that confine human beings into particular identities making them 'imaginary slaves of an illusory force' (Sen, 2007: 103). To counteract such an illusion, we need non-sectarian and non-parochial education that works against a fragmentary logic, contradictory to the unavoidable plurality of human nature (Ibid.: 119; 182).

If we consider cultural capability as an important dimension in education for counteracting such an illusion, how can schooling contribute to reinforcing the individual and group capacity of constructive voice and aspiration? (Brossard Børhaug, 2012) Culture is often considered to be a matter of the past and of common heritage (as it is explicitly said in the Norwegian curriculum discourse), and economics the science of the future. Such an interpretation is problematic (Appadurai, 2004: 60-62). However, an important concern is how to strengthen the capability of the poor, and by extension the marginalised groups, to find and cultivate their own voice, while avoiding a total loyalty to an oppressive culture or a total rejection of it. This requires the creation of a constructive dissensus in which the oppressed engage their own future by contesting the social, cultural and economic ideologies which jeopardise their space for agency and by supporting local cultural forces to cultivate greater aspiration in their own context (Ibid: 63, 66-67). Indeed, low capacity to aspire is a result of power:

46 *La marge qui tient la page* (Meirieu, 2012 :40.

the better your position is in terms of power, dignity and material resources, the more likely you will be able to turn your aspirations into outcomes. This capacity of aspiration can be considered as a navigational capacity where the more privileged members of society make use of their knowledge, experiences and opportunities in a more effective way than disadvantaged people.

The school has the important task of cultivating the capacity of voice and aspiration because they are nurtured by practice, repetition, and exploration. If not, the ability to express and aspire tends to be more rigid and binary and to develop scepticism, conformism, violence or too uncritical a compliance (Ibid: 69; Sen, 2007: 9). Therefore, voice and aspiration are essential to any anti-racist educational project and decisive in socially and culturally marginalised suburbs: 'When schooling fosters voice, here understood as the capacity to debate, contest, inquire, and participate critically, it simultaneously nurtures aspiration. Where children might be denied a capability of voice at home or in society, or where their aspirations might be cramped outside of school, there is then a particular ethical responsibility for the school to challenge exclusion, not to perpetuate it' (Walker, 2007: 184).

Unfortunately, the curriculum of civic education may not provide enough pivotal opportunities in order to exercise voice as an important cultural capability. Even though the French curriculum stresses the importance of the *argued debate*[47] in the classroom, we may wonder the real benefits of such a competency goal. Does the argued debate help to promote the pupils' capacity to engage in social, economic and political issues in their *own* cultural worlds (Rao and Walton, 2004: 24)? Or is it rather a sort of abstract intellectual exercise eventually reproducing some hegemonic concepts from the majority culture? Indeed, it is expected that French pupils learn to be active reasoning citizens and the argued debate is considered to be an excellent means towards this aim (Brossard Børhaug, 2008: 263-264). Still, much of the focus here is not put on the recognition of the individual's identity but rather on a more legal frame for discussing the citizens' duties and rights, societal rules and the institutions' legal action. Even though argued debate represents an innovative path in the apprenticeship to citizenship where pupils can learn to combine practical examples and theoretical knowledge in the classroom, there is much indication that the epistemological project entails civic monocultural morals based solely on the commitment to the majority's interest (Brossard Børhaug, 2008: 263-267).

---

47 *Les 'exclus de l'intérieur,* (Sayad, 2006 : 11).

Thus, for a curriculum to be a strong social conversion factor, it is important to have a curriculum which is both anti-racist and intercultural and provides many learning settings that allow discussing various valuable activities in multicultural society. Such curriculum could also counteract a broad compensatory pedagogy which compromises both aspiration and voice of minority pupils by depreciating their multicultural identity and by having negative expectations from them (Hauge, 2007). Consequently, it is fundamental to develop aspirational narratives through an intercultural curriculum and a classroom pedagogy that challenges pupils' responses such as silence, passivity and exit (Walker, 2007:184-185). However, present-time experiences are not sufficient to expand the individual freedoms. Better combination of concrete social and cultural aspirations ought to be combined with an interactive understanding linking together past, present and future for giving more genuine opportunities for the pupils to use own reflection, voice and hope in order to build self-governance and self-confidence in an unfair society.

An explorative anti-racist education

Coming back to my introductory argument, I would like to round up the complex argumentation about anti-racist education and the tension between excluding and including citizens in democracy by attempting to include in the curriculum discourse an apparently paradoxical reflection: the need for a combination of cultural (included religious) minority rights and a more visible ethical approach which would deconstruct the category of culture.[48]

If one considers a monocultural curriculum as an inhospitable environment for voice development, likely to generate lower aspiration capacity and limited effective agency, one would conclude that an intercultural curriculum would reinforce cultural and social capital, helping not only individuals but also groups to envision and shape their future in collaboration with the others (Rao and Walton, 2004: 25). To do so, cultural rights must be included in the discourse on human rights in a much larger scale than before (Touraine, 2005). A new paradigm has to be established, in which the citizenship of the subject is not only grounded on political, civic, economic and social rights, but also extended to cultural rights (Ibid.: 9-15). This analysis is confirmed by the declaration of Fribourg which states that 'cultural rights, as much as other human rights, are an expression of and a prerequisite for human dignity' and that their violation

48 *Débat argumenté*. One could also translate it in English as reasoned debate or rational debate.

'gives rise to identity related tensions and conflicts which are one of the principal cause of violence, wars and terrorism.'[49] However, Kymlicka's analysis of the international politics of diversity and the international organisations' contradictory choices shows the great complexity and controversy related to defining the content of minority rights (2007). Nevertheless, the discussion about the necessity for cultural rights brings about the dilemma on how to avoid a never-ending process in which all traditions are to be accepted on the grounds that they are cultural. How then can the school transmit a body of shared values and references? Another fundamental dilemma is how to prevent a potential disrespect of individual rights resulting from the confinement of the subject in its own group. Thus, cultural rights represent both the possibility of a democratic renewal and the possibility of an undemocratic closure. A critical debate on the implementation of cultural rights in identity work therefore entails a deep reflection on democracy. The capability approach can offer a useful conceptual vocabulary when discussing the capability to function as participative citizens in the multicultural community. French and Norwegian curricula for civic education are not dealing with the issue of cultural rights. Still, there is little doubt that anti-racist education and intercultural education as a whole will have to face this challenge, a fact that is already very noticeable in the case of the Muslim veil.

Since the human being is more than simple culture, one also needs to reflect on human difference not merely as a cultural dimension but also as an ethical one. In other words, racism as an ethical problem implies that anti-racism is an ethical activity. The philosophy of Lévinas reminds us of the fundamental uniqueness of each human being and its responsibility towards the *Other*, considered as a brother while remaining a stranger. Lévinas' philosophy questions our traditional understanding of the public sphere in producing rational thinking about the members of the community. Based on predefined notions, each person is categorised as belonging—or not—to a specific community and, that way, the public sphere appears to be closed to many human beings. Lévinas' understanding of ethical difference opens up the public room and produces a critical reflection on undemocratic and unethical forms of membership. This is not only of great importance in the action of working against totalitarian regimes

---

49 An intercultural/multicultural curriculum represents a complex thematic also influenced by the countries' specific history such as the work of James Banks in American context (2009b). I will here only shortly argue for the need for cultural rights and for an ethical reflection in an attempt to reflect further on anti-racist curriculum.

but also in Western democratic countries where arguments about capitalism and domestic culture give support to very restrictive immigration policies. The community has therefore a double structure: a social system based on justice and equal rights, and the asymmetric responsibility of the I towards the *Other*. Therefore, the contradictory tension between equality and difference is not only a political matter but also an ethical one, showing that equality cannot be understood without difference in our current democratic quest—with difference being understood as diverse identity belongings *and* as the uniqueness of every human being seeking to enjoy a creative meaningful life.

References

Alghasi, S., Eide, E., and Hylland Eriksen, T., (eds.) *Den globale drabantbyen: Groruddalen og det nye Norge [The global suburb: Groruddalen and the new Norway]*, Oslo: Cappelen Damm akademisk.

Alkire, S., and Deneulin, S., (2009) The human development and capability approach, in Deneulin S., and Shahani, L., (eds) *An introduction to human development and capability approach: freedom and agency*, Earthscan: London.

Allemann-Ghionda, C., (2009) From intercultural education to the inclusion of diversity: Theories and policies in Europe, in Banks, J. A., (eds) *The Routledge international companion to multicultural education*, New York: Routledge.

Appadurai, A., (2004) The capacity to aspire: Culture and the terms of recognition, in Rao, V., and Walton, M, (eds.) *Culture and public action: A cross disciplinary dialog in development policy*, Stanford: University.

Avenel, C., (2010) *Sociologie des 'quartiers sensibles' [Sociology of 'sensitive districts']*, Paris: Armand Colin.

Banks, J. A., (eds) (2009a) *The Routledge international companion to multicultural education*, New York: Routledge.

Banks, J. A., (2009b) *Teaching strategies for ethnic studies*, Boston: Pearson Education.

Bénichou, M., (2006) *Le multiculturalisme*, [Multiculturalism] Rosny: Éditions Bréal.

Biesta, G. J. J., (2006) *'Don't Count me in': Democracy—inclusion—education*, 34th Annual Conference of the Nordic Educational Research Association (NFPF), *Education Widens Democracy—Or?*, 10.03.2006, Örebro.

Biesta, G. J. J., (2011) *Learning democracy in school and society: Education, lifelong learning and the politics of citizenship*, Rotterdam: Sense Publishers.

Bleszynska, K. M., (2008) Constructing intercultural education, *Intercultural Education*, 19(6): 537-545.

Brossard Børhaug, F., (1999) Hvilke etiske prinsipper bør integrering av innvandrere bygge på? En teoretisk drøfting med utgangspunkt i Emmanuel Lévinas' tenkning [What ethical principles should the integration of immigrants be based on? A theoretical discussion on the basis of Emmanuel Lévinas' thinking], *Utbildning och demokrati*, 8(3): 85-111.

Børhaug, F., (2007) Kunnskapsløftets antirasistiske verdidiskurs. En drøfting av sentrale verdier i skolens antirasistiske verdigrunnlag [The anti-racist discourse of the Knowledge Promotion: A discussion of main values in the anti-racist value foundation of the school], in Hoff Kaldestad, I. O., Reigstad, E., Sæther, J., and Sæthre, J. (red.) *Grunnverdier og pedagogikk [Core values and pedagogy]*, Bergen: Fagbokforlaget.

Brossard Børhaug, F., (2008) *Skolen mot rasisme: En sammenligning av antirasistiske verdier i fransk og norsk læreplandiskurs [The school against racism: A comparison of anti-racist values in French and Norwegian school discourse]*, Thesis (Doctor rerum politicarum), University of Oslo.

Brossard Børhaug, F., (2012) How to better combine equality and difference in French and Norwegian anti-racist education? Some reflections from a capability point of view, *Journal of Human Development and Capabilities*, 13(3): 397-413.

Coulby, D., (2006) Intercultural education: Theory and practice, *Intercultural Education*, 17(3): 245-257.

Critchley, S., (1999) *The ethics of deconstruction: Derrida and Lévinas*, Edinburgh: Edinburgh University Press.

Derrida, J., (2000) *Foi et savoir: Suivi de Le siècle et le pardon* [Faith and knowledge: Followed by The century and forgiveness], Paris: Éditions du Seuil.

Diamant, C., (2005) *École, terrain miné, [The school, a mined field.]* Paris: Éditions Liana Levi.

Dubet, F., (2008) *La galère : Jeunes en survie ['La galère': Young in survival conditions]*, Paris: Points actuels.

Dubet, F., (2010) *Les places et les chances : Repenser la justice sociale [Places and opportunities: Rethinking social justice]*, Paris: Seuil.

Engen, T. O., (2010) Literacy instruction and integration: The case of Norway, *Intercultural Education*, 21(2): 169-181.

Gorski, P. C., (2008) Good intentions are not enough: A decolonizing intercultural education, *Intercultural Education*, 19(6): 515-525.

Hauge, A.-M., (2007) *Den felleskulturelle skolen, [The common cultural school]* Oslo: Universitetsforlaget.

Horst, C., and Pihl, J., (2010) Comparative perspectives on education in the multicultural Nordic countries. *Intercultural Education*, 21(2): 99-105.

Hylland Eriksen, T., (1997) Unge kreoler i en senmoderne verden: Ambivalens eller fundamentalisme? [Young creole in a late modern world: Ambivalence or fundamentalism?], *Ung i verden—ung i Danmark. [Young in the world—Young in Denmark]* [online], Copenhagen: Dansk Flygtningehjælp, folk.uio.no/geirthe/Kreoler. html [Accessed 1.3.2013].

Iteanu, A., (2005) A perfect individual: Violence and assimilation in the French suburbs, in Andersson, M., Lithman, Y. G., and Sernhede O., (eds.) *Youth, otherness and the plural city: Modes of belonging and social life*, Göteborg: Daidalos.

Kjeldstadli, K., (2008) *Sammensatte samfunn: Innvandring og inkludering, [Complex societies : Immigration and inclusion.]* Oslo: Pax forlag.

Kymlicka, W., (2007) *Multicultural odysseys: Navigating the new international politics of Diversity*, Oxford: Oxford University Press.

Laclau, E., og Mouffe, C., (2002) *Det radikale demokrati—Diskursteoriens politiske perspektiv, [The radical democracy—Discourse theory's political perspective]*, Frederiksberg: Roskilde Universitetsforlag.

Lévinas, E., (1982) *Éthique et infini: Dialogue avec Philippe Nemo, [Ethics and Infinity: Conversations with Philippe Nemo.]* Paris: Arthème Fayard et Radio-France.

Lévinas, E., (1993) *Outside the subject*, London: The Athlone Press.

May, S., (eds) (1999) *Critical multiculturalism: Rethinking multicultural and anti-racist Education*, Abingdon: RoutledgeFalmer.

May, S., (2009) Critical multiculturalism and education, in Banks, J. A., (eds) *The Routledge international companion to multicultural education*, New York: Routledge.

Meirieu, P., (2007) *Pédagogie : Le devoir de résister, [Pedagogy : The duty to resist.]* Issy-Les-Moulineaux: esf-editeur.

Meirieu, P., (2012) *Un pédagogue dans la cité : Conversations avec Luc Cédelle, [A pedagogue in the city: Conversations with Luc Cédelle]*, Paris: Desclée de Brouwer.

Ministère de la l'éducation nationale et de la recherche, Direction de l'enseignement scolaire, (2000) *Accompagnement des programmes: Éducation civique, juridique et sociale: Classe de seconde et de première, [Support programs: Civic, legal and social education subject for the two first years in upper secondary school]* [online], Paris: Centre national de documentation pédagogique, www.cndp.fr/archivage/ valid/14966/14966-8206-9262.pdf [Accessed 1.3.2013].

Ministère de l'éducation nationale et de la recherche, Direction de l'enseignement scolaire, (2001) *Accompagnement des programmes: Éducation civique, juridique et sociale: Classes terminales, [Support programs: Civic, legal and social education subject for the last year in upper secondary school]* [online], Paris: Centre national de documentation pédagogique, www.cndp.fr/archivage/valid/35185/35185-8207-9260. pdf [Accessed 1.3.2013].

Ministère de l'éducation nationale et de la recherche, Direction de l'enseignement Scolaire, (2003) *Éducation civique, juridique et sociale: Classes de seconde, première et terminale [Civic, legal and social education subject for the three years in upper secondary school]* [online], Paris: Centre national de documentation pédagogique, www.cndp.fr/archivage/valid/41098/41098-6083-18145.pdf [Accessed 1.3.2013].

Nussbaum, M. C., (2012) *The new religious intolerance: Overcoming the politics of fear in an anxious age*, Cambridge: Harvard University Press.

Observatoire de la diversité et des droits culturels, Institut interdisciplinaire d'éthique et des droits de l'homme, (2007) [Cultural rights: Fribourg declaration] [online], Fribourg: Institut interdisciplinaire d'éthique et des droits de l'homme, www1.umn. edu/humanrts/instree/Fribourg%20Declaration.pdf [Accessed 1.3.2013].

Pihl, J., (2001) Government discourse on inclusive education and its effects on the construction of 'The Other', *International, interdisciplinary conference about Genres and Discourses in Education, Work and Cultural Life: Encounters of Academic disciplines on Theories and Practices, 13-16.05.2001*, Oslo University College.

Pihl, J., (2010) Nasjonale minoriteter og det flerkulturelle Norge—Utsyn [National minorities and the multicultural Norway—Outlook], in Bonnevie Lund, A., and Bolme Moen, B., (eds.) *Nasjonale minoriteter i det flerkulturelle Norge [National minorities in the multicultural Norway]*, Trondheim: Tapir Akademisk forlag.

Poirié, F., (1996) *Emmanuel Lévinas: Essais et entretiens [Emmanuel Lévinas : Essays and Interviews]*, Paris: Babel, Actes Sud.

Portera, A., (2008) Intercultural education in Europe: Epistemological and semantic aspects. *Intercultural Education*, 19(6): 481-491.

Ricœur, P., (2005) *The course of recognition*. Cambridge, Harvard University Press.

Rao V., and Walton M., (2004) *Culture and public action: A cross disciplinary dialog in development policy*, Stanford: University.

Robeyns, I., (2009) Equality and justice, in Deneulin, S., and Shahani, L., (eds), *An introduction to human development and capability approach: freedom and agency*, Earthscan: London.

Sen, A., (2005) *La démocratie des autres, [Democracy and its global roots]* Paris: Éditions. Payot.

Sen, A., (2007) *Identity and violence: The illusion of destiny*, London: Penguin Books.

Skuttnabb-Kangas, T., Phillipson, R., Mohanty A. K., and Panda, M., (2009) *Social justice through multilingual education*, Bristol: Multilingual Matters.

Taguieff, P.-A., (2001) *The force of prejudice: On racism and its doubles*, Minneapolis: University of Minnesota Press.

Touraine, A., (2005) *Un nouveau paradigme: Pour comprendre le monde d'aujourd'hui, (New paradigm for understanding today's world)*, Paris: Éditions Arthème Fayard.

Unterhalter, E., (2009) Education, in Deneulin, S. and Shahani, L., (eds) *An introduction to human development and capability approach: freedom and agency*, Earthscan: London.

Walker, M., (2007) Selecting capabilities for gender equality in education, in Walker, M., and Unterhalter, E., (eds.) *Amartya Sen's capability approach and social justice in education*, New York: Palgrave Macmillan.

Walker, M., and Unterhalter, E., (2007) *Amartya Sen's capability approach and social justice in education,*. New York: Palgrave Macmillan.

Wieviorka, M., (2001) Qu'est-ce que le multiculturalisme?, [What is multiculturalism?] in: Jean.-Marc Roirant (eds) *Eduquer contre le racisme. Les idées en mouvements*, 87(3), Hors série. Paris: La ligue de l'enseignement.

Wieviorka, M., (2003) Qu'est-ce qu'une identité, une différence culturelle? [What is identity, a cultural difference?], in GREP Midi-Pyrénées (eds) *L'identité culturelle et le politique*, Toulouse: Le comptoir du livre, Collection 'Les idées contemporaines'.

Wieviorka, M., (2004) The making of differences, *International sociology*, 19: 281-297.

Wolff, J. and De-Shalit, A., (2007) *Disadvantage*, New York: Oxford University Press.

Øzerk, K., (1993) *Temaer i minoritetsrettet pedagogikk, [Themes in minority orientated Pedagogy]* Haslum: Oris Forlag.

Chapter 6

Cultural racism in liberal democratic education in Sweden

Åsa Möller

Introduction

This chapter examines the difficulties of pedagogy in Swedish schooling as a strategy for minimising ethnic differences in educational performances. More specifically, the purpose is to understand how pedagogy in Swedish education transforms in practice into forms of compensatory pedagogy that reaffirm the construction of racialised social differences in a way that is counterproductive to the intended purpose of creating social equity between ethnic Swedes and marginalised ethnic *Others*. The study is based on an ethnography carried out at a secondary school in an urban area with a large multi-ethnic population. Analysis of the data is informed by critical race theory and theories related to the sociology of school knowledge.

Segregation is one of the largest problems facing the educational system in Sweden today (Sernhede, 2009). Politicians, policy makers and practitioners are hard pressed to find effective and equitable solutions to the challenge of including minorities, immigrants and refugees into today's educational system. Over 100,000 people immigrated to Sweden in 2008. Approximately 29,000 refugees seeking asylum came to Sweden in 2011.[50] The non-Europeans who have immigrated to Sweden since the 1990s have come primarily from Iraq, Iran, Somalia, Afghanistan, Thailand and China. Despite large scale funding and intervention projects to improve integration through schooling, only forty per cent of students with foreign backgrounds were deemed eligible for upper secondary education in 2009. Swedish liberal social democratic politics have promoted policies and practices which often emphasised integration of minorities and immigrants into the mainstream education. Yet there are apparent discrepancies in learning outcomes and achievement that need to be addressed. However, it is not my ambition to address underachievement of the ethnic *Other*. It is my intention to examine cultural racism in the pedagogy to show

---

50 www.migrationsinfo.se/migration/sverige/asylsokande/

how cultural racism can be conveyed in pedagogical practice despite liberal and social democratic intentions.

The theoretical input to this chapter comes from critical race theory and sociological perspectives on education (Bourdieu and Passeron, 1977/1990; Leonardo, 2009). These theories provide a platform to critique approaches to multiculturalism that essentialise differences and defer social and political judgment. Together they provide the analytical concepts to examine how race is socially constructed, based on the premise that even though it is no longer a legitimate biological concept, race still has social and material consequences (Leonardo, 2009). A sociological perspective on race can provide insight into how race continues to stratify and classify people along the lines of culture. In conjunction to race a sociological perspective is needed in the pedagogical discourse in order to identify, describe and analyse learning processes that not only classify and separate people, but also reduces the subjects' choices of identifications and marginalises their social opportunities, on the one hand, and maintains social advantages on the other. Even though race is no longer a legitimate biological concept, it can be useful in conceptualising how racism is perpetuated in new forms even within a liberal democratic society such as Sweden (Pred, 2000).

Method

The research I have done is an ethnographic study of a public secondary school within an urban municipality in Sweden. I have chosen to do ethnography because of how it provides a means to link 'the particular expression of human agency to structural features of a cultural system'. I have primarily followed three year-nine classes over three separate years, and a fifth grade class for one semester, all at the same school. Students in Sweden finish their compulsory education in year-nine. These choices gave me the opportunity to study teaching and learning from multiple teacher perspectives over a long time with the same age group, the same core curriculum and the same learning goals.

The data provided for this chapter comes from participant observations, interviews and informal conversations with teachers, administrators and students. I have included data from classroom observations, an interview with one of the head-teachers, follow-up conversations with four teachers after their lessons in Art, Social Studies and Life Orientation and a focus group interview with five boys in one year-nine class. The empirical data presented is a combination of interview excerpts and field-notes from data produced for my on-going thesis which is an ethnographic study on knowledge construction and race.

My fieldwork was carried out in a town I call Woodbridge between 2006 and 2009. Woodbridge is a small community with a population of nearly 8000 people. It is nested on a plateau approximately a fifteen minute drive from the city centre. This community is part of a municipality that is divided into ten different districts. Woodbridge School is a multi-ethnic school with 359 students ranging in ages from six to fifteen years-old. Of these, only one per cent have both parents born and raised in Sweden. According to statistics, approximately fifty-nine per cent of the population in Woodbridge is born abroad, often outside of Europe[51]. Two-thirds of the students are registered for mother tongue education classes in twenty-five different languages.

Deficient or just different?

Woodbridge is a suburb within a larger municipality in Sweden that is characterised by what urban sociologists term *territorial stigmatisation* (see Sernhede, 2009; Wacquant, 2008). This implies an area or space that is seen as separate and inferior to the dominant society due to high unemployment, poor health and other indicators of poverty. It is a sub-urban area, an urban suburb that is not *urban* in a positive sense of modernism, sophistication and cosmopolitanism, but rather the type of urban associated to exclusion, stigmatisation and stereotypes of urban people who are working-class, people of colour (cf., Leonardo, 2009). Several Government funded programmes have been carried out in order to compensate for the negative social imagery associated to the area and to aid integration. In conjunction with this Woodbridge School fabricated an international and intercultural profile (Möller, 2010b). This profile emphasised local and international exchanges between schools, as well as, the individual development of the students' languages and cultures. This international profile was sponsored by government funding for urban development and integration of non-native people with immigrant backgrounds. It has also inspired other forms of pedagogy that focus on students' success in school and to enhance students' self-esteem, student-centered learning by focusing on what is working as opposed to what is not. Despite obvious socio-economic inequalities and differences, the discourse of difference in the following sections refers to difference as socially and/or culturally inherent.

51 Official statistics, 2009. (See Borelius, 2010, p. 14).

Leadership perspective of ethnic differences

The head-teachers in charge of the school are responsible for the formulation and implementation of the pedagogical discourse. Two head-teachers, Thorvald and Marie, worked together at Woodbridge during the time of my fieldwork. Thorvald had responsibility for the pre-school, the pre-school class and grades 1-4. Marie was responsible for the lower secondary school, grades 5-9. During fieldwork, I often spoke to them about the school's intercultural and international profile, its implementation, obstacles, as well as, their views on marginalisation and stigmatisation of the students in urban areas in general and students at Woodbridge in particular.

Prior to starting work at Woodbridge, Marie herself had worked with the development of a large government funded project called *Storstadssatsningen* (Eng. trans. urban investment) to improve integration in urban areas. In her own words the *Storstadssatsningen* was in part intended to compensate for a lack of common history and the lack of social networks amongst new groups of people living in urban areas:

> The *Storstadssatsningen* was based on taking a perspective from below. Working with active participation of the residents and working with people's involvement to compensate for the fact that people come from all different places: Norrland [northern Sweden], Iraq and Somalia and who do not have a common history or common network and that you can create a network within this little community, which then can have a huge impact on comfort and children's security.
>
> (Interview with the headmistress, Marie)

Storstadssatsningen was a municipally and nationally funded project that concerned issues of work, education, language and living conditions in urban suburbs that have large populations of people with immigrant backgrounds. The goal of the project was to improve living conditions in communities prone to problems related to social disparity. This was done by creating a sense of security and increasing the residents trust and participation in society, and by creating dialogue and growth in the community. More precisely the project intended to increase employment, reduce dependency on welfare and raise the levels of education[52]. In total a 345 million Swedish crowns were distributed

---

52 www4.goteborg.se/prod/storstad/dalis2.nsf/vyFilArkiv/Storstad.pdf/$file/Storstad.pdf

between four different communities within the same municipality. Of this 60 million went into improving employment and education in Woodbridge. The municipality estimates that co-financing of *Storstadssatsningen* amounted to 1.2 billion between 2000-2005.

Marie's involvement in *Storstadssatsningenen* carried over, in part, in her role as principal at Woodbridge. The school development plan was a direct result of the government funded project. The development plan contains two solutions to deal with segregation on the school level. One solution is to help non-Swedes build a so-called *dual identity* based on the concept of *biculturalism*. There is an embedded contradiction in the concept of biculturalism.

This concept is somewhat contradictory because the identity of 'Swedishness" is defined by who is not included in the category Swedish. Difference has to be constructed and maintained for the duality to exist. The bicultural solution in actuality upholds national, social and cultural differences as distinct and separate. The second solution is to strengthen skills in Swedish as a second language and maintain language skills in the mother tongue. The emphasis on language acquisition as the key to integration is overwhelming in integration politics and public debates (see Borevi, 2002; Milani, 2007). However, the emphasis on Swedish language acquisition places the solution to segregation firmly in the laps of the individuals who are living in segregated areas. This type of solution can be seen as shallow and simplistic because it neglects structural forms of discrimination that contribute to housing and socio-economic segregation of new arrivals to Sweden and the majority population (cf., Andersson, 1998).

The development plan outlines the pedagogical and curricular approaches used to aid and support language development for multilingual students and the importance for the individual to maintain a bicultural identity. The plan asserts the necessity of mastering the Swedish language effectively and adequately while also arguing for support of students' mother tongue. However, obstacles to the implementation of the development plan occurred when the project and the funding by the state to improve integration was discontinued.

The implementation of the school development plan had been put on hold because of the on-going economic crisis and redundancies within the municipality. The more pressing and primary concern for the teachers at Woodbridge School was their future employment. From an administrative point of view this inhibited discussions on teachers' values and attitudes towards multilingualism and bicultural education because teachers could not focus on school reform when their positions where threatened.

The employment of multilingual and bicultural teachers was a direct application of the development plan. Bicultural pedagogy was manifested in the actual teachers employed at the school, not in the pedagogical practice in ordinary classroom instruction. In other words, the multilingual teachers with non-native Swedish backgrounds, the pedagogues but not the pedagogy, represented a bicultural pedagogy. The forced lay-offs of bilingual teachers meant for the most part a stop to the implementation of this idea. Marie interjected that the only tools left to work with now were supportive and constructive attitudes towards students' multilingual ability.

> Now if we cannot have a an optimal model with bilingual education then, without bilingual teachers, we can at least have a positive attitude towards students' origins and have a supportive attitude of students' experiences and knowledge /.../ We know that in research in Sweden, in many different contexts, and internationally, that the monolingual majority teacher's attitude and approach plays a very important role for their self-perception. This, in turn, plays an important role in their [students] motivation and driving force to succeed in school. That is what we are left with right now you can say. (Interview with the headmistress, Marie)

The vision is to be supportive of the students' bicultural and bilingual ability. Yet, it is just this ambition and extension of the school development plan that is in jeopardy because of the financial crisis within the municipality. The potential threat of lay-offs at this time had imposed yet another hinder to implementing the school reform programme originally initiated by the *Storstadssatsningen* and outlined in the development plan. In other words, the bicultural policy ceased to exist without the presence of multi-lingual, non-native Swedish teachers employed at the school. What is left is a 'positive attitude towards students' origins' by the teachers in 'the monolingual majority'. In the interview with the principal (Marie) I referred to the emphasis on Swedish culture:

> There is still a strong emphasis on Swedish, Swedish culture and Swedish traditions and competencies ... I am aware of this and it is a long process to get all to 'join the train'. This is something that needs to be worked on constantly. We have been forced to focus on other issues /.../ This is something that must be worked on long-term with as I usually say 'a fool's stubbornness'. Slowly but surely turn the ship in another direction.

/… / We are simply not in that phase where we have a focus on that. It doesn't work like that. I have worked with the development of the municipal schooling for over twenty years and if there is something that I have learned is that sometimes it is necessary to reverse or at least cease. /…/ There are great changes underway, redundancies, in which people are affected down to the skin. Then it is very difficult to get attention for school reform work. (Marie)

The lack of inclusionary practices I observed was explained in terms of metaphors. Marie describes the process of acculturation and steps towards integration as a journey. She uses the metaphors 'join the train' and 'turn the ship' as descriptive expressions in which teachers' attitudes and perceptions are running parallel to, but not in sync with the development plan. The journey metaphors imply that there is a final destination in which acculturation can be achieved. Yet the emphasis on the process of acculturation and inclusion is more of an issue for the individual students' identity transformation than the perceptions and attitudes of the teachers to enacting biculturalism through pedagogy.

There is often talk about the students' need to get out of Woodbridge … You can see it like that, but I don't interpret it in that way. I could also see it that way with the view that I have. But I don't interpret it that way. I have seen at this school, during the time that I have been here, that many of our students are enormously ignorant about life outside of Woodbridge and they are also very insecure and afraid. They need a greater sense of security if they do not go with their parents and private networks outside of Woodbridge and experience different situations that are necessary to live in the Swedish society. They are poorly prepared for life in the Swedish society outside of the Swedish school. They really are in need of that, but finding the right form for this is not easy. (Marie)

The focus on mainstream culture is thus seen as a direct means of promoting integration and acculturation and is regarded as a direct necessity, as the students are perceived as lacking in knowledge and experience with the Swedish society and this ignorance and unaccustomed unfamiliarity is felt to be a major obstacle to integration and a deficiency that needs to be compensated for. As Marie expressed it in the same interview as above:

Many of our students are enormously ignorant about life outside of Woodbridge and they are also very insecure and afraid. (They need this knowledge) in order to live in the Swedish society.

But, this lack of experience and knowledge is not to be interpreted as a devaluation of their life experience in Woodbridge according to Marie, who firmly rejected the deficit perspective. She made this clear in the following way:

Instead of a deficiency perspective that they arrive here with a lack knowledge of Swedish, and that they lack knowledge that other Swedish students have who have gone to school; we can support their competencies, provide positive and high expectations and not neglect their experiences and their culture and their language.

It becomes apparent that life in Woodbridge is outside of, or at least not recognised as being part of the Swedish society. Students are expected to bridge this difference by compensating for their own 'lack of knowledge of how the Swedish society works, how it is, and getting into the habit of socialising with Swedish people' (Marie, headmistress). It is the students' lack of language skills and social savvy that is the obstacle to integration, not the way the mainstream society views people of colour, immigrants and communities such as Woodbridge. This is the essence of blaming the victim typology (Banks, 2008). Yet the question remains: Is this just a social and cultural difference? Defining Woodbridge inhabitants and the students of Woodbridge as different and separate from dominant social norms can be seen as a form of symbolic power and of a racialised social structure.

Symbolic power controls social divisions, labelling practices, criteria for prestige and status. It appraises whose capital (social, cultural, economic and symbolic) is being deemed legitimate (see Yosso, 2005). The criteria of legitimacy are arbitrary and relative to the pre-existing symbolic capital in use. Tara Yosso voices critique of *cultural capital* because of the presuppositions of white, middle class, male standards that form the basis of power. Transformation of existing conditions can only occur if symbolic capital already exists and if there is enough symbolic power to impose recognition (Bourdieu and Passeron, 1977, 1990). The students and inhabitants of Woodbridge are not in the position to redefine their existing social and cultural capital as valid and legitimate. Instead, their existing *social networks* are deemed inadequate and in need of compensation.

Contact with the world outside of Woodbridge and the mainstream Swedish majority is viewed as a solution to segregation.

In this construction of difference as a lack of contact with the mainstream there is an underlying presupposition and inference to race. In my own questions and Marie's answers there are references made to *Swedish people* and *Swedish society*. These labels are not neutral. They connote *whiteness* and white normativity[53] as an identity marker of 'Swedishness'.

The bicultural policy and employment of teachers with multi-lingual and non-native Swedish backgrounds tends to affirm a racialised difference based on inherent cultural traits. Even though these differences are not to be devalued they are none the less in need of compensatory measures.

Critical Social theorist Zeus Leonardo (2009) claims that race is a way of constructing group membership. Race, as a group identity, is a social construct assigned to and by different groups in the struggle for power and privilege. Leonardo asserts that race is an ideological construct that has material consequences. Even if race is not real, the privilege and/or social disparities between racial groups are. The concepts used in this paper such as *white* and *people of colour* are problematic because they infer essentialised differences, social identities, positions and ways of being in the world. It is important to note that these labels are not intended to refer to fixed categories, but rather to attributes, characteristics, and positioning that are socially constructed and maintained in social relations.

In sum, the leaderships' discourse on difference is in effect a direct devaluation of the Woodbridge experience. The diversity in language and culture and the lack of mainstream experiences are seen as the obstacles to integration rather than the belief that difference can be distinguished along the lines of culture. It is assumed that there is a dominant homogeneous Swedish culture that students must adapt to. Defining the inhabitants of Woodbridge as distinct and separate from native Swedes is problematic because it puts the burden of integration on the individuals defined as the *Other*.

---

53 Leonardo asserts that *whiteness* is an ideology not a verifiable, biological group of people, which confers power and privilege within a racialised social order (cf. Bonilla-Silva, 2005; Leonardo, 2009). These categories cannot be disconnected from the social context. As I see it the meanings and identifications given are inseparable from the social context in which they are created and the characteristics ascribed to them (Gruber, 2007).

Students lack mainstream experiences

In an informal conversation with Ingrid, the student guidance counsellor, I had a chance to speak with her alone about some questions I was harbouring. These questions had grown from her presentations with class 9E about future career and educational opportunities. Ingrid worked not only at Woodbridge, but served other schools within the municipality as well. I was curious to know her view of the students' needs and expectations in relation to students elsewhere. In our conversation, from my fieldnotes, Ingrid emphasised three aspects about the students' needs: 1) increased contact with the world outside of Woodbridge, 2) more contact with ethnic Swedes, 3) more exposure to the Swedish language.

> The students need more experience and contact outside of their own community (Swedish, *omvärldskunskap*). The students are isolated from the larger society. There are no ethnic Swedes here. They need to have more Swedish (i.e. input of the Swedish language) /.../ The school is tough because they lack contact with the larger society and community. They are isolated here, there is a lack of language skills and language experience. Parents here need a lot of support as well, to learn how the society works.   (Informal conversation, Ingrid, guidance counsellor)

Despite official policy *society* does not seem to include the culturally diverse, multi-lingual and multi-ethnic inhabitants of Woodbridge, who are viewed as isolated and lacking contact with Swedish people. The larger *society* that is being referred to is a homogeneous *Swedish* society. Woodbridge's multi-ethnic and poly-lingual population, which by and large includes people with immigrant backgrounds, is indirectly categorised as non-Swedish. The students of Woodbridge therefore *need* contact with ethnic Swedish people it is stressed, in order to succeed in school. This is similar to the assumption that black students in the United States would benefit from learning next to white students (Kozol, 1991; Foster, 1993) despite Marie's rejection of a cultural deficit perspective. The lack of contact with Swedish people is viewed as a deficiency that needs to be amended in order to acculturate (cf Banks, 2008, p. 53). The principal denied that the emphasis on mainstream Swedish culture is a direct devaluation of the area and the people who live there. Yet it is apparent that from the leadership perspective the students are described as 'ignorant and insecure and afraid ... of Swedish life and culture outside of Woodbridge'.

Indirect devaluation of Woodbridge

The territorial stigmatisation of urban poor is conveyed to the students of Woodbridge through an indirect devaluation of Woodbridge. Every year, eighth and ninth-graders receive information about future career and educational choices in preparation for secondary school. The individualised programme (IV) is an upper secondary programme for students not eligible for upper secondary school. The IV programme offered vocational training for students looking to get into food management. The programme was promoted as a preparation for work in the food industry, restaurants and cafés. My fieldnotes account for an observation of Mia, the head teacher, for class 9E when she informed the class about the programme. Mia read aloud an information sheet which stated:

> Individual Programme Café, restaurant and food industry in Woodbridge. This programme is for people ages sixteen to nineteen years-old who want to work in a café, restaurant or food industry. The course is two semesters and combines theory and work experience in our restaurant in Woodbridge.
>
> (Classroom observation, Mia, 9E, reads the hand-out for the food management programme)

Mia read the note which she had received from the student guidance counsellor. The deadline for upper secondary school applications had already passed, but the application deadline for this programme was extended. It was directed towards students who were not eligible for the national programmes and going on to the Individual Program instead. Mia, the Social Studies teacher explained to class 9E:

> *Mia*: Work is built on networks. But you have to be interested in working with food if you are going to do this. Right?
> *Åsa*: How long is it [the programme]? (Åsa)
> *Mia*: Two semesters. You could do it if you are tired of school. You can be tired of school and need a break for a year and then continue. I don't know, but society is to give you the best possible chances to get work, right? You can find new possibilities and new collaborative projects that can lead to something. It might suit someone. I personally think you should go on new adventures in the city. Right? But if anyone is interested you can get a hand-out from me.

Mia indicates to the class that the students need to widen their perspectives and not work in Woodbridge as suggested. The food management programme is specifically directed towards students attending Woodbridge school. In 2009 only forty per cent of the ninth-graders were eligible for the national programmes in upper secondary schooling. These results are typical for schools in metropolitan areas where a majority of the inhabitants are working class people of colour with immigrant backgrounds. Yet, they are astonishingly low compared to national averages. A majority of the students at Woodbridge could therefore not apply for upper secondary schooling because of their failure to meet the core subject requirements in Swedish, English and Mathematics. The head teacher suggests that this programme is directed mainly towards students who are tired of school, 'You could do it if you are tired of school', but an alternative solution could be to take a year off. This indirectly infers that low achievement is due to lack of motivation and that academic exhaustion can be cured by taking time off. Even though Mia informs the class about the programme and states that it might be suitable for someone she makes her preference known, 'I think you should go on new adventures in the city.'

The purpose of the programme is not directly negated. Mia answers that work experience is an important part of building a network and making new contacts. Getting a job is made through contacts emphasises Mia. 'Work is built on networks. You have to be interested in working with food if you are going to do this. Right?' said Mia. Its intention is to combine theory and practice, build a network and gain work experience, which are viewed as necessary aspects of working life and steps towards future employment.

The issue at stake is the location. The course is situated in Woodbridge. Despite the fact that many students could benefit from work experience, network building and training, it is not viewed as desirable to remain in Woodbridge. Even taking a year off is suggested as an alternative as opposed to working in the same community in which the students live. 'You can be tired of school and need a break for a year and then continue,' said the teacher. The desired preference, or norm, is life and work outside of Woodbridge. This norm, life and work outside of Woodbridge community, is a reoccurring theme in the discourse, policy and practice.

Compensating for ethnic differences

Above I have examined the social construction of differences in political and educational discourse and how differences are constructed in politics, attitudes and norms expressed by teachers and leadership Woodbridge school that directly and indirectly devalue the Woodbridge district because of the emphasis on the lack of traditional experience and lack of contact with native Swedes. It is assumed that there are distinct and separate cultures and a dominant homogeneous Swedish culture from which Woodbridge residents are excluded. On the basis of these differences, the present section examines education as a tool that is needed in order to compensate for changing cultural deficiencies. The bi-directional cultural policy is in fact reduced to compensatory education needed to bridge the gap between Woodbridge and mainstream Swedish society.

It is the intention of the school leaders and teachers to minimise the differences between the students of Woodbridge and the society at large. As I have discussed previously the students and residents of Woodbridge are already dispossessed, positioned figuratively and literally in a place of non-'Swedishness'. According to this rational, it is viewed as necessary to increase contact with the dominant Swedish population outside of Woodbridge in order to aid integration and acculturation to the mainstream society. As one of the principals said, 'They are poorly prepared for life in the Swedish society outside of the Swedish school. They really are in need of that [experience outside of Woodbridge], but finding the right form for this is not easy,' (Marie, principal). The following accounts point to the difficulties that occur when attempting to bridge the divide between the students at Woodbridge school and the dominant Swedish society. Life Orientation is a subject that has the intended purpose of reducing the divide by teaching Woodbridge students the correct form of social behaviour.

A lesson in 'Swedishness'

In the fall 2007, I made an observation during a lesson in Life Orientation with class 5B. This was a follow-up lesson for 5B's field-trip to the movie *Ratatouille* the week before. I had not followed the class on this field-trip, but did follow along to another movie a few weeks later. On that excursion I did not observe any kind of inappropriate behaviour. At the movie *Ratatouille* the class 5B had misbehaved by running in the aisles, talking loudly, throwing popcorn, taking extra soda pop from the dispenser without paying, running to the bathroom and going into other movies. In my fieldnotes, I observed two teachers, Martin and Ellinor, who held a lesson together on written and unwritten rules. This lesson followed-up the behaviour of some of the pupils during the movie *Ratatouille*. On the board Martin had written, 'rules and unwritten rules'.

> *Martin*:   What are the unwritten rules when you are at the movies?
> *Yusef*:   You have to sit still and not run to the bathroom 1000 times.

The students in 5B had behaved badly at the showing of the movie *Ratatouille*. Because of the disturbance some of the other paying customers had left and demanded a refund according to the teacher Martin. As a follow-up to this field-trip, the teachers planned a Life Orientation lesson that focused on making implicit social rules explicit. The students had also been threatened with not attending any more movies if their behaviour did not change. Martin the class teacher for 5B provided an example having to do with unwritten rules on limitations of refills. On the board Martin wrote:

> Unwritten rule
> 1 coffee 15 kr.
> 1 refill 5 kr.

Martin clarified the unwritten rule by explaining to the class:

> An unwritten rule is that everyone has to be quiet before going out on break. Is there anyone who knows what a refill (Sw: *påtår*) is? If you are at a Café and you pay for a cup of coffee or tea and you want some more then you can ask if refills are included. If they say 'yes' then it is included, but it usually means just one cup. You can't bring a thermos and shout to your friends 'Free drink! Come and get it!'
> (Classroom observation, class 5B, 2007-11-07)

Getting a refill is a key issue. Pointing out the difference between when a refill is charged and when a refill is free is a point that the teacher makes explicit as well as the limitation on how much of a refill is allowed. This lesson was about making implicit social rules explicit. It is assumed that the students lack an understanding of the social rules based on their unruly behaviour. The class was divided into three groups. Their assignment was to write down as many unwritten rules that they could think of. However, the boys in the group I observed came up with ten rules, prohibitions, on social conduct in public places. At this time, the boys knew, or had been made aware that shouting, throwing popcorn and 'stealing' soda pop were not allowed at the movies. Their list contained the following points:

Do not eat candy in school.

Do not point your finger in school.

Do not swear.

Do not shout in the movie theatre.

Do not steal soda pop.

Do not thrown popcorn at other people in the movie theatre.

Do not take other peoples places at a soccer game.

Do not ride your bike in the store.

Do not shout in the library.

Do not abuse books.

Do not throw rocks on other people's windowpanes.

(Classroom observation class 5B, 11/07/2007)

Three points on their list were in direct reference to the field trip to the movies: not shouting, not stealing soda pop and not throwing popcorn. Martin asked a few times initially how Swedish rules can differ from norms in other countries i.e. such as waiting in line is a Swedish custom. One boy mentioned that standing in line is a Swedish custom. Martin used an analogy of Swedes waiting in line compared to waiting in line in Germany where the rule is 'push your way to the front'. The Swedes are left waiting because they don't apply the same rules as German people when waiting in a cue. The unwritten rules, socially implicit behaviour and conduct, is connected to ethnicity and culture. It is implied that ethnic groups, i.e. Swedish and German, have different social rules. The inference here is that the students in Woodbridge are a separate ethnic group that needs to learn to apply Swedish ways. This point becomes more apparent in the next section on *Othering*. An implicit target of the lesson being self-management and self-government tactics (cf Bartholdsson, 2007). The self-management and government techniques, which are being taught, are equated with 'Swedishness' and Swedish nationality.

Martin rounded off the lesson by letting each group listen *quietly* while each group facilitator read their list aloud. Each group was given an evaluative comment i.e. 'I think that *do not cheat* is a good rule'. The teacher also pointed out the discrepancy between what we ought to do contrary to what people really do and that people don't always abide by social rules. After the lesson I asked Martin if the students know what the unwritten rules are when attending the movies and do not follow them, or if they simply don't know any better. The teacher replied:

They just don't know any better. Many of the students have never been to the movies before. They had no idea how to behave.

(Informal conversation, Martin, teacher, 11/07/2007)

In order to understand what lay behind the students' behaviour I asked Martin if this was due to non-compliance or with a lack of understanding. The teacher affirmed that it was inexperience and a lack of knowledge, 'They just don't know any better.' This view affirms the principal's statement that the students at Woodbridge are 'extremely ignorant' and inexperienced with life outside of Woodbridge (see Marie, principal, above). The teachers assumed that the students lacked both experience and knowledge of social conduct. The students' inability to demonstrate social skills was viewed as a deficiency that was remediated through the teaching of 'unwritten rules' such as when it is acceptable to get a refill. Lack of social and cultural skills were seen as a deficiency and used as the rational for the students' disruptive behaviour. Furthermore, the Life Orientation lesson associated social skills to ethnicity and cultural differences. There is an implicit assumption that the students are not just socially different, but also culturally different. That is to say the students' behaviour is not just bad behaviour, but also ethnically and culturally different. The following section reiterates the point that stereotyping of cultural difference is linked to expectations of deviant behaviour. Exhibiting 'cultural difference' is viewed as a provocation by the mainstream when mainstream norms, values, and behaviours are not validated or affirmed (Gruber, 2007).

All of the students were regarded as wanting knowledge of social skills in order to become more socially acceptable. The students' financial situation and lack of access to movie theatres in Woodbridge were not an issue. The movie *Ratatouille* was viewed at a new down-town movie complex. Tickets to a matinee range from 95-125 SEK. The additional costs of snacks can bring the total cost to 150 SEK per person.

The new surroundings and new circumstances were not viewed as an issue. Having access and money to buy soda pop and popcorn were not seen as a potential problem. The source of the problem was placed solely on the students and their behaviour. Not knowing how to behave at the movies and not having access to the movies were not viewed as consequences of economic inequality, but rather related to cultural deficiency.

The students were blamed for their lack of social skills and, in turn, this deficiency was related to cultural differences rather than to economic or social disparities that could hinder visits to the movies. Many other reasons could lay behind the students' unwillingness to comply with social norms, such as resistance and opposition to being *Othered*. In other words, the students may, like the lads in Paul Willis (Willis, 1977) study, be reproducing their own exclusion because of their pre-empted exclusion from Swedish society; unlike the lads however, there is no distinctive cultural identity to fall back on. This can be interpreted as an active *self-Othering*. Yet whether or not *Othering* is self-impose or inflicted by someone else the issue of inclusion and exclusion is still centered around the *Other* and not on the norms that reproduce power. The question of exclusionary norms and norms related to reproduction of power are peripheral and not problematised as central to the issues of acculturation, integration and segregation. The following observation illustrates the power of stereotyping in the reproduction of racialised norms.

Field-trips reaffirm Otherness

This section will continue to explore how field-trips contribute to the construction of difference. The aim of field-trips as I have already mentioned is to bridge the divide from Woodbridge to the society at large. However, encounters with the mainstream are not always a positive experience. 'Finding the right' form is not easy because of the advantages of being positioned as part of the dominant white Swedish society versus being positioned as the urban *Other*, the negative kind of urban, often leads to the unwanted discovery of social inequity and inequality. The sections below provide examples of how Woodbridge students are perceived as deviant and experience subjection (Phoenix, 2009) as the urban other when in contact with the mainstream.

The students at Woodbridge had previously been given assignments to do at the art museum in the city centre. They were to go to the museum on their own, without a teacher, and do an assignment there. This assignment was abandoned when the students from Woodbridge were not permitted to bring pencils with them into the museum. The guards at the art museum had told the students from Woodbridge to put away their pencils because they were afraid that the students would scribble (Sw: *klottra*) on things in the museum. Tom (the art teacher) explained that this was not the case with the Finnish students.

Up until approximately ten years ago there had been Finnish speaking students and Finnish classes at Woodbridge school. There are still Finnish speaking teachers but no longer any Finnish classes and only a handful of students with Finnish backgrounds.

According to Tom, the Finnish students and ethnic Swedish students had not been told to put away their pencils while doing art assignment at the art museum.

> The guards were on the students from Woodbridge to put their pencils away because they were afraid they would scribble on something. That was not the case with the Finnish students from the school or the Swedish students. Only our students were asked not to use pencils so we decided to drop it.
> (Informal conversation, 2009-05-20, Tom, art teacher, fieldnotes)

The nominal phrase 'our students' is in reference to the students at Woodbridge who by and large have immigrant backgrounds and are people of colour, that is to say not positioned as white. The identities Finnish and Swedish are code for whiteness. In Tom's account, race and racism, the colour and ethnicity of the students, is the basis of discrimination and the reason for discontinuing the art assignment in the art museum. The students of colour are suspected of deviant behaviour. It is assumed that inappropriate behaviour, scribbling on things in the art museum, is expected behaviour of non-white urban immigrant other. It is clear to Tom that the white students, Swedish and Finnish students, received preferential treatment, yet the terms race and racism are not brought up.

The response to racism is to refrain from visiting the art museum. The teacher's decision is to withhold exposure to this type of experience. This has consequences for students' learning and place in society. The consequences are twofold. First, the students are denied access to great works of art. They are denied the experience of learning and (re)producing knowledge about modern art history that is available to them first hand. The students of Woodbridge are denied the experience and resources outside of school because of discrimination. Mainstream white students, i.e. Finnish and Swedish students, are allowed access to and given the resources to (re)produced knowledge in locations outside of school. Neither do they experience collective stereotyping nor negativism attached to their social identity whereas the students of Woodbridge experience subjectification as the urban other when in contact with the mainstream.

Second, the colour-blind perspective, the pretence that colour does not or should not play a part in the exchange of goods and services, or any kind of social or interpersonal relationship (Leonardo, 2009) hinders acknowledgement of the social order and hinders addressing racism head on. The students experience racist practices, but are not given tools to fight social injustice or to help create greater social equity for people of colour. By not acknowledging or challenging racism the school in effect reaffirms the *status quo*. The students learn not to challenge the *status quo*, but to accept their position in society as the urban *Other*. Paul Willis' (1977) well renowned study is comparable in the sense that the school culture contributes to the reproduction of the social order.

Withholding the art museum experience is a form of institutional racism in and of itself because the students are denied access to resources otherwise available to mainstream Swedish students. Furthermore the issue of white normativity is not brought up or challenged. The colour-blind perspective—the belief that race does not, or should not play a role—reaffirms white normativity and the benefits of having a social identity that is not viewed as deviant or suspect. The learning process in this case can be viewed as epistemically violent because of the avoidance of addressing injustice and the subjectification of students' social identity as deviant.

Conclusion

This chapter has described an ethnographic study which illustrates the social construction of racial and cultural difference. I argue that there is a gap between the liberal and social democratic values in education and the way students with non-native Swedish backgrounds experience *Othering* and marginalisation. Despite good intentions, there is a gap between the perception of Swedish education as liberal and democratic and the social inequalities experienced by non-native people of colour with non-European backgrounds. I have interviewed the school leaders, teachers and students about social and cultural difference and observed classroom practices that demonstrate how students and teachers deal construct difference and manage these differences. Firstly, by constructing a discursive divide between the students at Woodbridge school and mainstream society and secondly, by constructing a policy and pedagogy to bridge this divide. This division is a form of *Othering* which functions to construct difference by maintaining a belief in cultures as distinct and separate. The bicultural policy reaffirms immutable and inherent difference which students must be compensated for in order for them to gain access to the socio-economic advantages of whites and native Swedish people (Leonardo, 2009; Mirza, 2006). It is the intention of the school to minimise the gap between Woodbridge and life outside of Woodbridge by bringing students in contact with the mainstream. The objective is to aid integration and assimilation through the acculturation and acquisition of Swedish norms.

According to the school leaders this is not intended to devalue the prior life experiences of the students in Woodbridge, but to aid integration with the society at large. However, from a critical race perspective the students and inhabitants of Woodbridge are denied full citizenship and recognition as members of society by being continually confronted by the message that getting out of Woodbridge and into the mainstream society, is not only possible if they try hard enough, but it is also the desired thing to do (King, 2004). The differences, the divide and the bridging can be seen as symbolic violence and representative of a racialised social order (Bonilla-Silva, 2005; Bourdieu, 1991). Whether or not adaptation and concession to dominant norms or resistance occurs the people and students of Woodbridge are pre-emptively excluded from the mainstream society on the basis of race.

The students are dispossessed, because they are from the outset positioned as non-Swedish and suffer the subjectification of a negative social stereotype. They must contend with negativism attached to their immigrant identity. The students must contend with subjectification when they comply with the expected norms and even when they do not. The students of Woodbridge experience subjectivity as the urban *Other* when at home in Woodbridge and when in contact with the mainstream *Swedish* majority. Despite the good intentions of liberal democratic education, this double punishment is characteristic of the symbolic and epistemic violence that students experience in Swedish schooling (Bourdieu and Passeron, 1977, 1990).

Although, there are no open references to race or racism to the empirical data presented, maintaining a colour-blind perspective is characteristic of liberal and democratic education (Leonardo, 2009). Other terms are used such as culture and immigrant. However, the label *immigrant* is a racialised term as is *Swedish* or *Finnish* as these labels are code for the binary opposites black/white, native Swedish/non-native Swedish. It is assumed that whiteness is characteristic of 'Swedishness'; whereas, people of colour must explain, reject or compensate for some kind of inherent difference. The students are expected to transcend the category immigrant by conforming to Swedish normativity. Yet, the issue of stereotyping, *Othering* and exclusion is not openly addressed. It is the students and multi-lingual teachers that are representative of cultural diversity and are responsible for integration and acculturation to the mainstream. More research on the construction of cultural differences and racism in liberal and democratic education is greatly needed (Tallberg Broman, 2002).

References

Andersson, R., (1998) Socio-spatial Dynamics: Ethnic Divisions of Mobility and Housing in post-Palme Sweden. *Urban Studies*, vol. 35,(3): 397-428.

Banks, J. A., (2008) *An Introduction to Multicultural Education 4th ed.*, Boston: Pearson Education Inc.

Bartholdsson, Å., (2007) *Med facit i hand: normalitet, elevskap och vänlig maktutövning i två svenska skolor, [With the facts in hand: mormality, pupil identity and male power.]* Stockholm: Socialantropologiska institutionen. Stockholms universitet.

Bonilla-Silva, E., (2005) Introduction— 'Racism' and 'new racism': The contours of racial dynamics in contemporary America, in Z. Leonardo, *Critical pedagogy and race* (ss. 1-36). Malden, MA: Blackwell.

Borelius, U., (2010) Två förorter, [Two suburbs.] *Ubildning and Demokrati*, 18(1): 11-23.

Borevi, K., (2002) *Välfärdsstaten i det mångkulturella samhället, [The welfare State and multicultural society.]* Uppsala: Upsala Universitet.

Bourdieu, P., and Passeron, J. C., (1977, 1990) *Reproduction in Education, Society and Culture, 2nd edition.* London: Sage Publications Ltd.

Essed, P., (1991) *Understanding Everyday Racism.* Newbury Park: Sage Publications.

Foster, M., (1993) Savage Inequalities: Where have we come from? Where are we going? *Educational Theory*, 43(1): 23-32.

Gruber, S., (2007) *Skolan gör skillnad, Etnicitet och institutionell praktik, [School making a difference: Ethnicity and institutional practices.]* Linköping: Linköpings universitet, Instituion för samhälls-och välfärdsstudier.

King E., J. (2004) Dysconciousness racism: ideology, identity and the miseducation of teachers, in G. Ladson-Billings, and D. Gillborn, *The RouteledgeFalmer Reader in Multicultural Education* (pp 71-83). London: RoutledgeFalmer Taylor and Francis Group.

Kozol, J., (1991) *Savage Inequalities. Children in America's Schools.* New York: Harper Perennial.

Leonardo, Z., (2005) *Critical Pedagogy and Race.* Malden, MA: Blackwell Publishing.

Leonardo, Z., (2009) *Race, Whiteness and Education.* New York: Routledge.

Milani, T. M., (2007) *Debating Swedish. Language Politics and Ideology in Contemporary Sweden.* Stockholm: Stockholm University.

Mirza, H. S., (2006) 'Race', gender and educational desire. *Race Ethnicity and Education*, 9(2): 137-158.

Möller, Å., (2010) Den 'goda' mångfalden. Fabrikation av mångfald i skolans policy och praktik. [The 'good' diversity: The fabrication of diversity in school policy.] *Utbildning and Demokrati*, 18(1): 85-106.

Möller, Å. (2012), What is compensatory pedagogy trying to compensate for? Compensatory stratgies and the ethnic 'other', *Issues in Educational Research*, 22 (1): 60-78.

Phoenix, A., (2009) De-colonising practices: negotiating narratives from racialised and gendered experiences of education, *Race Ethnicity and Education*, 12(1): 101-114.

Pred, A., (2000) *Even in Sweden. Racisms, racialized spaces, and the popular.* Berkely: University of Califormina Press.

Sernhede, O., (2009) Territoriell stigmatisering, ungas informella lärande och skolan i det postindustriella samhället, [Territorial stigmatisation, young people's informal learning and the school in post-industrial society.] *Utbildning and Demokrati*, 18(1): 7-32.

Skolverket., (1994) *Curriculum for the compulsory school system, the pre-school class and the leisur time centre Lpo 94*. Stockholm: Skolverket.

Wacquant, L., (2008) *Urban Outcasts. A Comparative Sociology of Advanced Marginality.* Cambridge: Polity Press.

Willis, P., (1977) *Learning to labour. How working class kids get working class jobs.* Westmead: Saxon House, Teakfield Limited.

Yosso, T. J., (2005) Whose culture has capital? A critical race theory discussion of community cultural wealth. *Race Ethnicity and Education,* 69-91.

Chapter 7

Divided city—divided school: Upper secondary school students and urban space

Jonas Lindbäck and Ove Sernhede

Introduction

The freedom to choose school in the Swedish school system can be viewed as an opportunity to overcome urban segregation. At the same time studies are saying that the freedom of choice increases segregation according to the pupils' performance and their social and ethnic background. In this context we find Berydsgymnasium[54] in the suburb of Beryd south east of Gothenburg interesting. This school has pupils coming from the whole city. Within the context of a larger ethnographic investigation we have interviewed twenty students at this school to hear their reflections on the segregated urban space and their views on the school as a meeting place. The interviews show how the divided and hierarchically structured urban space is a distinctive part of the students' conceptualisation of the world and that Berydsgymnasium does not overcome segregation. Even though it is open for students from all over the city, the most prominent feature of the situation within the school is how urban segregation and the distance between its different spaces is reflected in a way that also affects the relationships between the students. This situation is also highly prominent in inner city schools.

Beryd is a *Million Homes Project*[55] area consisting of several *vulnerable* city districts in south east Gothenburg. Every year, the upper secondary school in Beryd enrols students from all over Gothenburg and the surrounding municipalities. However, the largest student group comes from Beryd and adjacent city districts. It is a unique upper secondary school in the city of Gothenburg. For one thing, it is located in a poor, immigrant-dense suburban

---

54 To maintain confidentiality, all names of schools, places and persons in this text are fictitious. Gothenburg is the second largest city in Sweden.

55 The term *Million Homes Project* is used to describe the suburban mass housing built in Sweden during the period 1965-1974. The debate about *vulnerable* city district was introduced by *Storstadskommittén*, a committee established by the Swedish Parliament in 1995 to study big-city neighbourhoods.

City districts inhabited predominantly by people classified as having *low, very low and extremely low incomes* were defined as *vulnerable*.

area rather than in the inner city, where all the other upper secondary schools are found. Second, despite its location it attracts students from the more affluent inner city as well as from other, more established middle class neighbourhoods in Gothenburg. Beryd is an notorious part of the city. A striking proportion of the interviewed students from the inner city had never even visited the area before beginning school there. Since the introduction of free choice of schools, suburban area schools—from primary school to upper secondary school—have been drained of students who choose the more prestigious schools in the inner city.

In Beryd, we see the opposite pattern. There, we have an upper secondary school in a poor suburb that is chosen by students residing in the more affluent inner city. The primary reason is the high-class arts programmes (music, theatre and dance) offered by Berydsgymnasium. Thanks to their higher grades, however, arts inclined youth from the inner city have won the competition for admission places over many young people from Beryd. This has resulted in a school in which young people with different social, ethnic and religious backgrounds meet in their everyday school life. Gothenburg is a segregated city (Andersson, Bråmå and Hogdal, 2009), and here we find the prerequisites for an *integrated* school, but at the same time we see obstacles to integration. Our interest in Berydsgymnasium started from these circumstances and from thoughts about the school as a meeting place for young people with different experiences and backgrounds and from different places in or outside the city. In analysing the narratives of the students we find it necessary to go beyond the classroom. By using concepts and theories from the field of urban studies this article has as an ambition to understand questions and problems related to educational research.

The organisation of the investigation and research questions

In this paper, we wish to emphasise two different tendencies or patterns that have emerged since the introduction of free choice of schools at the upper secondary school level and that are now manifesting themselves at Berydsgymnasium.

One of these patterns concerns students who choose to attend Berydsgymnasium even though they do not live in that city district and despite the criticism and the negative portrayal of the suburban schools and these districts. The other pattern concerns youth who have grown up and lived in Beryd, who have chosen an inner city school, but who have concluded after some time that they did not make the right choice. Therefore, they have returned to Beryd and the upper secondary school there. In their initial choice to leave Beryd they have often been influenced by criticism voiced against suburban schools such as Berydsgymnasium.

The study is divided into two parts, though there are not razor-sharp lines between them, and they intersect in some places. In the first part, we will encounter young people who live in other parts of Gothenburg, but who nevertheless choose to attend upper secondary school in Beryd. We will also meet students who reside in Beryd and have chosen to go to school there. Here, we are interested in the school as a multi-ethnic meeting place. We wish to examine students' attitudes towards this aspect and towards the school's actual spatial structure. Through the students' narratives, we would like to create an understanding of what importance urban segregation has for their attitudes towards and reflections on their own school, the suburb and the city as a whole. How are these two spatial dimensions—the division of the urban space and the division that structures the school's inner space—related to each other and how do they influence each other? What is the significance of these two divided worlds for how young people interpret and relate to the surrounding world?

In the second part of the article, the focus is on the youth who return to Beryd. What was it that made them choose an inner city school in the first place? For what reasons do they later elect to leave that school? What are these students' reflections on and experiences of changing schools? What are the factors or motives that guided their decision to change paths and return to the suburb? For many of the students from Beryd, the choice of a school in another part of the city may offer a chance to leave their neighbourhood, thus breaking with the segregating patterns that divide and categorise the city today. At the same time, however, choosing to leave the suburb to attend a Swedish high-status school may involve difficulties in finding one's place in a new social and cultural context. How do their encounters with the new inner city school environment take shape? In what ways does shifting between suburb and inner city give rise to questions concerning identity and space, belonging and kinship, and opportunities and limitations as regards climbing the social ladder or becoming integrated into Swedish society?

In both parts of the study, we investigate how, in their narratives, young people relate to the inner city, suburbs and schools and to their experiences of these spaces. In this way, we hope to create an understanding of how the hierarchies of urban space act on and affect the individual. Before making room for the students' narratives, we will take a retrospective look at Beryd to briefly orient the reader to the city district and the history of the school.

City, suburb and school—a brief exposé

All over Western Europe we can see an on-going development that segregates and separates the big cities' immigrant-dense housing areas from the rest of society. New patterns of unemployment, marginalisation and the effects of what has been defined as territorial stigmatisation (Wacquant, 2008) has a direct impact on the everyday life and self-esteem of residents in these areas as well as on the climate and culture of learning in the schools. The concept of territorial stigmatisation aims to describe the process by which certain city areas are depicted as lawless, dangerous and unattractive, in a way that could be described as a symbolic degradation of these areas. Unemployment, urban segregation and stereotyped images of the suburb are all part in creating this territorial stigma. This stigma creates a sense of personal indignity that influences interpersonal relations and negatively affects opportunities in school and the labour market (Wacquant, 2008). Related to this is the concept of *othering*, which describes how people from these suburban districts are made different and alien in relation to the dominant society (Wacquant, 2009). The suburbs where we have conducted our study are all to some extent part of these processes of territorial stigmatisation.

When we use the word suburb in this article we are referring to a residential area on the outskirts of a city or large town, as in English, but the connotations are not equivalent to those of the English term. In standard English, a suburb is a place where principally upper-middle and middle-class people live. In English, a suburb is any residential area near to, basically within commuting distance of, a large city, and it constitutes in one sense a separate residential community with some political autonomy from inner city neighbourhoods and usually a lower population density. In the United States in particular suburbs tend to be generally wealthier areas than average in a city region with a prevalence of detached single-family homes due to their development from the upper-middle-class community fractions in the late nineteenth century and the post-World War II economic expansion. This is not the case in Sweden and is certainly not a characteristic of the regions we have done our research in. These suburban areas have more in common with poorer inner city or urban areas in Great Britain or the United States, than they have with the more wealthy suburbs in the same countries.

In our description and analysis the concept of space takes on a central role. But it is not defined as a merely descriptive concept of geographical character, rather it should be viewed as intertwined with the social, political and economical dimensions and hierarchies of society (Lefebvre, 1991). Space embodies and enforces relations of power, and we can therefore talk about a 'spatialised social power' and it is the power relations in the construction of space and not only space in itself that needs to be observed (Massey, 1999 p. 291). Space is constantly being constructed, and it is both 'socially produced and socially productive', and therefore it is central in exercises of power and in the production of social relations, identities, etc. (Lindgren, 2010 p. 36; Foucault, 1999). In our study we can see how the students are relating to the different aspects of space, and the ways in which space is filled with meaning, constrains and possibilities.

A short historical recapitulation

In the 1980s and 1990s, the U.S.A. and Western Europe went through a substantial process of economic transformation. At the same time, great changes in the social and political climate were taking place. The welfare state that had been built up in many countries during the decades following World War II was now under fire. A large number of researchers all over the globe consider this change as a revolution from above (Harvey, 2007; Wacquant, 2008; Hall, 2011). In Sweden the neo-liberal changes became apparent in the 1990s, and many Swedish researchers consider this period as an *epoch shift* (Bengtsson and Wirtén, 1996; Lindberg, 1999).

One aspect of this shift can be found in increased social polarisation, widening income gaps and increasingly tangible housing segregation, particularly in the big cities (Sernhede, 2002). The negative aspects of the shift are most evident in the multi-ethnic suburbs surrounding metropolitan areas. The Swedish school, which during this period went through a major change, from one public school for every one to a market driven, free choice schools system, has met big difficulties in counteracting segregation and territorial stigmatisation. The free schools choice has created a segregated school market where the pupils from the poor, immigrant-dominated areas in the suburbs are the losers. Here, school fails to live up to the educational goals and school no longer offers these pupils an entryway into Swedish society (Bunar, 2001; Runfors, 2003). The school is not the primary and obvious arena in which suburban youth can develop self-esteem, knowledge and an understanding of the age in which they live. There are those who claim that the municipal schools in the suburbs may instead be reinforcing feelings of alienation and experiences of not being part of Swedish society (Parszyk, 1999; Runfors, 2003; Sernhede, 2011). The relationship between space, schooling and students' possibilities has also been of international interest (see, e.g., Journal of Youth Studies, 2009).

Patterns of segregation and lack of equality are as evident as ever in the city, and differences between city districts are obvious. Ethnic heterogeneity is striking in the *Million Homes Project* suburbs. Of the entire population in city districts such as Rosengård in Malmö and Hjällbo[56] in Gothenburg, sixty-one to sixty-two per cent were born abroad, and many others have their roots outside Sweden. Unemployment is high, disposable income is below and ill-health statistics are above the average for the country as a whole. Among students living in Rosengård who graduate from nine-year compulsory school, only forty-eight per cent are qualified for upper secondary school. The corresponding figure for Hjällbo is sixty-three per cent (Ungdomsstyrelsen, 2008). This situation places heavy demands on the schools in these areas. Beryd can be compared to city districts such as Hjällbo and Rosengård on many levels. When discussing the upper secondary school in Beryd it is therefore important to bear this picture of the city district in mind as well as the fact that a significant portion of students in the district never even begin upper secondary school.[57]

The opening of Berydsgymnasium

In many of the *Million Homes Project* suburbs the social institutions that were planned for, such as community health centres, schools and libraries, were often never realised. In Beryd, however, things were a bit different. At the end of the 1970s a cultural centre was completed. In 1985, the doors of Berydsgymnasium were opened for the first time. And just at that time, the library was opened. Berydsgymnasium came to be a place to which young and radical teachers with visions were often drawn. In the 1960s and 1970s, the most expansive and successful years of the welfare state in Sweden, the schools and education were considered arenas for creating a just society and social citizenship (Beach et al., 2003). These ideas probably remained among many of the teachers who came to Beryd in the 1980s. There was a belief in the future and an enterprising spirit at the school—a wish to make a difference and to influence developments in the district and in society at large.

Håkan, a teacher who was present during the school's first years, described how the school and its climate were characterised by 'a kind of pioneering spirit.'

56 Rosengård and Hjällbo are two of many suburbs that were built during the *Million Homes Project* and that today are populated by a high number of disadvantaged people.

57 Some of these students simply quit school, others study to qualify for upper secondary school another year for example.

There was a group of teachers and staff from the inner city who wanted to 'show that you can have a good senior high school out here in a poor suburb like Beryd,' he said. The social fervour present at the time of Berydsgymnasium's opening can still be felt today. Teachers and staff still show great devotion to their students. This can be seen in the hallways and is apparent in the interviews with students. Over the years, however, neither the school's resources nor the influx of students has followed this level of commitment. After the school's popular start and strong position during the 1980s and into the 1990s, setbacks began to appear in the mid-1990s.

The introduction of a new school system in the early 1990s called *free* or independent schools (Government Bill No. 1991/92:95), gave parents and students the right to choose between municipal and independent schools. This reform is financed through the taxes, so the parents have the possibility to place their children in any school of their choice. According to the Board of Education (1996), this freedom of choice reform was meant to promote, among other things, 'increased diversity and pedagogic renewal' (p. 11), but also to give students and parents the opportunity to leave a school they found unsatisfactory. However, freedom of choice was restricted by the proximity principle, according to which the schools were obliged to give precedence to children living in their catchment area. Karin, a member of the school staff since the start, described the second half of the 1990s as 'pretty tough and difficult.' Many new students arrived who had immigrant backgrounds and traumatic experiences of war and conflicts and who needed extra support. At the same time, Karin said, the school's reputation was beginning to give way.

A changing school in a changing world

Developments at the upper secondary school in Beryd can be related to the overall changes in society that we mentioned earlier. The economic decline during the 1990s entailed substantial cutbacks for the schools and childcare systems. Combined with the reorganisation of educational policies, these events resulted in increased segregation and differentiation in the school sector, especially in the metropolitan areas (Broady, 2000). During the 1990s, ethnic segregation became increasingly salient both in society at large and in the schools. This further added to the segregation based on gender, achievement and social background that already existed in the Swedish schools (Swedish Government Official Reports, 2000:39).

The changed rules for admission to upper secondary school, introduced in big city municipalities around the year 2000, could therefore be seen as an opportunity to overcome the restriction of the individual created by urban segregation. The new rules abandoned 'the proximity principle' in favour of 'the grade principle.' This put an end to the first option of neighbouring schools and allowed all students to compete on the basis of grades (Söderström and Uusitalo, 2005). However, the new system has turned out to be problematic; new patterns of stratification have meant that certain schools and programmes are only attended by students with high grades. Although Stockholm has experienced great mobility between districts and schools, this very mobility has led to an increase in social, achievement-related and ethnic segregation across various schools (Söderström and Uusitalo, 2005). The same can be said about the situation in Malmö and Gothenburg.

Urban segregation and the stigmatisation of the suburbs contributed to Berydgymnasium's declining reputation as well as the student base during the late 1990s. However, the most significant changes were brought about by the new admission rules in 2000. The number of applications for admission to the school sank at that time, as many students opted for municipal schools or independent schools in other parts of the city. Moreover, the proportion of independent schools has increased markedly since the 1990s. In 2010, for example, forty-seven per cent of all students in Gothenburg attended independent schools. Thus, the competition between schools has increased.[58] An increasingly acute situation at the beginning of the 2000s caused the Board of Education politicians to decide on a new direction for Berydsgymnasium. In the autumn of 2005, the school's new profile was implemented. Each student was to choose a major field of study based on his or her area of interest, whether it be law, soccer or textile design. Although this fresh start did lead to an upswing, the school continued to struggle to compete with other schools. Bridging the mental, geographical and symbolic distance to the inner city is an continuing challenge.

Method and participant selection

In order to better understand and interpret the place where students spend a large part of their time, we first carried out participant observations at the school. Using this form of ethnographic work, we attempted to create a picture for ourselves of the relations and circumstances that exist at Berydsgymnasium

58 According to Gunnar, project leader at Gothenburg's Educational Administration. Interview on March 23, 2010.

(Willis, 2000). This insight into the school also gave us a better foundation for conducting the interviews. Because we were interested in the students' thoughts, reflections and experiences of, among other things, changing schools and the city, qualitative interviews were a natural choice as they are able to convey a multifaceted and complex picture. Such interviews enable us to approach the students and look at how they conceptualise their environment. In this way, we can hopefully create a greater understanding of their lives and experiences.

Prior to the interviews, we made a strategic selection. We contacted teachers in the school's social science and music programmes. We visited the school to introduce ourselves and to explain why we were interested in meeting with students and listening to their narratives. The reason for choosing the social science programme was that those classes contain the majority of returning students as well as students who live near Berydsgymnasium and have gone there all along. The music programme, on the other hand, was where we found the most students from the rest of Gothenburg. Thus, the two programmes provided a distribution of students, those who commuted *to* and those who lived *in* Beryd, as well as those who had *returned* to that city district. All in all, we interviewed approximately twenty students at the school, half of them girls and the other half boys. Apart from the student interviews, we carried out seven interviews with teachers, school staff and officials in the educational administration. The purpose of these interviews was to get a better picture of the school and the changes it has undergone—as well as to understand how the teachers view their work and see the school as a multi-ethnic meeting place.

Before conducting the interviews, we informed the students, teachers and staff about their anonymity, and about the study and its purpose. All names of students, schools and city districts are fictitious to eliminate the risk of disclosing the students' identity. The interviews were conducted individually. The interview structure was relatively open so as to encourage narration and give the students opportunities to express their own thoughts and reflections. The questions addressed in the interviews varied somewhat between the two parts of the study. They dealt with issues such as school environment, reasons for choosing and changing schools, relations to Beryd and the city, as well as with issues of identity and family. All interviews were audio-recorded, transcribed and later analysed.

For the analysis, we applied a narrative approach (Johansson, 2005). Emphasis has been placed on the narratives in relation to the social, cultural and spatial context surrounding the students (Bourdieu and Wacquant, 1992). Narratives give context and meaning to our life and help us understand our experiences and the world around us. Thus, they contribute to forming the identity and reality that we, as narrators, make our own. Analyses of these narratives help us to understand how the individual conceptualises him-/herself and the surrounding world.

Choosing Berydsgymnasium

Beryd and adjacent city districts such as Askerby and Sörbo were built during the time of the *Million Homes Project*. Today, these districts are characterised by extreme ethnic heterogeneity, a high rate of unemployment, high ill-health statistics, a large proportion of public assistance recipients, and a high degree of social exclusion (Göteborgssamhällets utveckling, 2009). This ethnic heterogeneity is apparent in the schools of the *Million Homes Project* suburbs as well (Bunar and Kallstenius, 2007). In some classes, the proportion of students with a native language other than Swedish is close to one hundred per cent (Bunar, 2005). Thus, urban segregation is reflected in the schools, and, in the long run, this situation threatens to reproduce the rifts and differences between social groups (Bunar, 2001). The aim was that this picture of a segregated educational system would be counteracted by the changed admission rules. As noted, the new rules have resulted in increased mobility between schools, but at the same time new patterns of segregation have emerged (Söderström and Uusitalo, 2005). One consequence of this segregation is that schools in the poor, immigrant-dense suburbs have been branded as inferior, giving them a low status and a bad reputation (Bunar, 2001). This is true of Berydsgymnasium as well.

Whether you come from Beryd or the inner city, attending Berydsgymnasium means being compelled to respond to people's negative images of and attitudes towards the school. This issue came up in many of the narratives, including Bijan's, who attended the social science programme since his first year in senior high school.

> When you tell people you go to Berydsgymnasium, they look at you funny, as if you were an idiot or whatever, as if you're slow [...] Those are the kinds of prejudices they have against the school, that it's not great here.

Bijan felt there was an idea circulating that students at, for example, Sommerska senior high school in central Gothenburg, were better than students in Beryd—a theme that Yousef also took up. Yousef is in the same class as Bijan. He felt that many parents did not want their children to attend Berydsgymnasium. Even his mother had misgivings in this regard. 'They have it drilled into their brains that Beryd is bad, that it's shit, better in the city, to get a real education,' he said. Thus, our mental maps can govern our perceptions of and ideas about the city, city districts and schools. The notion of Beryd as a place for a well-functioning, successful senior high school or as a good educational environment does not fit in with the image of the *vulnerable* suburbs.

When we met at the end of May, 2010, Maryam was about to graduate from the senior high school in Beryd where she lives. A few years earlier when Maryam was about to apply for admission to senior high school, she wanted to 'make a fresh start, get to know other people, how they live and their attitudes towards life.' But that was not the only reason she turned to the inner city schools.

> The reason I didn't start out at Berydsgymnasium from the outset was that there were prejudices against it. That there were tons of immigrants, that there was always trouble, that the police practically lived here [...] Those were prejudices, I heard them and listened to them.

Maryam's conceptions of Berydsgymnasium are reminiscent of depictions of suburban schools—depictions partly based on negative images of the suburbs and the associations with crime, 'immigrant gangs' and alienation these images evoke (Sernhede, 2002). Her statement can be interpreted as part of an overall discourse in which these schools are described as culturally different, low achieving and rowdy, a characterisation that further contributes to lowering their status and worsening their reputation (Bunar, 2001). The students in our study often stand up for their neighbourhood and their school, criticising the negative media accounts. At the same time, it may be difficult to avoid being influenced by such representations, as in Maryam's case.

Before Addo, who lives near Kyrkoplatsen[59] in western Gothenburg, began studying at the school's music programme, he thought 'maybe it would be a little more like a suburb style school than it was, you know.' But when asked he could not really elaborate on what he meant. His picture of Berydsgymnasium exemplified how the school is unavoidably associated with the district, thus becoming part of the symbolic charging the district has as a suburb and as another place. This symbolic charging of Beryd helped to shape Addo's picture

---

59 Kyrkoplatsen is an area quite close to the city centre with a mix of middle class and working class population. The housing contains both early twentieth century buildings and buildings from the 1950s.

of the school, a picture that would later change in relation to the reality he encountered. To the question of whether the school was as he had envisaged, he quickly replied, 'Well no, that was just some weird picture I had before I'd been there. […] It disappeared right away after I got there, those thoughts.'

Many of the student narratives show clearly how territorial stigmatisation and the stereotyped images of Beryd are mingled with the school. Prejudices against the school are seen in notions of it being a rowdy and disorderly environment with irresponsible students and poor opportunities to really invest in one's studies. This changes, however, when one comes face to face with reality. 'I've been happy here at Berydsgymnasium. And it hasn't at all…the prejudices that exist, they don't make a bit of sense, they weren't right at all,' said Maryam. Her statement is not unique. In many of the narratives, we can observe how negative notions of the school became positive after students began their studies there.

The suburb

For many of the students who did not live in Beryd, the encounter with the district and the school challenged their ingrained opinions. For Hanna, a music student living with her parents on Samsö an island close to Beryd, it meant creating a new picture of the city.

> … I understand that Gothenburg is very segregated. Just look at Samsö, nobody there comes from anywhere else, or how should I put it. […] Well you know, they call you like a *slonk*[60], that's a person who lives in the city, if you live in Kristinedal and come out here. And I guess that doesn't sound so great to everybody. You know, that sort of thing. And in Beryd you're maybe the only blond person on the bus. So, yeah it's divided really.

In her encounter with Beryd, the differences between the city's different spaces became apparent to Hanna. That was 'when I realised for the first time' how segregated the town is, she reported. For Hanna, her time at the school meant changing her routes through the urban space. She discovered new neighbourhoods that had previously been hidden to her. The city's rifts suddenly became part of her daily bus journey.

However, students living in Beryd described the experience of segregation even more clearly. The city's invisible boundaries, the polarisation and the prejudices against the suburb and its people are all part of the lives of these young people.

60 A *slonk* is an offensive term for someone that doesn't live on one of the islands close to Beryd.

Bijan came to Beryd while he was in elementary school. Before then, he had lived in Denmark, the country to which his parents had emigrated from Iran. In Beryd and the adjacent districts there are 'mostly foreigners all the time,' he said. But 'if you walk around near Trädgårdsstaden you won't find anybody with black hair, you'll only see Swedes all the time and the nicest cars, homes for fourteen million.' This experience of Gothenburg as an ethnically and socio-economically stratified city is in reasonably good accordance with reality (see, e.g., Göteborgssamhällets utveckling, 2009.)

Estrangement and prejudices follow in the footsteps of urban housing segregation, which helps to reproduce stereotyped images of the suburb as a menacing and different place. Bijan, however, questioned this depiction of Beryd.

> The thing is that we have that sort of reputation here, that we've been told we're different. [...] Okay, I admit that a lot of stuff happens here, a lot of crime, there's a lot of that. But things like that happen everywhere. But I can't say either that it's safer here than in, maybe, Hövå or Halså or Tyveda or Tallbacka. It's the same there as here. The chance of getting robbed or beaten up there is just as great as here. Regardless of skin colour, ethnicity and all that.

Bijan felt that, owing to stereotyped descriptions of criminality, people in the suburbs are stigmatised as different, as aliens and 'something else' in relation to the surrounding society. This experience of being unjustly judged and labelled reflects the geographical and mental polarisation taking place in the urban space, where some people are reproached because they live in a certain place or because they have the wrong skin colour or ethnic background. The way in which the image of Beryd, and many other suburbs, is reproduced on the basis of the same discursive form—in which certain images, signs and symbols are recurrent elements—promotes this development. Territorial stigmatisation has thus become more fixed, not least because of stereotyped and negative media representations that make it more difficult to put across alternative views and descriptions (Ericsson et al., 2000). We can see how a stratified urban space is created in which city districts are assigned different levels of status and significance, contributing to Bijan's experience of not being considered an equal.

Meetings and distinction—side by side

One of the first times we visited the school we met David, one of the teachers, who showed us around. He guided us from the east hallway, where students in the business training programme spent most of their time, through the social science hallway in the middle of the school, and then on to music and the other arts programmes in the west part of the school building. These three large hallways form parallel aisles that are linked together by smaller corridors and that make up the school's framework. The very heart and centre of the music programme is the Hall, with its stage, sofas, rehearsal rooms and studios. As we were passing by, a couple of students were plucking on their guitars on one of the sofas, while others were having a conversation close by. The feeling was more that of a youth recreation centre than of a classroom. Addo told us that, during his three years at the school, there 'has been such a damn good atmosphere.' Other music programme students also expressed this feeling.

The social science programme students we talked to, both those who had attended senior high school in Beryd from the beginning and those who had 'returned,' had many positive things to say about the school. Fatima said that she was 'much happier here than I was at Kanal school,' and that the atmosphere in the class was 'much better.' The teachers at Berydsgymnasium were described as personal, friendly and warm. Shirin said that the teachers were good at giving support when it was needed. These sentiments remind us of how suburban school teachers have been described in previous studies (e.g., Schwartz, 2010).

But the positive atmosphere and closed friendship mentioned by the students did not apply to all relations at the school. This became very clear when we spoke with students in the music programme. Tobias described the situation as follows: 'The music programme and all other arts programmes, they are terribly isolated from one another and from Berydsgymnasium as a whole. They're like small cells that don't communicate with each other.' Similar stories emerged in the other students' narratives. Before Hanna came to Berydsgymnasium, she thought that there would be a 'togetherness with everybody in a way. But it's like social and natural science for themselves, then it's us in music completely separate.' Talking about the Hall, she said:

> … we just hang out there. There aren't many other places to hang around
> except there…well, near the entrance maybe. […] A lot of those *wallah*[61]

---

61 *Wallah* in Arabic means '(I promise) by God.' The students may have been born in the Middle East, or the expression may reflect the syncretic culture of the suburb where particularly words and languages are mixed (Sernhede, 2002).

kids hang out there, ha ha, [...] You know, it's not like I'd sit down there and say 'what's up'. No I mean really, it's just so separate.

Here, the spatial and mental division of the school becomes evident. The little café and the tables at the entrance are places where Hanna does not feel at home. That is the *Others'* place. It is a *different* place, separated from her place—the Hall. The Hall has become the music students' own sphere, but in this way it also becomes an isolated space.

Clara, another music student, felt that their isolation was unfortunate, but despite the lack of encounters, she did not experience any tension between the different programmes. But the rifts between students and programmes do exist. 'And then we have pass cards we use to get in through the doors, and those only work in our two hallways,' Clara reported. The spatial and mental rifts are thus reinforced by the actual boundaries established by the pass cards needed to enter one's own hallways. Students' opportunities to meet and socialise across programmes are also limited by the few meeting places available on the school premises. Yousef expressed his feeling that there is no 'really good meeting place' where students can get together, talk and relax between classes. The Hall appears to be such a space for the music students, but there is no comparable space available to the remaining students.

The west· central and east hallways

In the narratives of the social science students, the school's spatiality takes on an even clearer form. Yousef related:

... you could say that the school is divided into three parts, one part is for us in the business training programme, and students from other countries who are learning Swedish, they are in the same hallway, they are often the unsuccessful students, if you see what I mean. So that's where all the *blattar* [62] are too. Here, in the central hallway where we're walking, that's for the social and natural science programmes. Both Swedes and immigrants are together there, so that's the best place to be. Especially us in the social science programme, we think this is good, because we have to get to know different people from different cultures and backgrounds, and that's what we get to do here in Beryd, in the

---

62 A slang term in Swedish referring to people with a non-European, non-Caucasian background who live in Sweden. It is similar to the British English slang term *wog*.

central hallway. Then there's the last hallway, that's mostly music and all those practical programmes. [...] There are mostly girls there and Swedes, they don't come from Beryd, they're from outside Beryd, far from here, I think. And some of them are really rich even, you wouldn't think they'd go to school here, but they do. They pretty much always stick together. So there are three groupings.

As we can see, the different hallways are just as much about the students' study programmes as they are about identity, status and perceived future prospects. Yousef's words illustrate how students in the different hallways are attributed different roles, from unsuccessful to 'really rich.' Some even appear to be so rich that, according to Yousef, one might wonder whether they really should attend this school, perhaps because they don't fit into the image of what Berydsgymnasium or the suburb represents. But the statement also illustrates the polarisation between rich and poor that exists in the city. This polarisation is temporarily transcended at Berydsgymnasium between some of the students and at some places in the school.

However, the roles and the ways in which they are attributed to different locations in the school are about 'blattar' and 'Swedes' alike. The groupings at the school are constructed along these dividing lines, which help to create a divided space that is intersected by both socio-economic class affiliation and ethnicity. Different kinds of groupings are probably a rather common phenomenon in many schools, but at Berydsgymnasium it is in a fairly obvious way. And a way where the internal conditions at the school partly reflect the social geography of the urban space, as well as the segregation that contributes to estrangement and the gulfs between city districts and people.

Still, the social science programme stands out as a possible meeting place in an otherwise partially segregated school landscape. It is a place where students from different parts of the city and with different backgrounds can get to know each other. Ibrahim reported that everyone in his class got on well, 'so it doesn't matter if you're Swedish, Arabic or Albanian.' Integrating trends thus exist side by side with those that segregate.

The returning students

The image of Berydsgymnasium was one reason why students from Beryd did not choose to go there. However, there were many things about the inner city schools that were attractive. The desire to get to know new people and the excitement of going into the city centre were factors that caused Fatima and Amina to apply to these schools. But one of the most frequently mentioned reasons was the ambition to 'take school seriously,' as Shirin put it. Shirin, who is in the same class as Fatima, came to Beryd at the beginning of junior high school after having grown up in Falun, a middle-sized city in the middle of Sweden. To her, school had primarily been 'a place for having fun,' but in senior high school she wanted to devote more time to her studies, she said. The fact that her big sister did not think she should go to school in Beryd also influenced her choice of another school.

The advice offered by friends, family or relatives as well as the influence exerted by parents seems to play a rather important role in some students' choice of school. For others, such influences are of less significance. Grades and getting a good education may sometimes be the strongest factors, particularly in Fatima's case. She began her high school studies at Kanal school, but her father thought she should choose another school.

My dad really wanted me to go to Berydsgymnasium. He wanted me to go to school here in Beryd as usual, and then get a good education. Being well-educated is very important to us. So, Beryd doesn't have the world's greatest reputation, he wanted us to go to school here anyway and get a good education so people would realise that it doesn't matter which school you go to, you can get good grades and be well-educated anyway.

During her years at Berydsgymnasium, Fatima has indeed earned very good grades. But changing the image of the school is a difficult and slow process, and the school's teachers and principal bear witness to that. Mats, the teacher responsible for marketing the school, said:

We are seriously affected by the loss of goodwill Beryd incurs each time there's a negative headline in the newspaper. [...] the average parents of a child considering attending our school asks questions they would never ask about our competitors, if you see what I mean. And it's difficult to wash these things away. [...] its a steep hill that others don't have to climb. We have to prove that it's peaceful and friendly, cosy and safe here, things other schools don't need to spend their time on.

Berydsgymnasium is forced to grapple with the media representations and negative images of the school that have been created. How the school is portrayed and opportunities to present a favourable picture of it became increasingly important after the introduction of freedom of choice and the resulting competition for students between schools. 'When the proximity principle was repealed and we began with regional admissions, that's when we noticed the decline at Berydsgymnasium,' said Urban, one of the teachers. 'That is when ambitious parents 'sent their children to independent schools and schools in the city,' he went on to say. However, the senior high school in Beryd is waging an uneven battle against the other schools, the reason being the negative attitudes that exist concerning both Beryd and the school. 'As the competition increases, so does the problem,' added Mats.

The schools in the city centre

Whereas schools situated in the city suburbs, such as Berydsgymnasium, are frequently encumbered with a negative stamp and a poor reputation, the opposite is generally true of the inner city schools. These schools can often live on their past history, their good reputation and their place in the urban geography—factors that help explain why Shirin, Fatima and other students applied for admission there. Lindbygymnasium and Kanal school are the two most popular senior high schools among the students we have spoken with. In 2010, both had the highest proportion of applicants per student place in the municipality of Gothenburg. In contrast, Berydsgymnasium was third from the bottom in terms of number of applicants per place. It should be noted, however, that Berydsgymnasium usually has an influx of students during the school year, some of whom are the *returners* we have met with. Lindbygymnasium offers theoretical programmes only. Kanal school, on the other hand, has a greater variety; apart from theoretical programmes, they offer, for example, a healthcare programme.

Both Maroun and Ida attended Lindbygymnasium for some time. According to Ida, studying at that school involved a great deal of work and stiff demands were placed on one, especially by fellow students. After slightly more than a year at Lindbygymnasium, she changed to Berydsgymnasium. At the time of our meeting, she was a third year student there. Yet study tempo does not stand out as the main reason for changing schools. Instead it seems as though the school environment, teachers, interaction with fellow students and general contentment are important to a student's chances of keeping up with schoolwork.

One view that frequently recurs in the student interviews is that the inner city school teachers are perceived as distant, cool or solely professional in their relation to students. This point of view was expressed by, among others, Fatima, who attended Kanal school.

> I thought the teachers were very cold. I could have, my educational adviser for example, I had her four times a week [...] almost every day, right, but when you met her in the hallway she didn't even say hello.

Amina, who also attended Kanal school, was on the same track. In her experience, the teachers could not even remember the students' names, and she never made any real contact with them. 'Not like here, here you get to know the teachers. Here you joke around with your teachers, but over there it was really, like, strict,' Amina said. The strained relations with teachers at Kanal school contrast with the more relaxed atmosphere prevailing among students and teachers at Berydsgymnasium, as reported by Amina. This theme recurs in several of the student narratives.

Alienation at school

Feelings of non-belonging or alienation are expressed to varying extents in several students' narratives. Fatima sometimes felt 'that I don't fit in with them [...] after all they were Swedes and kept to themselves.' She thinks that the reason for this was that she came from Beryd. Almost everyone she socialised with at school came from suburbs in southwest Gothenburg. It is reasonable to assume that experiences of alienation partly derive from existing images of and prejudices against the suburbs and the people who live in them. Representations of the suburbs create an imaginary charging of place that influences how people think and talk about these areas (Dikeç, 2007). This is manifested in suburban students' encounters with inner city schools.

In Maroun's experience, 'everybody had a really bad picture of Beryd'—they thought it was a *ghetto*, he explained. 'Aha, you're from Beryd. I'm not gonna mess with you,' that's the way it was,' he continued. The fear encountered by Maroun emanates from the menace and danger that are associated with the suburb and that are based on stereotyped images of its residents as being criminal, dangerous and different. Because images such as these are reiterated in public discourses on poor suburban areas, these places become demonised and associated with insecurity and fear. This constitutes a process of othering, through which primarily suburban young people are considered different and alien in relation to the surrounding society (Wacquant, 2009).

Like Maroun, Jalil often had to deal with prejudices against Beryd during his time at an inner city high school. His experience was that the other students changed their attitudes towards him when they discovered where he lived.

> Lots of them didn't think I was as smart as everybody else just because I came from here. You could say I was sort of the underdog in my class. But I didn't feel like one. I only got bad grades because I wasn't happy there. And at first, I got just as good grades as the others, if not better.

At Lindbygymnasium, Jalil was the only student from Beryd in his class. Most students lived in the inner city, and he felt he didn't *click* with them. They did not have the same sense of humour and they had different pastimes. 'It just didn't work,' he reported. Jalil's feeling of not *clicking* with the inner city youth was a matter of not sharing their interests and cultural references—things he did share with young people from Beryd, like for example football, the way to dress oneself, and the things he laughs at. Place was the common denominator. His studies went very well at first, but 'then it just got worse and worse because I started cutting class, I didn't have the energy to go to school.'

The social environment at the school and the feeling of alienation affected the students' opportunities to complete the studies they had begun. Proponents of strong currents in today's school debate claim that it is up to the individual to study more, harder and better, that the individual must assume responsibility for his or her own life, choices, successes and failures. However, this way of looking at things ignores the context of the individual. School achievement often requires more than simply an instrumental relation between the student and the subject matter to be learned. No individual is an autonomous and solitary being; everyone is dependent on the people and contexts surrounding him or her. When we talk about contextual influence and 'peer effects,' we are referring to the social environment and other students' potentially positive influence on the individual's school achievement. Hopes for this type of positive influence from classmates at a certain school may affect the choice of school as well (Bunar, 2009).

Lindbygymnasium, Kanal school and the other inner city senior high schools can be described as positive social environments in which students display good results. This, in turn, can be taken as a reason for these schools' popularity. But in Jalil's case, and in other cases, the social environment did not have a positive effect on his studies. On the contrary, it was the very *cause* of his achieving less well than he did later on at Berydsgymnasium. Even if Fatima, Jalil and the others were motivated and ambitious students with very high grades, they were not able to find their place in the schools they chose. The teachers and students at these schools neither confirmed nor strengthened their self-esteem, and the school climate did not reinforce their desire to learn. This, then, had consequences for their school achievement as well as for their contentment with themselves and their lives.

The outstanding reason for students' choice to return to Beryd was their feeling of alienation—of being different. These feelings were associated with notions of the suburb and 'Swedishness', and with what these notions are supposed to represent. This had consequences for the interaction, or rather lack of interaction, between students. Fatima said that she could hear 'the Swedes at Kanal school talk about '*blattarna*', like we do, where we talk about our own people'.

The students' narratives also show how their person is tied to their place of origin. This place—the suburb of Beryd—stood in their way in the new school environment. Alienation can be viewed as a feeling of being in the *wrong* place. The students from Beryd talked about how they mostly socialised with other *immigrants* and about their feelings of not fitting in. The school space is thus ethnified through the invisible but no less tangible boundaries drawn between 'Swedes' and 'immigrants', between those from the inner city and those from the suburbs. Something that is true for both the inner city schools and the school in Beryd. The urban space's social, mental and physical boundaries emerge as real obstacles to meetings and contacts between students in these schools.

Summary and conclusions

Segregation in Gothenburg is not showing any signs of weakening. On the contrary, it has increased during the past few years (Göteborgssamhällets utveckling, 2009). As a consequence, trends towards division and categorisation of people and places have become an increasingly tangible part of life in the city. New patterns of inequality and gulfs create a hierarchisation of the urban space that contributes to the spread of estrangement and the othering of groups, such as those with a different ethnic background. Stigmatisation has become a conspicuous aspect of daily life in these city districts. It affects life in every respect, from job-seeking and contacts with social authorities to everyday encounters with people (Wacquant, 1996, 2008).

Segregation and polarisation of the urban space find expression both at Berydsgymnasium and at the inner city schools, even if their forms of expression may vary. For a student from the stigmatised suburb, going to one of the inner city schools involves a change of place and environment that gives rise to questions about identity and about existing notions of *Swedes* and *immigrants*. The social and economic hierarchies in the city are also exposed and displayed. But regardless of whether or not one has studied in the inner city, most young people from Beryd are well aware of the existence of different social worlds within the same city, and they know about the reputation of their neighbourhood. Now they have from their own self-experience got some more knowledge of what it means to live in a divided city.

The interviews with youth from the suburbs shows that the encounter with the inner city schools has not occurred without friction. Moreover, everyday life at Berydsgymnasium partly recreates the patterns of segregation we see in the city as a whole. These young people's narratives make it evident that the ways in which the city's spaces and people are described, categorised and positioned are not harmless acts. They affect the image of these spaces, their inhabitants and how people relate to them (Dikeç, 2007). This becomes particularly apparent in connection with the students' encounters with schools in the inner city. Their experiences of not being treated like a 'Swede' and of being repeatedly viewed as the *Other* are associated with the individual's place in the urban space. 'As soon as you tell somebody you come from Beryd, then [...] you notice that that person changes his or her attitude towards you,' said Jalil. Identity is in a way inscribed in the place itself. From this point of departure, our pictures and representations of the city create a sort of 'mental map' (Lindgren, 2010; Soja, 2000) that governs our perception of the city's different spaces, places and people. A 'mental and spatial separation and a spatial hierarchy' are established in the city (Alinia, p. 65) and are reflected in the schools as well. This is clearly visible in the way that Berydsgymnasium mirrors the social and the physical segregation in the city *inside* the school itself. The internal architecture of the school in Beryd, the physical dimension of space, contributes to the constructing of boundaries between different parts, classes and students in the school. But the segregation inside the school is also an effect of the mental or social dimension of space, how different parts, classes and students in the school are ascribed different meanings. The physical and the social space are in this regard constructed in a dialectical relationship where they enhance each other, thus creating the segregation in the school. And this is not true only for Berydsgymnasium, similar kind of patterns and divisions between students is also apparent in the inner city schools.

Based on the students' narratives, we can establish that several interacting processes contribute to difficulties in creating *multicultural* encounters in the schools, whether they are in Beryd or the inner city. At the same time, the narratives on Berydsgymnasium show how spatial and imaginary boundaries can be—for some of the students—partly transcended in favour of new ways of interpreting and understanding the city's different spaces and people, and thereby challenging the segregated minds. To achieve this transcendence, however, the school system must support meetings between students, and move beyond the practice of boundary marking that now exists within schools. This fixing of boundaries may be even more distinct in the inner city schools. The students' narratives about these schools reveal the difficulties in creating a truly democratic school in which all share the same opportunities, and their ambition to overcome the urban segregation through choosing an inner city school are instead contributing to their feeling of alienation. A picture emerges in which the city's spatial dimensions and the importance of space and place are central to our understanding of the conditions that students in the Swedish schools are wrestling with and of the challenges facing the freedom of choice principle, the schools and the city.

References

Andersson, R., Bråmå, Å. and Hogdal, J., (2009) *Fattiga och rika—segregationen ökar: Flyttningsmönster och boendesegregation i Göteborg 1990-2006. [Poor and rich—increased segration: Movement and domicile segregation in Gothenburg 1990-2006.]* Göteborg: Göteborgs Stadskansli.

Beach, D., Gordon, T. and Lahelma, E., (2003) Introduction—Marketisation of democratic education: Ethnographic insights, in Beach, D., Gordon, T. and Lahelma, E., (eds.) *Democratic education: Ethnographic challenges*, London: the Tufnell Press.

Bengtsson, H. A. and Wirtén, P., (1996) *Epokskifte: en antologi om förtryckets nya ansikten, [An epoche shift: an anthology on the new face of oppression.]* Stockholm: Rabén Prisma: Tiden/Athena.

Board of Education (1996), *Att välja skola: Effekter av valmöjligheter i grundskolan, [Choosing schools: Effects of possibilities of school choice in the comprehensive school.]* Skolverkets rapport nr. 109 (The Swedish National Agency for Education, Report no. 109).

Bourdieu, P. and Wacquant, L., (1992) *An invitation to reflexive sociology*, Cambridge: Polity Press.

Broady, D., (2000) *Välfärd och skola: antologi från Kommittén Välfärdsbokslut, [Welfare and school: an anthology from the Welfare Committee.]* Stockholm: Fritzes offentliga publikationer.

Bunar, N., (2001) *Skolan mitt i förorten: Fyra studier om skola, segregation, integration och multikulturalism, [Suburban schools: Four studies about school, segregation, integration and multiculturalism.]* Stockholm: Symposion.

Bunar, N., (2005) Valfrihet och anti-segregerande åtgärder, [Fredom of choice and anti-segrational measures.] *Utbildning & demokrati*, 14(3), 75-96.

Bunar, N., (2009) *När marknaden kom till förorten: Valfrihet, konkurrens och symboliskt kapital i mångkulturella områdens skolor, [When the market came to the suburbs: Freedom of choice, competition and symbolic capital in schools in multicultual areas.]* Lund: Studentlitteratur.

Bunar, N., and Kallstenius, J. (2007) *Valfrihet och integration i Stockholms grundskolor, [Freedom of choice, competition and symbolic capital in Stockholm's schools.]* Stockholm: Utbildningsförvaltningen, Stockholm Stad.

Deboard, G., (2006) Introduction to a critique of urban geography, in Knabb, K., (ed.) *Situationist International Anthology*, Berkeley: Bureau of Public Secrets.

Dikeç, M., (2007) *Badlands of the Republic: Space, politics and urban policy*, Oxford: Blackwell Publishing.

Ericsson, U., Molina, I. and Ristilammi, P.-M., (2000) *Miljonprogram och media: Föreställningar om människor och förorter, [The Million Homes Project and the media: Representations of people and suburbs.]* Norrköping: The Swedish Integration Board; Stockholm: The National Heritage Board.

Foucault, M., (1999) Space, power and knowledge, in During, S., (ed.) *The cultural studies reader*, London: Routledge.

Government Bill No. 1991/1992:95, *Om valfrihet och fristående skolor, [On freedom of choice and independent schools.]* Stockholm: Government Offices of Sweden.

Göteborgssamhällets utveckling 2009 (2009). Göteborg: Stadskansliet.

Hall, S., (1992) The West and the Rest: Discourse and Power, in Hall, S. and Gieben, B., (eds.) *Formations of Modernity*, Cambridge: Polity Press.

Hall, S., (2011) The Neoliberal Revolution, *Soundings*, 48: 9-27.

Harvey, D., (2007) *A brief History of Neoliberalism*, Oxford University Press: Oxford.

Johansson, A., (2005) *Narrativ metod och teori: Med livsberättelsen i fokus, [Narrative theory and method: Life stories in focus.]* Lund: Studentlitteratur.

Journal of Youth Studies (2009). Special issue on Young People, Class and Place, 12(5).

Lefebvre, H., (1991) *The production of space*, Oxford: Basil Blackwell.

Lindberg, I., (1999) *Välfärdens idéer, [The idea of welfare.]* Stockholm: Atlas.

Lindgren, J., (2010) *Spaces, mobilities and youth biographies in the New Sweden: Studies on education governance and social inclusion and exclusion*, Umeå: Department of Education, Umeå University.

Massey, D., (1999) Spaces of Politics, in Massey, D., Allen, J. and Sarre, P., (eds.) *Human Geography Today*, Cambridge: Polity Press.

Parszyk, I.-M. (1999) *En skola för andra: minoritetselevers upplevelser av arbets—och livsvillkor i grundskolan, [A school for others: the experiences of minority pupils and work and education conditions in the comprehensive school.]* Stockholm: HLS.

Runfors, A., (2003) *Mångfald, motsägelser och marginaliseringar: en studie av hur invandrarskap formas i skolan, [Difference, contradiction and marginalisations: an investigation of how immigrant citizenship is formed in school.]* Stockholm: Prisma.

Schwartz, A., (2010) Att nollställa bakgrunder för en effektiv skola, *Utbildning & demokrati*, 19(1): 45-62.

Sernhede, O., (2002) *AlieNation is My Nation: Hiphop och unga mäns utanförskap i Det Nya Sverige, [AlieNation is My Nation : Hiphop and young men as outsiders.]* Stockholm: Ordfront.

Sernhede, O., (ed.) (2011) *Förorten, skolan och ungdomskulturen: Reproduktion av marginalitet och ungas informella lärande. [The suburb, the school and youth culture: The reproduction of marginality and youth informal learning.]* Göteborg: Daidalos.

Soja, E. W., (2000) *Postmetropolis: critical studies of cities and regions*, Oxford: Blackwell.

Swedish Government Official Reports, (2000:39) *Välfärd och skola: antologi från Kommitén Välfärdsbokslut, [Welfare and school: An anthology from the Welfare Committee.]* Stockholm: Fritzes offentliga publikationer.

Söderström, M. and Uusitalo, R., (2005) *Vad innebär införandet av fritt skolval i Stockholm för segregeringen i skolan?*, IFAU: Rapport 2005:2.

Ungdomsstyrelsen, (2008) *Fokus 08—om ungas utanförskap*, www.ungdomsstyrelsen.se/ publikationer/fokus-08 [Accessed 12 February 2013].

Wacquant, L., (1996) Red belt, black belt: racial division, class inequality and the state in French urban periphery and the American ghetto, in Mingione, E., (ed.) *Urban Poverty and the Underclass*, London: Blackwell.

Wacquant, L., (2008) *Urban outcast: a comparative sociology of advanced marginality*, Cambridge: Polity Press.

Wacquant, L., (2009) *Punishing the poor: the neoliberal government of social insecurity*, London: Duke University Press.

Willis, P., (2000) *The Ethnographic Imagination*, Cambridge: Polity Press.

www.ingramcontent.com/pod-product-compliance
Lightning Source LLC
Chambersburg PA
CBHW061738270326
41928CB00011B/2290